HOW
TO BE
HAPPY

Pat Adams

HOW
TO BE
HAPPY

TITLES LTD – DOUGLAS – ISLE OF MAN

TITLES LTD, 19 Peel Road, Douglas, Isle of Man IM1 4LS.

First published by Titles Ltd, Douglas, Isle of Man, 1997.
Reprinted 1998 (February).

A CIP catalogue record for this book is available from the British Library.

ISBN 1-901636-00-3.

Printed and bound in Great Britain by Page Bros of Norwich.

Contents

PART ONE

Clearing the Path to Happiness

In this book, I am going to give you the basics of a way of living so as to achieve happiness. This, of course, begs the question, "What is happiness?". When you have it, you will recognise it. If you have not got it, then you are aware of the lack of it. But it is not quite that simple. Happiness is often confused with joy and with pleasure, but one can be terribly unhappy and yet still experience some pleasure in some things; and, equally, being happy does not mean that you will be incapable of feeling pain, even emotional pain, in some circumstances.

The best definition I have come across is that happiness is a state of non-contradictory joy, but you should not, even at this stage, be in any doubt as to what happiness is. As Louis Armstrong said when he was asked for a definition of jazz, "If you gotta ask, you ain't never going to know!" Happiness is like a sneeze, impossible to describe satisfactorily, but absolutely unmistakable.

I will offer no more in the way of definitions for the time being. Let us get to the important business of being happy. First and foremost, we have to deal with the barriers to happiness.

1

"Happiness is often conceived of as a state hermetically sealed off from difficult feelings. But ... happiness, cut off from the digestion of our other feelings, is synthetic."

Susie Orbach

Chapter 1

The Barriers to Happiness

There are two basic kinds of barriers to happiness. Some are the same for everybody (no-one can be truly happy if racked by guilt, for example) whereas others are very individual. For example, some people are happy with very little money, while for others shortage of cash is a real problem. These barriers, whether universal, as I shall call the first type, or individual, as I shall call the second, are never completely permanent – even if they feel like it! There is always hope, always some choice to be made, which will either get you past the barrier or which will destroy it completely; either way, there is always a way forward.

We will see later that a great deal depends on your individual power to choose, but for the time being, let us start with the ...

Universal Barriers

Of these, the first to discuss is ...

Barrier no. 1: guilty conscience

No-one can be happy with feelings of guilt, but it is important to distinguish between guilt which you feel because of something which you have done which is really evil and guilt feelings which you have for some other reason. We will deal with each of these later: for now it is enough to know that if you really have done something wrong, then it is a good thing that you feel bad about it and there is a way forward to a happier life in which you won't do *that* again. Also, if you feel guilty but can't identify any particular thing that you have done wrong which explains it, then the chances are that someone has been manipulating you – and there are ways to deal with *that* too.

Barrier no. 2: loneliness

Being alone is one thing; being lonely is altogether another. It is quite possible, and terribly painful, to be lonely when in company. Loneliness is when you lack real relationships with real people. We need other people, and superficial relationships are insufficient to meet that need. In many circumstances, superficial relationships are appropriate, but they are not sufficient on their own.

If you are lonely, as opposed to just happening to be alone at the moment, it is virtually certain that either you lack relationship building skills, or you are afraid of the implications of building close relationships and are therefore avoiding them. Either way, change is possible. Fear of relationships is understandable but it can be overcome and it is worth overcoming. And skills, even skills like relationship-building, can be learned.

Barrier no. 3: helplessness

It is often said that power corrupts and absolute power corrupts absolutely, but I have heard the opposite point made, *i.e.* that powerlessness corrupts. When we feel powerless and helpless, we are on a nasty downward slope. The feeling of helplessness is actually a feeling that one has no power of choice.

This is always an illusion. Even if you are imprisoned and under threat of violence, you always have some element of choice. It is the power of choice which is the quintessentially human property that makes us different from all the rest of the animal kingdom. There will be much more on this later in the book; for now it is enough to note that there is always hope because some power of choice always remains to you, no matter how bleak things might appear.

Barrier no. 4: inner conflicts

Do you ever find yourself feeling that you hate yourself? Do you ever find that you say one thing and then do the opposite? What about your heart "ruling" your head? Are you shocked at your own inconsistencies? Do you disappoint yourself, let yourself down?

Any of these things mean that you have some sort of inner conflict. Inner conflicts are amongst the hardest problems to overcome. What really takes work is identifying the root cause of the conflict and resolving it, and then finding that there is another conflict with another cause, and so on ...

The good news is that, although such inner conflicts fall into my category of universal barriers in that they can stand in the way of happiness for anyone, it is also true that everyone, even really happy people, have some degree of inconsistency and inner conflict. In other words, if it is really bad, you need to fix it (and you can!) but you don't need to root out every last weed of this kind. If you were to do so, you would probably end up being boring, which would never do at all.

Barrier no. 5: repressed emotions

Almost everything that happens to us warrants some sort of emotional reaction. It is proper to feel what is going on as well as to see and hear it. It is not always right to express our emotions at the very moment that we feel them; small children and animals can do this, but not adult human beings. Instead, we suppress our feelings for the time being, and give vent to them later.

That is all very well, but it can go wrong. If we suppress our emotions and don't ever let them out, then we are repressing them instead; in other words, we bottle them up. What happens then is that at another time, on some other emotional stimulus, we have an "outburst", and the bottled up emotion comes out, often violently and in an inappropriate way. This usually leaves us feeling out of control and downright unhappy.

What is worse is that it is quite common for people to repress emotions at a very early age and then suffer in adulthood from inappropriate emotional reactions which they cannot easily explain. The resulting misery is a common cause of unhappiness. Unfortunately, this is one area where self-help is only of limited effectiveness: good counselling, not necessarily from a professional, is virtually essential.

Two things should be obvious, though. Firstly, as an adult you can stop making matters worse; you can choose deliberately to suppress your emotions at times but never to repress them altogether. Secondly, even if you have profound problems of this kind it is possible to deal with them.

Barrier no. 6: poor self-image

It is impossible to be truly happy whilst thinking of yourself as stupid, ugly and incapable. Note that the important thing here is what you think of yourself, not what other people think of you, and especially not what other people thought of you, or said they thought of you, a long time ago.

Now why do I mention this last bit? How could what people said a long time ago matter to your self-image now? This is a good question, but the fact is that most people's self-image problems, especially those to do with abilities rather than appearances, date back to childhood.

Children are less capable than adults at almost everything. Unfortunately, adults (especially parents) have a nasty habit of pointing that out. "Don't touch that, you'll only break it!" "You'll fall off!" "Let me do that, you don't know how!" "You wouldn't understand." "It's too difficult for you." Can't you hear them going on and on about how incapable you are?

A great many physical self-image problems come from things said (or chanted) by siblings and peers, such as playground taunts. If they called you "Fatty" at school, the chances are that you will spend much of your adult life worrying about your figure, regardless of how you actually look.

No-one can be really happy with a poor self-image, but self-image problems are usually easy to overcome once their cause is recognised.

Barrier no. 7: lack of self-worth

If you have no sense of being a valuable member of the human race, you will not be happy. If you have this kind of feeling of lack of self-worth, it might simply be a matter of inadequate self-image, or it may be that you are capable of making some sort of contribution to the welfare of the human race, by productive work, for example, but instead you are taking more than you are giving.

If you are taking more than you are giving, and you are capable of giving more than you take, you are bound to be unhappy. We are social animals, and we depend on each other. Each person depends on the work of the others to help keep the human race going. Nevertheless, the human race can and does keep going with a significant proportion of the members relying on the efforts of others, without making much effort of their own.

If you are one of those who relies on the work of others, without making a genuine contribution of your own to the health, wealth, and well-being of the rest of the human race, you will have very little sense of self-worth, and you will not be happy.

Barrier no. 8: aimlessness

If you drift through life aimlessly, you will not achieve happiness. Happiness is, in part, a consequence of achieving rationally chosen goals.

If you do not have goals, everything you do will be purposeless, and such action without purpose does nothing to make you happy, in fact quite the opposite. If your goals are not chosen with proper care and thought, they are likely to be inconsistent and may even be destructive: either way, they will not help you to be happy. Finally, just having goals is not enough to ensure your happiness: you have to do what is necessary to give yourself the best chance of achieving them; the alternative is purpose without action, otherwise known as laziness, which will never help you to be happy either.

The good news is that, whatever your circumstances, you can make rational decisions about what you want to achieve, and then you can get on and do what is necessary to achieve it. This process of setting goals and working towards them will, provided that it is carried out intelligently, help you towards happiness.

Individual Barriers

There are also a number of common barriers to happiness which are not so universal, in that there are people who manage to be happy in spite of having these particular problems. I call them individual barriers because any individual (maybe you) can be prevented from attaining happiness by these things.

Real problems and phantom problems

What exactly do we mean by the word "problem"? The best definition I have come across is Gerald Weinberg's; he defines it like this: "A problem is a difference between the situation as observed and the situation as desired."

Everybody has problems of one sort or another. In fact, it is healthy to have some unfulfilled desires and something to aim at. If you never wanted the situation to be different from how you observe it to be, you would stagnate quickly. When something is not how you would like it to be, this is a real problem, but it is not of itself a barrier to happiness. It can become a barrier to happiness if you come to believe that it can never be solved or otherwise overcome.

By "solving" a problem, I mean changing the situation so that the new situation matches your desires. By "overcoming" it I mean changing something else so that you no longer have the mismatch between what you observe and what you desire. It is possible to change your desires, and some of this book will be about that, but what about changing your observations? In other words, what about seeing things differently?

Why should you wish to see things differently? This brings me to the title of this section, "real problems and *phantom problems*". A phantom problem, as defined by Weinberg, is when the situation is as you desire, but your observation of it is wrong. I would like to extend this idea to its obvious opposite; when the situation is not really how you desire it, but you believe that it is – this is delusion!

For some people, a phantom problem can be a barrier to happiness, but it is often fairly easy to overcome. Delusions, on the other hand, do not stop you from feeling happy in the short term, but their long-term consequences can be devastating. Eventually, the truth will become apparent, and the fact that you have been living with delusions will be inescapable, and this can destroy your happiness, which was itself a delusion. To minimise the potential for such devastation, you must recognise and overcome any delusions you have.

Phantom problems and delusions are to be approached in the same way. It is vital and urgent that you learn to see reality for what it really is. Much of this book is about honesty and realism, because both are needed for true happiness.

Money worries

There are people who do not worry about money. They seem to be in the minority. Most of the rest of us worry about whether we have enough for the moment, or enough for the future. Of the minority who are confident that they have enough or more than enough, many worry about whether they are using their money responsibly.

The really interesting thing is that, while money worries of one sort or another are almost universal, not everyone is prevented from being happy by the fact of having money worries. In fact, many money worries amount to phantom problems, but that is not the point. The point is that there is something about money, something uniquely human because no other species has it, which makes it very important to us.

I believe that it is right that money should be important to us and that those who deny this are denying a fundamental aspect of humanity and civilisation. In fact the whole matter of being happy about money, regardless of how much you actually have or owe, is so important that the whole of Part Five of this book is dedicated to just that subject.

For now, though, I just want to press home the point that, if you have money worries, you are not alone (far from it!) and that money worries need not prevent you from being happy.

Relationship worries

Almost everything I have said about money worries could equally well be said about relationship worries. Perhaps it is worth mentioning the fact that relationship worries are not uniquely human. Many animals put a great deal of effort into finding the best mate they can, and many also have to worry about territorial disputes with their neighbours, or about their position in the pecking order.

In short, everyone has, has had, or will have some cause to worry about a relationship at some time. Of itself, such a problem need not be a barrier to happiness. My view is that where a problem with a relationship appears to be such a barrier in its own right, the explanation is often the other way around: a person who is living their life in such a way as to preclude happiness consequently tends to have relationships which are so screwed up that they appear themselves to constitute a barrier to happiness.

If I am right, then the approach to these relationship worries is radical: change the way you run your life, along the lines shown in this book, and then observe your relationships improving. This applies to everyone, whether you find your relationship worries a fundamental barrier to happiness or not.

Job worries

Are you earning your living? I am not asking whether you are being paid enough to live on; that would be a completely different question, although people often confuse the two. What I am asking is whether you are working and giving value for money for your work. If you are, then your job worries (if any) are probably phantom problems, because even if you lose your present job, your attitude will probably help you to make a living some other way.

If you are not earning your living, then, unless you are in some way disabled, there are probably some changes for you to make before your job worries will stop being a barrier to happiness for you. If you are disabled, then you have a different set of problems (which may or may not constitute a barrier to happiness for you), but you could still also have the same kind of work-associated barriers to happiness that an able-bodied person might have.

Health worries

People who worry about their health are not necessarily hypochondriacs. People who live their entire lives without any health problems at all are very rare and it is reasonable to be worried about your health at some time in your life. This need not be a barrier to happiness.

If you are convinced that the only reason you are unhappy is that you are ill, you must ask how it is that some people manage to be happy despite illness. In the final analysis, this may boil down to the great question of death, and how you are going to face it. If the mention of the subject frightens you, do not run away from it. It will come up again later in this book and I shall contend that true happiness is impossible without a satisfactory approach to the big question of death.

Your choice of rules

In one of his books, Anthony Robbins claims that if you are unhappy then it is simply because of the rules you have chosen, rules by which you will choose to be happy or not. Although I think he oversimplifies, I have to agree that he has a point. People really do say to themselves things like, "I shall never be happy until ... " and their happiness then depends on just how they have phrased the "until" clause for themselves.

Robbins makes the excellent point that the phrasing of the "until" clause is a matter of choice, and some people choose impossible preconditions for themselves and consequently doom themselves to lives of unrelieved unhappiness, unrelieved, that is, unless and until they discover that it was a matter of choice all along, and go on to make a different choice.

Now I agree that happiness is largely a matter of choice. A great deal of this book is about how to make choices in a such a way as to lead you to happiness.

However I do not accept that the only choice to be made is that of rules, because there do exist the universal barriers to happiness I mentioned earlier. These, in effect, amount to in-built rules about which one has no choice.

Nevertheless, the choice of rules, in the sense that Robbins means, is a real choice and one that does have a bearing on your happiness. It is a very individual thing, though, and different people erect for themselves different such barriers to happiness.

Chapter 2

Removing Barriers

If you have one or more barriers to happiness, as described above, then the first thing to do is to deal with them. That is not the whole story; after having dealt with the barriers, there follows the task of building happiness into your life, but you will get virtually nowhere with that whilst you still have the barriers in the way. The barriers either have to be removed, or, failing that, you have to get past them somehow.

This chapter is about removing them, if you can. You have to change something, so what can you change, and how can you change it?

Whatever you want to change, the one thing you must do is to behave in such a way as to bring about the change. This applies not only to the great changes which will revolutionise your life, but also to completely trivial things. If you are sitting reading this book feeling that you would like a cup of coffee, just feeling that you would like one won't achieve anything: you have to get up and put the kettle on, or at least persuade someone else to bring you a cup.

Sitting and feeling changes nothing: you have to do something, and what you do has to be chosen so as to help you to get what you want, but do you know what you want?

Defining your Goals

One of the themes of this book is that happiness comes from working towards rationally chosen goals, and attaining them without cheating. There is much more on choosing, setting, and achieving goals later in this book, especially in Chapters 25 and 26, but at this stage we are only looking at overcoming barriers to happiness, and there are just a few aspects of this large subject to look at in this context.

There are three fundamental steps to goal-setting. First, decide what you want to achieve in your life. Second, work out what you have to do in order to achieve that. Third, work out what you need to have in order to be able to do what you have to do.

What do you want to achieve?
This is the biggest question of your life. Only you can decide on what you want to do with your life, and you cannot become happy having defaulted on that decision. If you do not decide on what you want, you will drift through life never being sure exactly why you do anything, and reach the end feeling you have wasted your time.

Since it is such an important question, it is worth spending time answering it, and being careful about the details of the answers you give yourself. You cannot say that you are too busy to think about this question, because nothing is more important than answering it, and nothing is more urgent. It is certainly worth missing a few hours of television, and you could even take some time off work for it.

You will almost certainly find it useful to write down all the things you might like to achieve, no matter how trivial, no matter how grand, no matter how easy and no matter how difficult. Do not rule anything out simply on the grounds that it seems too ambitious.

Amongst the things you have written down will be your most precious ambition, the one thing you most want. You may be clear about what this is, but if not, consider each potential goal, keeping in mind the question, "What for?" Eventually you will find what you really want to do. For example, you may think you want to be rich, but when you ask yourself what for, you may find that it is so that you have the time and other resources necessary to do something else, and it is that something else which is the ultimate goal. Eliminate anything which precludes that principal goal. Concentrate on that principal goal, the main ambition of your life

Having written down everything you want and eliminated anything which conflicts with your main ambition, look for any other contradictions, any mutually exclusive goals, resolving these conflicts of interest by deciding on what you really want.

What are you going to do?

When you have a clear idea of your aims and goals in life, you are in a position to work out what you have to do in order to achieve them. This takes a certain amount of effort in thought and planning.

Do not shy away from this effort, and never fear that you will not be able to work out a way of achieving your goals. If there were no way of achieving them, you would not have thought of them as goals in the first place. However, you will not achieve them if you do not take the trouble to work out how you are going to. It is not realistic to expect to achieve anything without putting in the effort of working out how.

The process of working out how you are going to achieve your aims may be complex. You will find more guidance on this in Chapter 25. Whether or not you find it a straightforward task, the effort should lead you to a list of things to do, each of which is clearly within your ability.

Having worked out how you are going to achieve your goals, you must then have the self-control actually to do what you have concluded is necessary. This is one of the central themes of this book, and we will return to it again and again.

What do you need to have?

To form a list of things you need, go through your list of things to do, and ask yourself if you have all the resources you need to do each item on the agenda. Remember that resources are not just objects in the material world, but also money, skills, relationships and time. From this process, you will get a list of resources you need or will need at some future time.

Getting what you need is a sub-goal, or perhaps a set of sub-goals. If you are going to spend money on acquiring the things you need in order to achieve your goals, you must first have the money! If you are to remain happy, there is just one rule which applies to the acquiring of money: you must get it honestly.

To do anything, you need your own strength, physical, mental and emotional. When you have taken to heart everything in Part Two, you will know how to build these resources and to draw on them. When you are setting goals for yourself, take account of your personal resources, and especially of any such resources which you have not yet properly developed. Developing your personality in order to achieve some other worthwhile aim will help you to be happy.

Will you be able to achieve everything you want without the help and co-operation of other people? I rather doubt it. As we will see in Part Three, it is not difficult to get other people to work with you, provided always that you take their values into account, and that you do not try to get anything from them by any unfair means.

When you decide on your goals, and make your plans for achieving them, remember always that time is one of the resources you will need. Achieving any goal whatsoever takes time. Any time you waste pushes that goal farther and farther away. If you don't use a minute at its appointed time, it deteriorates into an inaccessible part of the past immediately and irretrievably. The issue is how you apply each minute. Keep your goals constantly in mind, and you will find yourself applying your time to the attainment of those goals; do otherwise and you won't. There is enough time available. If there weren't, you would never have thought of the goals in the first place, as it is not in our nature to conceive of the impossible. The resource is there; all you have to do is to use it, and not let it perish. Using time purposefully is the way to happiness. Wasting it is not.

Changing your Behaviour

Whatever you want, it is always true that ...

You can do things differently
However you have lived your life in the past, whatever choices you have made, whatever course of behaviour you have followed, you can do things differently from the way you have done them in the past. This is hardest of all if you are in the grip of a compulsion, such as an addiction to drugs, alcohol or gambling, but at some level within you there is the capacity for change, the ability to choose to do things differently.

To change anything, you must change!
The important thing to accept is not just that change is possible and that changing your behaviour has implications for everything in your life. No, the important thing is to accept that you can change aspects of your character which underlie the things you habitually do. In other words, you can change.

Not only can you change, but if you are to remove any barriers which are preventing you from being happy, you must change. This is not always easy, but who said it would be?

Whatever you want to change, whether it is as trivial as the setting of a thermostat or as fundamental as a complete reform of your own character, the same three things underlie the power to change. The words may be unpopular, but don't let that put you off. They are discipline, thought and control. In decreasing order of unpopularity ...

Discipline

We are not so much concerned here with discipline in schools or in the military, as with self-discipline. If you are subject to military discipline, for example, you are allowing yourself to be controlled by your superior officers. Thus discipline amounts to control, and self-discipline really amounts to self-control. If you do not have self-control, this begs the question of who controls you if you don't.

Do you actually want someone else to control you? Maybe you do, because it saves all that effort of making your own decisions, taking responsibility for your own actions and generally living your own life as a human being. I will come back to this in Chapter 7, but for the time being, I will just assert that unless you take responsibility for your own life, you will never find happiness in it, not least because you will be incapable of removing your own barriers to happiness.

Taking it as read then, that the person in charge of your life is you, what are you going to do with it? To answer this question, you need ...

Thought

I am often amazed at how unpopular thought is. Whatever you want, you have to do something to achieve it. How do you know what to do? If you just believe what someone else tells you, you might be lucky and get what you want some of the time, but there are bound to be times when the someone else whom you believe either hasn't fully understood you, or doesn't really care, or actively wishes to prevent you from achieving happiness. Then you get hurt.

The only way of preventing this is to do your own thinking. That is also the only way in which you choose your behaviour: even if you have opted out of self-control, that opting-out was a consequence of some form of thought.

This, then, is the real purpose of thought. You think in order to be able to choose what to do. Having chosen, you then need ...

Control

Human beings control things. No other animal does this. Even the intelligent sheepdog which appears to control a flock of sheep is itself controlled by the shepherd. Who controls the shepherd is up to the shepherd.

We control things by means of our bodies. We control our bodies by means of our minds. How well we control our bodies is in part a matter of heredity, and in part a matter of choice. I am typing this text rather faster than many people would be able to manage because I have chosen to learn how to operate a computer keyboard. On a sports field, my performance would be less than impressive because I have not chosen to learn certain other skills. To some extent such choices are influenced by our natural mental and physical characteristics, but only to some extent. There are, after all, disabled athletes, who put to shame those of us who have no physical disabilities but who still have no athletic prowess to speak of.

To summarise the last few paragraphs, to change anything requires control of the physical world, which in turn requires skills, which require thought and self-control, or discipline.

All that may be obvious enough but it does not seem to be sufficient. People can know what they want, think out how to achieve it, be in possession of the relevant skills, and still not do what has to be done. Why not? Usually because of fear, most commonly fear of what other people will think.

Other people's reactions

We are naturally concerned with what other people think. Some people argue that no-one should ever care what other people think, but this is just too simplistic. It is one of those aspects of life where the right answer is a middle course between two extremes. So let us look first at the extremes and see why, in this case, a middle course is better.

On the one hand, if you are concerned solely with what other people think, especially if it is what just one other person in particular thinks, then either you are being effectively manipulated or you have opted out of responsibility for your own life. Either way, you are not in control of your own life.

On the other hand, someone who never ever cares what anyone else thinks clearly has a personality disorder. There are a number of psychological conditions with this extreme form of solipsism as a symptom, but it is not the purpose of this book to discuss mental illness. More to the point, people who are not mentally ill but who have very little regard for the thoughts and feelings of others tend to be social misfits, and not very happy.

Thus you need a healthy regard for other people but also an ability to make your own decisions (rationally taking into account the feelings and opinions of others, only in so far as they are relevant) coupled with an ability to follow through on what you have concluded and decided. The only really effective way to do this is to know why you have reached the conclusions you have, so that you can defend them against people who may disagree with you, and also so that you can change your mind rationally if you are presented with new information which you had not taken into account before – especially if the new information is presented by people who disagree with you and that information can be shown to be correct.

If all this seems difficult, it is just because you are not in the habit of thinking for yourself. The important thing is to do your own thinking, make your own decisions and then act on what you have decided. This is an absolutely necessary combination if you are ever to change your own behaviour and thereby remove your own barriers to happiness.

Changing your Circumstances

One of the most important consequences of changing your behaviour can be a change in your circumstances. I mentioned earlier that many people find that problems associated with their financial state, their work or their relationships can present barriers to happiness. The next thing to discuss is how you change your circumstances. This is always achieved by means of some sort of change of behaviour, but we need to be more specific than that.

The surest sign of needing to change your circumstances is the feeling of being "stuck". So, what does it mean to be stuck, and how do you get unstuck? When you feel stuck, it is because it seems to you that you have very few choices. Indeed it may be true that your choices are limited. The most important aspect of poverty, and probably the thing which most makes poverty miserable is the lack of choice which it entails. (Conversely, wealth can bring its own problems associated with too much choice, but that is another matter.) Lack of choices, whether because of poverty or for any other reason, is demeaning and unpleasant simply because the power of choice is so central to being human.

The key to getting unstuck is to make choices which lead to new situations where greater choice is possible. The process then snowballs. That can be hard to believe at times when you feel as though you have no freedom of choice. Nevertheless, no matter how things feel, there is always some choice, but ...

What choices do you have?

At the most basic level, you always have the choice of focus. That is, except when overcome by physical pain or immediate fear of violence, you have the choice of what to think about, the choice of what to concentrate on.

This is not always easy. In fact it can be very hard when things have happened which go round and round in your mind, leaving you preoccupied and worried about things you cannot control. When you feel crippled by emotional pain, it can be very hard indeed to get your mind off the hurt and on to something else. I am not suggesting here that you should repress your feelings and distract yourself from them; rather, I am pointing out that, even when things are very tough, you can still choose what you focus on.

Now, what should you focus on in order to increase your power of choice in the longer term? And how can your choice of focus make a difference anyway?

Move towards what you want, not away from what you dread

There is a subtle feature of the working of the mind which seems to have been discovered by all successful people, whether they have been intellectually aware of it or not, and which has been missed by most other people. By "successful" here, I do not just mean wealthy, I mean to refer to people who achieve what they want to achieve. Some writers have rather ironically referred to this as a great secret; it can't be a secret when it has been published so often, but so many people have missed it that it can seem as if the people who understand it are keeping it secret from the rest. Anyway, here it comes!

The secret is that the subconscious mind tends to direct a person's behaviour in such a way as to bring about circumstances like those which the conscious mind thinks about and visualises. The process is not quick, but it seems to be inevitable. What this means is that if you think constantly about the disasters which might befall you, you will increase the probability of falling victim to them, whereas if you are always looking forward to a better future, then a better future will come. We will come back to this in greater detail in Part Five.

For now, the important point to grasp is that in order to increase your power of choice, the most important first step is to concentrate on just that question. Ask yourself constantly what choices you can make which will themselves lead you to circumstances where your power of choice is greater. Do not spend time thinking about what you want to avoid or get away from because it won't help; spend time instead thinking of what you want to move towards, and keep asking yourself how you can get there.

Remember always that if you keep asking yourself "Why can't I ... ?", you will eventually find an answer, but if you constantly ask yourself "How can I ... ?" you will find a much more useful answer.

Look under your feet

When asking yourself these useful "How can I ... ?" questions, be wary of answers which involve too much immediate change. Most of the best changes in life are achieved by a large number of rather small steps, rather than by a single huge one. Remember that you are looking for choices which will lead you on to a greater power of choice.

When you discover the underlying principle of this, it can be tempting to give up your dead-end job, sell everything you own and move to another continent to seek your fortune. This is not necessarily the wrong answer, but the sense of freedom may be illusory. If you feel stuck in a dead-end job, you may not be anything like as stuck as you feel, and the job may not be that dead-end really. It is more likely that the attitude you have had to work is what has caused you to stagnate thus far.

You can change your attitude. It is, after all, almost entirely a matter of choice of focus. Changing your attitude will change your behaviour, and changing your behaviour will lead to a change in your circumstances.

You may be wondering why I entitled this section "Look under your feet". There is a story about a man who had a moderately successful farm in South Africa, but who wanted to be richer. He had heard of people making large amounts of money by prospecting for diamonds, so he sold his farm and went looking for diamonds. By the time he died in abject poverty, the man who bought his farm had become very rich as a result of all the diamonds found on the farm. Where the first man went wrong was that he didn't look under his feet.

Always be on the look-out for the opportunities which are right under your nose (or feet); don't miss them because you are looking too far afield, or just because you are not looking. It all depends on your choice of focus!

What are you going to do?

Well, what *are* you going to do? It is not for me to answer that question for you. This is not a recipe book. Nor is it an instruction manual. It is up to you to choose not only what to focus on, but also what to do. When you ask yourself,

"What am I going to do?", ask yourself not just rhetorically, but expecting an answer. Keep asking yourself this question, whilst bearing your goals in mind. The answers will come, and they will be your answers, and then it is up to you to do what you know that you have to do.

Do it, and your choices will expand. You will get unstuck. The barriers will vanish.

Chapter 3

Surmounting Barriers

But what about the things you really can't change, the barriers which are beyond your power to remove? It is, for example, completely impossible to change the past, so if what has happened in the past is a barrier to happiness for you, then you have a different kind of problem, which means that you need to find a different kind of solution.

While a change of behaviour can remove a barrier, if the barrier as it stands just cannot be removed, then you have to get over it, under it, around it or through it somehow. Surmounting a barrier, as I call it, amounts to no longer treating it as a barrier. Again this comes down to a matter of choice and sometimes the choices are very hard and sometimes you have to change your whole view of Life, the Universe and Everything. Of course, that is really a matter of choice of focus, and you always have that choice, even if it means seeing things differently from how you have seen them in the past.

We will come later to the interesting business of how to adopt a new and better world view. For now, I just want to look at those barriers which you have rather more obviously chosen for yourself, and how you can choose to get over them.

Firstly we need to recognise that a major cause of unhappiness comes from a sense of failure, that is from a feeling that you have never achieved and will never be able to achieve your goals. I have already mentioned the fact that changing your behaviour in a relevant way can bring you closer to your goals, but sometimes the goals themselves are wrongly chosen in that they are unattainable for one reason or another. In such a case, you will need to change them.

Changing your Goals

It is no small matter to change your goals in life. There are a number of books on the market which go into the matter of goal setting, but most of the authors seem to think that many people have no goals, that they just drift through life aimlessly. While it is true that many people do seem to drift aimlessly, I don't think this is because of a lack of any goals; rather, it is because of badly chosen goals. A badly chosen goal, to my mind, is one that does not help you to be happy.

The first way of choosing your goals badly is to do it unconsciously. If you have never stopped and asked yourself where you are going in life and why, you are pretty well doomed to an unsatisfying existence. Worse than that, you will probably find yourself (if you dare look inside) filled with inner conflicts. We will deal with all these things later in the book.

The other way of choosing your goals badly is to do it consciously. Obviously, one does not deliberately choose unhelpful goals, knowing them to be that, but it is impossible to get everything right all of the time, and one has to have the humility to realise that one might have chosen wrongly and then to have another try. This is just a matter of changing one's mind after finding new information. If I come across new information which shows that I was wrong about something, I change my opinion; what do you do?

If at first you don't succeed ...

The first and most obvious clue to a badly chosen goal is a sense of failure. Such a sense of failure is almost in my category of "universal barrier", but not quite. A sense of failure is usually a barrier to happiness, but it need not be. It can depend on how you choose to let the past affect you.

So what do you do if you have this sense of failure? Firstly, you must ask yourself what exactly you have failed at, and why. This calls for hard thinking. Did you really want whatever it is you have failed to achieve, or was it just that you hadn't identified what you wanted? Was there something else you wanted which got in the way of whatever it is you're missing? Was it just that you didn't find an effective method of getting what you wanted, and now you have to find a better method? These are just a few of the searching questions to ask yourself, and you must find the others for yourself.

W.C.Fields once said, "If at first you don't succeed, try, try again ... then give up; it's no use making a damn fool of yourself!" He had a point. In fact, he had more than just one point. The profound part of his remark is the hidden point that people can be driven beyond what is sensible, not just by a misplaced determination not to give up, but also by the old words of a familiar proverb beating away in their heads.

How, then, do you decide when it is right to give up?

Realism

Firstly, if any of your goals is actually unattainable, in that it requires a change to the laws of nature or a miracle, then it is time to get over that barrier by dropping that goal. You are bashing your head against a brick wall, and already making a fool of yourself.

I am not talking about things which you genuinely believe for rational reasons are attainable even though the body of learned opinion is against you. People like the Wright brothers would never have achieved the great things that they did if they had taken too much account of those who said it was impossible for man to fly in a heavier-than-air machine.

Be realistic too about timescales. Some things take decades to achieve. Don't give up just because you have spent years on something and not achieved it yet; but do give up if it is obvious to you (not in someone else's opinion) that you are not getting there. If you have tried honestly, there need be no shame in admitting defeat, and it can leave you free to achieve other, maybe better, goals.

Material goals

The area in which people seem most commonly to make mistakes over their goals in life is that of material wealth. There are many ways to make mistakes in this area, not least of which is the mistaken belief that the possession of a certain standard of living will itself lead to happiness. You will find much more on this subject in Parts Four and Five but, for now, I just want to mention the particular matter of unattained or unattainable material goals amounting to a barrier to happiness. This should never be a problem if you choose your goals intelligently. In fact, if you find that it is a problem, then it is virtually certain that you have not chosen well, and you need to change your goals.

Your goals should be chosen in such a way that working towards them helps you to be happier and actually reaching them is not an anti-climax. If a goal fails those two tests, change it, and that way you will overcome a barrier: the material world will be unchanged, but you will no longer have that barrier between you and happiness. All you will have done is made a choice and changed your focus, and yet your life will be fundamentally improved. This theme is central to this book, and we will come back to it again and again in different guises.

Non-material goals

Do you want to be a better person? Probably, but what do you mean by better? If you want to become more caring, more reliable or more expert in your profession, progress will usually help you to be happier. However, it is possible to make your own self-improvement goals into a barrier to happiness for yourself. This can come about if your objective is to become better at what you do, but what you do is itself preventing you from being happy, if, for example, your profession itself is destructive of your happiness.

The goals you set yourself for the development of your character are at least as important as any material goals, and they are within your power to change in just the same way. Be very careful how you set such goals, as they have a profound effect on your happiness, but do not be afraid if you discover that you have chosen them badly, because change is always possible.

Changing your "Rules"

I mentioned earlier that I think the idea that your happiness is entirely dependent upon your choice of rules is oversimplified. That does not mean that I think there is nothing in it, quite the contrary, but I want to put a somewhat different slant on this basic idea. (Most of the ideas here are taken from Anthony Robbins' book, "Awaken the Giant Within", published by Simon & Schuster, 1992, a book well worth having on your shelf.)

The way I see it is that people's "rules", in the sense that Anthony Robbins uses the word, are just one type of barrier to happiness. This barrier is one that they have chosen to erect for themselves. This may not be a bad thing in itself, because the technique of setting up such a barrier consciously can even be a useful method of self-motivation – I think there are better ones, but that is a different matter. Let us look now at these rules, what they are, how you choose them (when you can), how and when to change them.

What has to happen?

The first step is to ask yourself what has to happen in your life in order for you to feel good. By "feel good" here, I do not mean "feel that you are a virtuous person", I just refer to having some pleasant feeling about yourself, some sense of joy or pleasure. Robbins suggests asking yourself this question under four headings: success, love, confidence and excellence in any area of your life.

Your answers tell you a great deal about yourself. Realising that the rules you have are of the form, "I only feel good when ... ", or "I won't be happy until ... ", and that your rules are not the same as everyone else's, can show you that you have chosen your rules yourself; maybe you have chosen them less than fully consciously, but nonetheless you have chosen them and they are yours.

A new standard

Realising that you have chosen your rules can give you a huge new power, the power to choose new ones. You can therefore set yourself a new standard for your life. At the most basic level, you can say, "I will feel good whatever happens." This is probably going too far, because in the limit you could talk yourself into feeling good despite constant criminal behaviour: for a while you would succeed but ultimately you would destroy yourself.

The point, however, is that you can choose to feel good despite some things about which you have always felt bad in the past. You do this by breaking your own rules, or rather by changing your rules.

Rules you can never break or change

As I hinted above, there are rules which you can never break with impunity. These have to do with universal moral standards. They are so fundamental to human life that they are essentially impossible to change.

There have been attempts to codify them, from the Ten Commandments, to a much more recent idea that the only thing ever to be ruled out absolutely is the first use of physical force or threat of physical force.

At this point, we are in danger of confusing the two senses of the word "rule". They are related, in that the rules you have for allowing yourself to feel good are intimately related to your rules about proper behaviour, and they also underlie most good legislation. Now, it is possible, and in some cases right, to break the laws enacted by government, and still to feel good about yourself; but it is never possible to do something which you know to be wrong (no matter what the law of the land says) and yet to be happy about it.

You know that violence is basically bad and that so is cheating of all sorts. They can never lead you to happiness if you are a human being, so do not kid yourself that you can set up your personal rules in such a way as to allow them.

Rules you must change

While it is true that there are some rules which cannot be changed, you may have some rules which you must change. Rules like, "I never feel good when

I'm sober", or "I'll feel happier when I'm richer" are horrendously dangerous. The first of these is obviously terribly destructive, and you can generalise it to apply to any addiction. The second is a bit subtler; the difficulty with it is that, being open ended, it is a prescription for unlimited greed with no prospect of satisfaction. Be very sure to understand here that I am not arguing against financial goals, which can be very useful. It is the unlimited, open ended nature of this rule that makes it a killer; you could equally well have, "I'll be happier when I'm thinner", which is a prescription for anorexia nervosa.

Any rule you have which leads to a vicious circle of any sort *must* be changed! Now!

The danger of accepting someone else's rules

For a while, until quite recently, there was a rule of behaviour widely accepted within parts of the Western World, that you should never in any circumstances eat meat on Friday. This led to many millions of people adopting as their own rule, "If ever I eat so much as a morsel of meat or any form of meat extract between midnight on Thursday night and midnight on Friday night, I will be racked by guilt feelings, at least until I have been formally absolved of my sin by a priest." This is now seen, even by the church which set up the first rule, not to be useful.

Perhaps it is worth mentioning that this particular silliness was not quite as daft in its origins as it would seem at first sight. The original idea was that fasting could be a useful exercise in self-discipline, helping to build self-control, which is undoubtedly good and useful. The difficulty is that when people have guilt feelings foisted upon them by means of such an arbitrary rule, it is not *self*-control which is built; what is built is a means by which the people who feel obliged to obey the rule are controlled by those who feel empowered to make the rule. Many bad laws enacted by the world's governments are also founded on this principle.

Beware, therefore, of adopting rules other than those which you have worked out for yourself. Other people's rules are what they use to control you: they may claim – and they may even believe – that they have your happiness as a goal when they ask you to obey their rules, but no-one can have a greater interest in your happiness than you have yourself.

Therefore, make your own rules, change them when it is useful to do so, and obey them the rest of the time. Obey them by means of your own self-control. The alternative is to accept someone else's rules, and thus someone else's control; and this can put your happiness at great risk.

When rules clash

Another thing you may find when you examine the rules you have (or even new ones you are about to adopt) is that a contradiction in them means that you will never allow yourself to be happy. It is not helpful to have a rule which prescribes good feelings in one situation and another which precludes them in the same situation.

For example, if you have a rule which tells you that you can only feel good about your sexuality if you can seduce anyone you like, but another which tells you to feel bad if you are unfaithful to your wife or husband, then you have a combination which leads to internal conflict. As we have seen, internal conflict is a barrier to happiness.

When you find your rules clash, review them and scrap whatever is unhelpful.

Chapter 4

Choosing to be Happy

No matter what your situation, happiness is within your power of choice. This can be very hard to believe, especially when you have a lot of pain, but the power of choice is always there.

Power of Choice

The power of choice, the fact of not being an entirely deterministic machine, is what makes you a human being. If you really have no such power, then you have been thoroughly dehumanised, but the very fact that you are reading this book proves that that has not happened to you. You can choose to close your eyes now, or maybe throw the book away. Or you can choose to read on.

When choice is limited

A desperately poor man once said to me, "When you've got no choices, you don't think; you feel." He thus summed up brilliantly the danger of the situation he found himself in. Having come outside the scope of state benefits, he was for a few weeks entirely dependent upon charity. Fortunately the particular charity supporting him got him to think for himself again and in due course he found work and was able to support his family again. If he had got stuck with the idea that thought was outside of his scope of choice, his situation would doubtless have remained hopeless.

Think!

I pointed out earlier that the choice of focus always exists. The very act of thinking involves a choice, the choice of what to think about – and it is on this choice that all others depend.

Choose!

Having used the basic power of choice of focus to choose what to think about, the next step is to use the power of thought to work out what to do. You have to choose what to do.

Act!

Having chosen what to do, you have to choose to do it. This may seem unspeakably obvious, but it is where many people fail. The reasons for this are very deep and subtle (and I won't go into them in detail here except very briefly). Thus far, all choices have been internal; when it comes to action, the changes which result from these choices can be observed, not only by other people, but by parts of yourself which may not care what you think, but which object to any change in what you do.

Be patient

It is hard to change. It is easy for me to sit here hitting keys on a keyboard and unctuously pouring out words about the power of choice and so on, but actually doing things significantly differently in your life is not easy. The chances are that it will take you time to learn to do things differently. There are some short cuts, but it still remains true that change is difficult. It follows that you will disappoint yourself now and then. Be patient with yourself, and don't give up.

Your Choice of Rules

As I explained earlier, it is up to you to decide the preconditions for you to feel pleasure or emotional pain. Equally, it is up to you to decide what your personal code of ethical conduct is to be. These two sets of rules are intimately related, in that if you break the latter, the former will come into operation and make you feel bad.

The point you must grasp is that, subject to a few limitations, the particular set of rules which you adopt is up to you. It is your choice.

Immutables

Having said that it is up to you to choose your rules, I have to point out that human nature is such that certain choices preclude long-term happiness. You cannot lie, steal, cheat or murder your way to happiness. You cannot use fraud or manipulate other people by means of their emotions or weaknesses of any sort and still achieve long-term happiness.

I am not moralising here. I am just telling you what doesn't work. These things are immutable.

Acceptance

It is also impossible to achieve happiness when your rules require as a precondition of happiness that something completely impossible occur. Amongst my acquaintances, there are at least three happy people who suffer permanent disabilities of one sort or another. One of these was greatly saddened when she was forced to give up a most rewarding career because of constant ill-health, but she was nonetheless able to choose happiness, because she did not choose to make it a rule for herself not to be happy without a career.

You may not be disabled, but if, for example, you can't be happy until the past is changed, you're stuck until you change your rules. Some things just have to be accepted even if they are unsatisfactory. I don't mean that you shouldn't want to change things. It is perfectly natural to be happy and yet to want certain things to be different. What I am getting at is that you must accept that not everything is possible.

There will always be something you would like to be different from how it is and you must accept this fact and not let it become a barrier to happiness for

25

you. Expecting the universe to share your perfectionism is bound to lead to disappointment.

Trying to do everything

You are likewise stuck if you have chosen a rule which says you can't feel good until you have achieved all your goals and also a set of goals including at least one which is bound to be forever beyond you. While working to change the things you can change, you must accept that you can't do everything at once and there are some things you cannot do at all. Do not let this fact stop you from doing what you can, and never let it make you feel unhappy about what you can't do.

It is up to you

Your future happiness, which is what this book is about, is up to you. You choose what to think about. You choose what to do. You choose to do it. You choose what to feel about the results. You even choose what to feel about things which happen outside the scope of your control or outside your sphere of influence.

The last of these is the hardest to accept, the hardest to believe. There is a subtlety here. With almost all the others, the choice is more immediately obvious. It is less obvious that in the longer term you choose your feelings.

If someone you love dies, you will feel sad, and you could be very offended by the suggestion that this feeling is within your control. Of course you feel sad, but it is worth asking why. The basic reason is that you cared about the person and it is natural to grieve when you lose someone you care about. But you chose to let that person close to you, you chose to be vulnerable for them: this is not a bad thing, but it has consequences – and now you are feeling them. That is life and that is the risk you took.

It can be good to risk being hurt, and it can be a good thing to feel the pain in consequence of such a risk. This need not destroy your happiness; in fact, quite the contrary, as we shall see later. What is more, how long you feel the pain even of bereavement is up to you to some extent. As we shall see in the final chapter of the book, even the most intense emotional pain need not destroy your happiness if you decide that it will not.

The Implications of Choice

I opened this chapter with a section about the power of choice, and it is important to recognise that the ability to choose is power, and power implies the ability to choose; the two things are virtually identical. This section might, therefore, equally well have been called "The Implications of Power".

There is an old saying, which only has an element of truth in it, that power corrupts. The important thing to recognise is that power of any sort, that is the ability to choose, has consequences; it has implications.

Responsibility

The first implication of the fact that the exercise of power has consequences is that the exercise of choice requires responsibility. In other words, if you choose to do something, the consequences are your responsibility. This is true whether or not the consequences were what you wanted; you have responsibility for your mistakes too. Some people think that they can get out of this by submitting themselves to someone else's control; then they can plead "only obeying orders", but the truth is that the decision to obey was theirs and the responsibility for the consequences is theirs too.

Putting this even more strongly, you are responsible for the consequences not only of your actions, but also of your inaction. If you choose to do nothing, that is your choice, even if it comes from defaulting on a decision.

Any attempt to deny responsibility for the way you choose to live your life will backfire on you sooner or later. Such a denial is essentially incompatible with long-term happiness. If you think about it, you will realise that it would amount to an attempt to deny your own humanity, and you can't do that and expect to be happy!

I would argue that it is not power in itself which corrupts, as the old saying suggests; rather it is the irresponsible use of power that corrupts.

Freedom

Freedom and power are very similar concepts. They both mean the ability to do what you want. They both also depend for their meaningfulness on the concept of choice. If you can choose, you are, to the extent that you can choose, free; and likewise to just that extent, you have power.

Much of this book is about how to make choices that increase your ability to choose, so that you can ultimately choose a way of life that will lead you to happiness. This is also the path to personal freedom.

Real feelings

One of the strangest things we human beings do is to seek artificial feelings. This is called entertainment. Sometimes it can be a useful tool for learning what our own feelings might be in situations we have not yet encountered, but more often than not it degenerates into escapism.

Why resort to escapism? Is it to avoid real feelings, when the feelings you would feel if you dared would be so unpleasant? Surely there has to be a better way. There is. The better way is to have your own feelings, and good feelings too. This is possible: real feelings are a consequence of choice, and if you make good choices, you will feel good and it will be real.

Ever greater choice

It is said that success breeds success, and that nothing succeeds like success. For a long time, I thought this was unfair. Why should the rich grow richer? It seems so unfair, especially when it looks as if the rich are getting richer at the expense of the poor. In fact it is neither fair nor unfair, it is just inevitable that success breeds success. It is also not true that all rich people get richer; it tends to be only those who work hard who get richer (often building businesses which employ people who might otherwise be poorer), while those who squander their wealth tend to get poorer.

Why am I suddenly on to the subject of wealth and poverty at the end of a section on the implications of choice? Is it not clear that power, freedom and wealth are related? Except for people so addicted to money that they cannot use it but can only accumulate it, wealth brings freedom and power.

As with money, so too with the power of choice. If you choose to work with it rather than squander it, if you choose to use it to build your power of choice, as it were to invest it for the future rather than just use it for a short-term fling, it will grow exponentially and indefinitely.

It is your choice.

Changing Things

You are choosing happiness. This has to be an improvement. An improvement is a particular kind of change.

Now change happens all the time; we live in a dynamic universe, in which nothing at all is static. Things which appear static are just changing too slowly for us to notice, but they are changing. The way in which almost everything is changing is called decay, or change for the worse, and it is a consequence of a basic law of physics known as the second law of thermodynamics. This law says, in effect, that, left to themselves, things will tend towards disorder.

Improvement is the opposite of this, and ...

Improvement requires control

Unless the principle of natural selection is at work eliminating things which don't work, any improvement in anything requires conscious control. This means that if anything is to improve in your life, you had better be in control of it yourself. Any alternative to this is unlikely to lead to better things for you.

Self-control

The first thing you have to control is yourself, because it is by means of yourself that you will control anything else that you do control. In fact, as we shall see, self-control is the only real form of control that exists; control of anything else amounts to an extension of self-control!

Controlling the material world

If and only if you have achieved self-control, you can look towards having some degree of control over the material world. The most impressive achievements of control of physical matter are to be found in high technology, in factories and in research laboratories. All of these things depend upon people with a high degree of self-control, the necessary precursor of control of any sort.

Remember, though, that no control is absolute. I am no great lover of sport but I believe there is a lesson to be learned from games such as darts. The very greatest players never have absolute control of what they are doing. They just do their best to maximise the probability of the outcome they seek.

That is all you can ever do: behave in such a way as to maximise the probability of getting the outcome you seek. And like a good darts player or engineer, your success will depend ultimately upon your self-control. But however good your self-control, your control of the exterior world will never be absolute.

Influencing people

One of the reasons your control of the world can never be absolute is that it is impossible to control other people. Not only is it impossible to achieve, but it is also not really desirable to try.

It is reasonable and right to try to influence other people with your ideas if you believe your ideas are right but trying to control them (usually done by trying to influence their feelings) is manipulation. Manipulation of this sort might help you reach certain goals, but as a technique for helping you reach happiness, it is a non-starter. This is because knowing that you have reached your goals at the expense of someone else's happiness, which is the consequence of manipulation, will preclude your own happiness. It is one of the universal barriers I have mentioned before.

Accepting Things

Now, I have said that while you must be in control (especially of yourself), your control is never perfect. Does this mean that the idea of control is an illusion, that you have no power of your own, that your life can have no lasting effect? Certainly not, although there are some people who would like you to believe that, so that you will resist less when they try to manipulate you; some of the most dangerous religious cults seem to depend on convincing their adherents that they are powerless and unworthy to think for themselves.

Never let anyone persuade you that your decisions make no difference, because it is obvious from a quick look at the world around you that it has been changed as a consequence of people's decisions, so anyone trying to persuade you that *your* decisions are worthless must be trying to get you to believe a lie for some reason, and that reason is very unlikely to be to your advantage.

On the other hand, you must accept that you cannot do everything, that there is a limit to what you can achieve. The actual limit is almost certainly way beyond what you now believe, but it is still as well to be aware that the actions you take are always directed at increasing the probability of the outcome you require, not absolutely ensuring it.

Giving up?

Does this mean giving up? If you can't be sure of achieving what you want despite your best endeavours, why bother trying to do anything? To answer this, consider the trivial things you do in an ordinary day.

One of the first things I did this morning was to switch on an electric kettle. A few minutes later, there was boiling water available; I had achieved my objective (actually a step towards a greater objective, coffee). I did not stop to agonise over the undeniable fact that switching on a kettle does not absolutely guarantee a supply of boiling water: kettles do occasionally fail, so do mains electricity supplies, I might have had a heart attack or a stroke before the water boiled; things like this really do go wrong from time to time, but that doesn't mean we should give up trying!

It is the same with less trivial matters. I am not going to give up writing this book because it is not certain that it will be published. I want it published, and I will do the best I know how to maximise the probability of it being published. That is how things are achieved, by people who don't give up just because the desired outcome is never absolutely certain.

Limitations

You have to accept that your control of things is never absolute, but not be put off doing what you believe to be right because of this. You also have to accept limitations of all sorts.

Most of this book is about change, how to change yourself and the environment which surrounds you so as to maximise the probability of your long-term happiness. There are some limitations to this process of change which, in the nature of things, cannot be completely overcome and just have to be accepted.

The first of these limitations is your start point: while you can change a great deal and you can transform your life, given time, you have to start where you are and it is no use wasting energy wishing that that wasn't where you were starting; just get started and soon you'll be somewhere else anyway.

The second limitation is time. Time is the most precious commodity which exists. It is also the most perishable: if you don't use a particular moment it is wasted immediately and forever. While this is a limitation of sorts, it is also a motivator for obvious reasons. The down side of this is that it is possible to waste a lot of time agonising over how you could better have used the time you have already wasted! Everybody wastes some time, so don't waste any on thinking about what you have already wasted: just use what you have as best you can.

There are also physical limitations of all sorts. The most obvious of these is that the human body is a delicate machine with rather limited capabilities, and yet it is all we have with which to achieve everything we want to achieve. Some people spend (or waste?) their whole lives trying to extend the capability of the body, by fitness régimes of one sort or another. While it is a wise idea to keep your body in good working order, you have to be realistic about it, accept that its capabilities are limited, and work within those limitations.

Happy with problems?

I mentioned earlier that a problem can be defined as a difference between the situation as desired and the situation as observed. On the face of it, that would seem to be a barrier to happiness, but it is not so. If you are unhappy, that is by definition a problem, but having a problem does not mean you are unhappy.

Happy people have problems too. The only people with no problems are either dead or just dead from the neck up; they are certainly not real, live human beings. We want to change things; this is in our nature. We recognise that things do change, and we don't want them to change for the worse, as they will if we do not take steps to control them. Problems are therefore a natural part of human life.

I am arguing here that it is necessary to accept that you will have problems. This is not the same as saying that you cannot solve them. Solving them is a most rewarding part of life, but once you solve one problem, you will be faced with another, and with it the potential joy of solving it.

Poor but happy?

One of the commonest problems in life is shortage of money. Having money can bring extra freedom and power, and, of course, shortage of it can reduce your freedom.

When I point out the relationship between freedom, happiness, power and wealth, I am not suggesting that in order to be happy you must also be rich. Chronic poverty is a cause of unhappiness, but happiness does not depend upon having great wealth. What it does depend on is a willingness to cope with what you have or with what you are fairly confident of soon being able to have.

One of the most interesting and challenging things said by Jesus was when he mentioned the "poor in spirit" as being blessed or happy. Unfortunately, it is not entirely clear what he meant by this phrase. People will argue about this for ever, but I think he probably meant that a precondition for happiness is the ability to accept that whatever is enough to get you through today is actually enough.

This is a particular case of the general principle that it is possible to be happy with problems. If you would like to have more in the way of money and material wealth than you have, then you have a problem. Having that problem need not of itself make you unhappy. You can at the same time accept that things are not as you would wish, and still do something about changing them. There is no contradiction here, and once you have grasped that, you are well on the way to being happy.

"Happy are those who hunger and thirst for what is right. They will be satisfied."

Jesus of Nazareth

PART TWO

Being Happy
With Yourself

Other parts of this book deal with how you can be happy with other people, with the material world, with money and so on. Without this part, they are completely worthless. Likewise, there are many books on the market which purport to tell you how to get rich and so on, but it is useless to be rich if you are not happy with yourself. So, although we are still quite near the front cover, we have reached the most important part, because everything depends on what follows in the next few chapters.

Now, to be happy with yourself, you must first know who and what you are, and also that you can change yourself if you want. Throughout your whole life, you will need self-knowledge.

"*I had in five or six days got as complete a victory over conscience as any young fellow that resolved not to be troubled by it could desire. But I was to have another trial for it still; and Providence, as it generally does, resolved to leave me entirely without excuse.*"

Daniel Defoe

Chapter 5

Self-knowledge

In order to get anywhere, you first have to know where you are starting from and where you want to end up. Not only that, but you must also keep track of where you are along the way. On the great journey of life, what you will need is self-knowledge.

You can adopt one of three approaches to the subject of self-knowledge: you can work hard to achieve it; you can work hard to avoid it; or you can just not bother.

If you don't bother trying to achieve self-knowledge, you will inevitably notice some things about yourself, and what you will tend to notice most are those aspects of your character which cause you pain. This may cause you to associate emotional pain with self-knowledge, and thus you may be tempted to strive to avoid self-knowledge, because of the pain which you fear comes with it.

If you strive to avoid self-knowledge, you will never completely succeed, and, insofar as your efforts are successful, they will have the damaging side-effect of blocking out parts of your personality. This never helps you to be happy. In particular, if there are aspects of your personality which cause you emotional pain, these are the very ones which you need to change, and you cannot change them without being fully aware of what they are.

Therefore, the only sensible course is to strive to achieve self-knowledge.

Do not be Afraid!

The first thing to do is to overcome the fear of self-knowledge which comes from the association of self-knowledge with pain. It is not so terribly hard to overcome this kind of fear; as we shall see, one of the best-established methods of dealing with fear can work pretty well with this one.

What is there to fear?

Can you answer this question? What is there to fear in self-knowledge? Pain, of course, but it is useful pain, the kind that gives you valuable information. I have never heard of anyone wishing they had not improved their level of self-knowledge. There is a saying that, where ignorance is bliss 'tis folly to be wise, but it just doesn't apply in this field. So how can we understand this fear?

You will not hurt yourself

The fear of pain is, of course, fear that you might damage yourself. You may find the process of gaining self-knowledge uncomfortable, as you have to admit

35

to yourself things that you might have preferred not to be true. When something is uncomfortable it can be a warning that it should not be pursued, so you might feel that because it is uncomfortable, the process of increasing self-knowledge is harmful in itself.

This is an illusion which it is very important to recognise. What is hurting you is not the process of gaining knowledge but the nature of the knowledge itself. The truth, which is so hard to grasp and yet so vital for the journey towards happiness, is that the pain is good and useful. It is hard to grasp because I seem to be contradicting myself, entitling this section "You will not hurt yourself" and then going on to talk about the process being painful.

The important distinction to grasp is that pain is not damage, but a signal that damage exists or might be about to occur. As a signal, pain is one of the most useful things a creature can have: any animal which lacks the ability to feel pain is very vulnerable. This is the point. If you try to mask your pain or run away from the feeling itself rather than from its cause, you will be worse off and in greater danger of damage than if you face your pain and get it to tell you what its real cause is.

When it comes to seeking self-knowledge, you look inside yourself and you will doubtless find certain aspects of yourself which you would like to be different. This is painful. It is a useful pain because it signals to you the need to change something. Look harder and you will find what you need to change. Change it and you will feel better.

Now what are you afraid of?

How to overcome fear
The oldest trick in the book, when it comes to handling fear, is to do the thing you are afraid to do. Face your fear, go through it and conquer it. Trying this with legitimate fears can amount to foolhardiness; there would be very little to be said for walking alone at night through a city centre notorious for muggings just so as to overcome your fear. With irrational fears, it is ultimately the best way; not that I am recommending to all claustrophobics that they should immediately go for a long walk in the country: such things have to be built up to gradually.

With self-knowledge, though, there is no reason to hold back. If you find yourself just too hard to face alone, get a good friend or even a trained counsellor to help you to talk about yourself to whatever depth you can cope with. Other people can help too if you find yourself going round and round in circles rather than getting any deeper.

We will come later to more detail on just how you can acquire and deepen your self-knowledge. For now, I just want you to grasp the basic idea that it can't hurt you even if it is painful and the best way to overcome the fear of it is to do what you fear (introspection) and then to enjoy ...

The pay-offs
The first benefit of introspection is the good feeling you have (if your rules allow) of having done what you feared despite your fear. Next comes the good feeling of having new knowledge. These feelings are not particularly great in

themselves, but they can be very useful because of the immediate positive feedback you can give yourself for having done something that is good for you. Enjoy them because they are helping you on the road to happiness. They are immediate, they are good, and they are useful, but they are not the objective.

The objective is the big pay-off. The objective is happiness, and lasting happiness at that. Self-knowledge is necessary to reach this. If you find yourself running away from yourself, remind yourself of this objective, find what you need to change, change it and make things better. Remember, you must know where you are in order to know in which direction to go, so as to get to where you want to be. This is true all the way.

Achieving self-knowledge is an unending task and it can be hard work and it can be painful, but it is all worthwhile. If ever you doubt this, remember the objective, remember the pay-off.

It Takes Time

Do you know anyone well? Any really good friends, people you trust? What about your parents, your children, if you have any, or your siblings? How long have you known these people? Can you claim to know someone you met yesterday? How well?

To get to know a new acquaintance takes time. In just the same way, it takes time to get to know yourself. In both cases, you must be aware that the person you are getting to know is changing all the time. This ability to change is one of the reasons why the process of getting to know someone is unending; the other reason is that people are just too complicated ever to be fully understood.

There is something of a paradox here. If it is impossible to understand someone completely, why should we try? Isn't it pointless to embark upon an endless task, to set out on a journey with an unreachable destination? It would be pointless if the destination were the objective, but in this case the objective is to get closer, not to arrive. In the same way as with any process of self-improvement, progress is what matters, not achieving any particular goal.

What about getting to know yourself, then? Just as with getting to know anyone else, you have to spend time with yourself, and that does not mean sitting in front of your television watching the big match.

How to get to know yourself

In order to get to know people, you talk to them and you listen to them and you observe what they do in various circumstances. After a while, you can predict to some extent how they will react to things, what they will say on certain subjects and how they might behave in new situations.

What about getting to know yourself? Should you talk to yourself? Isn't that the first sign of madness? Listening to yourself sounds even crazier! Observing yourself sounds rather a bizarre idea at first too. But actually these are just the things you need to do.

How much time?

The simple answer to the question of how much time to spend on this quest of self-knowledge is, rather obviously, as much as possible, but that is not a very useful answer for me to give you. Clearly you have other calls on your time: you have to eat and sleep and you probably have to earn your living too; you must also have some time for socialising.

What I recommend is two things. Firstly, set aside several days once or twice a year in which the pursuit of self-knowledge will take precedence over everything else. Secondly, develop a new discipline of spending at least half an hour a day in silence with nothing to distract you.

The first of these is one of the most profitable ways of using a holiday. If you get a couple of weeks off work each year, you will probably want to escape to a more beautiful part of the world for a short while. There is nothing wrong with that. Some people, however, try to use this time to make their habitual escape from themselves more effective, and that is a recipe for longer-term misery. They distract themselves from their pain by means of the excitement of skiing, surfing, scuba-diving, rushing around an endless series of visits to ancient monuments, churches and stately homes, or just seeing new sights, any new sights, sounds or experiences; in fact they seek anything to distract themselves from themselves. Do not fall into that trap: it takes a lot of effort, is directed at achieving the opposite of what is really desirable, and it never works properly anyway.

The second, spending half an hour a day in silence, involves developing a new habit, which may in turn involve breaking some old ones. This can be very hard, especially if you are used to filling each waking minute with something. "Does it have to be every day?", I hear you ask. No, but the days when you don't manage it should be very much the exception. Does it have to be half an hour? No, but most people who have tried this find that that is a useful minimum: occasionally less will be sufficient, but more often, especially at first, you will need quite a bit more.

How to make, beg, borrow or steal time

Where are you going to find half an hour a day? Do you watch television? If so, there is your answer. I know someone whose life was revolutionised by the simple step of taking the television off the table on which it normally stood and hiding it under the table for just six weeks. The idea was that six weeks later, it could come out from under the table and resume its former position of power, but its owner found so much more in life that it was over a year before it resumed its place on the table, and then it was for less than an hour, just for the sake of one particularly good programme.

Another friend of mine who was fortunate enough to have a house larger than he really needed had a television room quite separate from the living room. This room had no carpet and no heating and no furniture apart from a few hard upright chairs and an old black-and-white television. For the sake of a really good programme, he or any member of his family might put up with the discomfort, even wearing overcoats in winter if necessary. The beauty of this idea was that they could watch anything they wanted to but the television did not dominate their lives.

I am not necessarily suggesting that you do something so extreme as to displace the one-eyed god from its hallowed shrine in the corner of the living room and desecrate it by putting it under the table or putting the poor thing in a cold room on its own. No, all I am suggesting is that you deprive it of its power for half an hour. If you can't bring yourself to switch it off and stay in the same room with it late in the evening, go to another room, or go to bed early and get up half an hour earlier to enjoy your silence then.

If you don't watch television and you think that finding half an hour a day might be hard, I have to observe that you are reading this book. This suggests to me that you may do a lot of reading. If you read a great deal but you do not take time to reflect on what you read, much of the time you spend reading is wasted. At the end of this sentence, try putting this book down and doing nothing for half an hour.

Now you are back with me, I might just say something about workaholics. If you don't watch television, you don't spend much time reading books and still you think that finding half an hour a day could be really difficult, then either you have the most amazing social life (which could be a problem in itself) or you are "too busy". If you are too busy, then either you have allowed people to manipulate you into doing much more than your share, (in which case it is vital for your future happiness that you stop, disappoint a few people in the short term and give yourself some time now) or you are working all the hours God sends, and then some. This is what workaholics do.

If you are working that hard and yet you have taken the time to look at a book called "How to be Happy", there are a couple of points you need to grasp instantly. The first is the distinction in business between essential actions and business details. Essential actions are those things which make money for your enterprise; business details is the rest. If all your time is spent on the former, you must have already learned to delegate the latter and you must be making enough money to pay for that; now could be the time to delegate some of the essential actions. If, on the other hand, much of your time is going on business details, just stop wasting it, and do something really useful instead for half an hour a day; you will soon see how to use your time much more efficiently. This brings me immediately to the second point to grasp: a very successful businessman was once heard to say during one of his frequent long holidays, "I couldn't possibly do all my work in twelve months a year, but I can do it in ten!" Time out from your busy schedule, if only spent pondering how you spend the rest of the time, could be the best investment you ever make. I recommend half an hour a day, plus a few whole days once or twice a year.

What to do with the time

There are all manner of ideas around as to how your quiet time should be spent. Some people recommend prayer, others meditation (transcendental or other-wise). Do you need a mantra? What about self-hypnosis? Yoga? All of these ideas have their own value, but I don't think it is useful at this stage to talk about techniques. I will therefore not prescribe exactly how you should sit, what noises you should make or what edifying images you should call to mind.

Remember that your objective here is self-knowledge. Remember, too, that if you don't like what you find, you can change it!

When you are alone in silence, you will discover certain things about yourself. Notably, you will discover how happy or unhappy you really are. The chances are that you will find that you are fundamentally unhappy, or at least that there are things you are unhappy about; else, why would you be reading this book? Having this unhappiness come to the surface may make you feel miserable; the pain may even make you cry. If it does, remember, as you weep, that pain is useful: it tells you that you need to do something different.

Am I suggesting that your objective should be to shut yourself away in private for half an hour's crying every day? No, I am not. What I am saying is that, if that is what happens at first, it is not necessarily a bad thing.

So what is supposed to happen? What are you supposed to do with this time? It doesn't actually matter, as long as you do not distract yourself from yourself. When you are getting to know someone else, there is no prescribed order in which you must talk about things or do things together; the important thing is being there, talking, sharing things. Likewise, when getting to know yourself, only one thing is really important: Be there!

You will find, in the quiet, that memories bubble up from the past, that dreams, ideas and even fears for possible futures come to mind, and also that you become aware of yourself as you are in the present. All of these things are good (even if some are unpleasant) because they are telling you about yourself ... who you have been, who you could and should be, and who you are.

Who are You?

The first and most important thing to grasp, when it comes to the question of who you are, is that there is no single, static, unchanging, unchangeable answer. Quite the contrary, in fact: the only people who are not changing are dead. Life involves change, you are changing all the time, and so is everyone else.

This section is therefore more to do with where you are now on a journey which takes your entire lifetime. Much of this book may be seen as being to do with choosing the direction you want to go, and then going. The question of who you are is the same as the question of where you are on your life's journey.

You are what you do

I think it was Aristotle who said something to the effect that a man is the sum total of all his actions. You do what you do because of who you are ... and what you do is the best pointer anyone can have to who you are. The old sayings, "Handsome is as handsome does" and "Actions speak louder than words" have arisen because what you do is so much more important than what you say (although what you say is part of what you do).

Not only can other people tell a great deal about who you are from what you do, so can you! In your quest for self-knowledge, you can learn about yourself by observing yourself. When you sit quietly at the end of the day, remember all the things you did that day, and if necessary ask yourself why you did them; include the things you said, and why you said them. Try also to develop the art of observing yourself during the day: try to imagine how other people are perceiving you. Remember that it is self-knowledge you are seeking.

You and your social environment

Your relationships form part of your identity. Although you cannot choose your family or your place of birth, you have chosen your friends, and the place where you now live is almost certainly a consequence of choices you have made. I find it very interesting, therefore, that some people choose to define themselves according to their family or their place of birth.

Your great-grandfather may have been a most remarkable man, but that does not make you who you are. Even if you are the kind of person who talks a great deal about your family connections, it is not your family connections which make you who you are; the fact that you choose to talk about them so much does go a long way to defining who you are!

To a great extent, you are defined by the choices you make, and these choices show up in your relationships. If you care more about the relationships which you did not choose than you do about those which you did, are you really being yourself? If you are not being yourself, who are you, and can you ever be happy?

The worst type of person who defines himself by accident of birth rather than by choice is the extreme nationalist or racist. Do you ever hear the words "fascism" and "happiness" in the same context? People who have lost themselves into such political extremism or racial hatred often seem to be very unhappy. I think I can see why: they don't even know who they themselves are; if they did, they would change. Because they do not see themselves as anything more than a member of a particular tribe, they cannot see members of any other tribe as being individuals.

Such suppression of individualism is also common to oppressive régimes, where "stepping out of line" may amount to a political crime. Oppression can only grow where individuality is suppressed. Lack of self-knowledge is therefore dangerous in a free society: it tends to lead to the society becoming less free. In a less free society, lack of self-knowledge is even more dangerous: in fact, knowing exactly why you do everything which you do do can help you to avoid imprudent expression of individuality. Furthermore, the spread of self-knowledge and individuality can only work towards the eventual freeing of society.

You are unique!

Getting back to you as an individual in your own right, let us ask a few basic questions about your personality. Are you an extrovert or an introvert? Do you look at things carefully before forming an opinion about them, or do you rely on your initial impressions? Do you make big decisions on the basis of careful thought, or on the basis of what you feel is right? What about your reactions when other people do things you don't agree with ... do you condemn them or try to understand them? What about your answers to these questions ... are you consistent, or do you say that it all depends on context? Are you sure of your opinions? Are you a helpful person? Are you efficient, effective and successful? Are you a very special, unique individual? Would you describe yourself as wise? Are you loyal and trustworthy? Is everything OK in your life? Are you a powerful person? Are you content?

There are no right or wrong answers to all these questions. Different people have different answers. The answers can even change for a given individual from day to day or from situation to situation. This is the essence of being human. Normality involves being different from other people, and different from yourself as you were yesterday. To be a perfectly balanced individual, always able to give the same "right" answers to all the above questions, would be very weird indeed.

You are an individual person, different from everyone else, and you are changing all the time. That is normal!

Who you really are

You are an assemblage of processes, some of them conscious, others sub-conscious or unconscious. When all these processes stop, you die. (According to people who believe in life after death, each person contains at least one conscious process which never completely ceases to exist, but that is another subject, to which we will return in Part Six.) This book is about your conscious and sub-conscious processes, and how you can manage them so as to enhance your happiness.

If you have more than one conscious process, does this mean that you are more than one person? To some extent it does. Does this mean you are schizophrenic? No, but the mental illness known as "multiple personality disorder" seems to me to be the far end of a spectrum, at the other end of which would be another kind of illness. This other kind of illness might be called "single personality disorder", much commoner in the boringly predictable "one-dimensional" characters of badly-written fiction than in real life.

Along this spectrum would be not just an increasing number of personalities, but, more importantly, an increasing separation of them. Can you see yourself as somewhere on this spectrum? Inside you, there are several conscious and sub-conscious processes, each of which has some degree of awareness of the others. The path to happiness involves increasing the level of awareness and resolving any conflicts there may be between these processes. The opposite direction, denying the conflicts and increasing the separation by suppressing awareness, leads to deeper misery and eventually to mental illness.

So who are you really? Is there one supreme mental process, the one with the sense of continuing consciousness, who is reading this book and who is you? Maybe. What about all the other mental processes you have? They are part of you too. If you don't like all of them as they are, do not deny their existence: recognise them, and then learn to change them.

Who do You Want to Be?

One of the mental processes going on inside your cranium is constantly thinking about the question of who you want to be. You may not always tune in to this process and become aware of it, but it is there, and you can pay attention to it if you choose, bringing it to the forefront of consciousness, as it were. If you doubt this, you could try some deliberate constructive daydreaming, imagining life as you would like it to be, including imagining yourself as you would like yourself to be. How would you look to others?

The image you project

Now, how do you actually look to others? Are you projecting an image which fits with your idea of the person you would like to be? Or are you letting people see you as you really are now? Or are you projecting an image which is neither of these?

Some people choose to project an altogether false image: they live a lie in this way. Why, and what are the consequences of this lie? The nice thing about a false image is that if people don't seem to like it, you know that it is not you that they dislike! You're safe behind your screen. Lies, however, virtually always have bad consequences; so what is the bad consequence in this case? Simply, in the same way as you are protected from being really disliked (because nobody knows the real you hiding behind the image), so too are you prevented from being really liked, for exactly the same reason. At worst, it is possible to lose your sense of identity.

Projecting a false image is not necessarily a bad thing overall. While you are sorting your life out, the protection it gives you has a lot to be said for it; you can be very vulnerable at times, and it may well be worth the disadvantages I have just outlined to gain the space you need to change yourself; but this is really only true if you are at least being honest with yourself about who you are, how you want to change and who you want to be. Later, you will be able to be honest about who you are, and you will gain hugely from that.

Who do you Want to Be?

When you are honest about who you are, both to yourself and to the rest of the world, the image you have of yourself and the image you project will naturally match up.

Let us return now to the dream you have for how you will appear in the future. How do you want to be able to see yourself? I can't answer this for you. I can't even give you much in the way of guidelines, other than to say that you will probably want to be, and therefore to appear, happy, confident, and well able to deal with the world as you find it. These things are fundamental: finer details are up to you.

I urge you again to dream of how you would like to appear both to yourself and to others (there being no difference).

Deserving the self-image you want

Now, if you have a clear idea of how you would like to appear, of the self-image you would like, you have an idea of the person you would have to be to deserve that image.

"Deserve" is not an easy word. "Deserving" used to mean getting the consequences, good or bad, of one's actions. Nowadays, we have the idea of "a deserving case", usually taken to mean someone in difficult circumstances (which may or may not be of their own making), who "deserves" help from a charity or from the state.

I want to go back to the old meaning of the word: it seems to me that the only way in which an image can be deserved is if it reflects reality accurately. It follows from this that if you want to have a particular kind of image, in the eyes both of others and of yourself, you must actually be the kind of person you wish to appear to be. For this, you might have to change yourself so as to become the kind of person you wish to be.

Form Follows Function

The other side of this idea is that, in the final analysis, whether you like or not, you will appear to be what you are; in other words, you will end up with the image you deserve! You can't fool all of the people all of the time, and, if you fool yourself, you will make a fool of yourself in the long run. No false image can be maintained indefinitely without someone seeing through it. If you continue to project a false image, you will be recognised as the kind of person who projects that kind of false image. The irony of this is that that recognition is genuine!

Do you wish to be seen as the kind of person who projects a false image to the world? No? If not, the answer is easy: Don't be the kind of person who projects a false image to the world! The only real alternative is ...

Being genuine

It is not easy to be genuine. Firstly, you have to know yourself, and that, as we have seen, takes work. Secondly, you have to be honest about yourself to other people as well as to yourself, and honesty also involves hard work, as we shall see later. Thirdly, you put yourself at a greater risk of certain kinds of emotional pain.

This is what seems to frighten people most about being genuine. If you are honest and open about yourself, and someone whose opinion you care about reacts adversely to you, it hurts, and the pain can be enough to frighten some people off being genuine, so let us consider this in more detail.

Vulnerability

Imagine the scenario: you have just told a friend whom you value your heartfelt and honest opinion about something that matters to you very much, and he laughs at you and ridicules what you have just said .... OUCH!

Here's another: you're in love, but you haven't admitted it to your beloved yet, you think the moment is right, you say the words, and then you find you were wrong, ... OUCH!

I could go on giving example after example; indeed, whole books have been written on this kind of theme, thousands of them! But you get the idea: be genuine, make yourself vulnerable, get hurt, resolve never to be open, honest, genuine and vulnerable again, thereby avoiding pain. The catch is that if you resort to this strategy to avoid pain, you will lose more than you gain.

The thing to grasp – and it is very hard to do so – is that pain is useful. Pain is your friend. Pain tells you things. What emotional pain tells you is that something is wrong. Unfortunately, it does not tell you exactly what is wrong. To benefit from emotional pain, you must think, and think deeply, about the real cause of the pain. (Physical pain is usually easier: it comes from the damaged part and tells you not to do again whatever you did to cause the damage.) If, when you experience emotional pain, you simply avoid whatever immediately preceded the pain and appeared to cause it, you can make some terrible mistakes.

One of the commonest of these terrible mistakes is to abandon genuineness on finding that the concomitant vulnerability increases the likelihood of feeling emotional pain. What you have to do instead is to find the real cause of the pain – which is doubtless some aspect of your character or behaviour – and change that.

When you have done that, you will have one obstacle fewer on your path to happiness.

Chapter 6

Conscience

If you are going to be happy with yourself, you must have a clear conscience. The word "conscience" once just meant "self-knowledge", but, like many other old and important words, it has taken on other connotations, some of which are destructive, but many of which are in fact good. For this chapter, I want you to set aside what you think you know about the concept of conscience, and look at the whole thing afresh.

Don't be Put Off by the Word

The human conscience seems to have had a bad press in recent decades. The word itself sounds old-fashioned. The concept seems outdated. The whole idea has become contaminated. We will come soon to the reasons why your conscience is a vital tool for you in your quest for happiness, as well as a most fundamental part of you. Before we get to the good bits, though, let's look at some myths which seem to have damaged the idea of what a conscience is.

It's a pain

What does a conscience do? It pricks! The idea has got about that this is the whole story, which it isn't: the rest of the story is summarised in this chapter. It is, however, true that a guilty conscience can be painful. This has made it unpopular.

It is a slightly strange thing that the conscience, as an essential part of a human being, is unpopular because it can be painful in certain circumstances. It is as if heads were unfashionable because one can sometimes have a headache.

It's a nuisance

Something which can hurt and which has no obvious purpose is clearly a nuisance. Some people regard the conscience as a nuisance for exactly this kind of reason. Not understanding the purpose of the conscience, they are not happy people.

A nuisance is something to get rid of, if at all possible. Can you get rid of your conscience? It is very difficult! Should you? I think not; it does, after all, have a purpose, or, rather, several purposes. Something which can hurt, but which has a real purpose, is not really a nuisance, but an asset to be treated with care.

It gets used to manipulate you

One of the oldest and most successful ways of manipulating someone is by means of false guilt. The idea is to change someone's perception of right and wrong in such a way that they feel guilty if they don't do what you want. Since it is the conscience which is perceived in the short term as the source of the painful feeling of guilt, people who have found themselves manipulated in this way tend to train themselves to ignore messages from the conscience: they do this in a bid for freedom, but in fact freedom is not what they get.

We will come back to the terrible subject of manipulation later. For now, just take it that manipulation does not lead to happiness either for the manipulator or for the manipulated. If you find yourself the victim or intended victim of a manipulative person or régime, never risk your future happiness by numbing your conscience; there are much better ways to deal with the problem than that!

It's best ignored

If your conscience is a pain and a nuisance and it gets used to manipulate you, it looks like a liability, doesn't it? The obvious answer is just to ignore it, especially because it tends to work less effectively if it is consistently ignored. This is what many people seem to choose to do, but it is a mistake.

It can be a source of pain, I agree, but the pain is useful pain: it tells you to do something differently; it is therefore not just a nuisance, but an asset. As for manipulation, by the end of this book, you will have learned enough that you need never be a victim of it again. So, do not ignore your conscience; you need it!

How it Really Works

So far, the only aspect of the conscience we have taken into account is its capacity to give you that form of emotional pain called guilt. Everyone knows what it is like to be pricked by a guilty conscience, even people who have worked hard to numb theirs. Unfortunately, many people, if not most, have never discovered that there is much, much more to the conscience than this ability to transmit the pain of guilt. So what else can it do, and how does it really work?

It tells you what to do

How do you know what is the right thing to do? If you do something which is wrong, your conscience will let you know by means of the guilt feelings we have discussed, but, before that, you will still know which course of action is right, and which is wrong. You will know before you are committed that a particular course of action will lead to feelings of guilt. More to the point, you will know that an alternative course will not lead to such feelings.

That knowledge of the right course, the one which will not lead to guilt, also comes from the conscience. In fact, it is the most important function of the conscience. It is even true that if you manage always to follow the positive prompting of the conscience, you need never again experience the conscience in its popularly understood guise as a source of pain.

If you remember nothing else from this book, do remember to follow the positive promptings of your conscience. This is the most important sentence of the entire book.

It tells you what to avoid

If you do something which is really wrong, someone gets hurt, maybe you, maybe someone else. If there is no victim, there can be no crime. While that is fundamentally true, your conscience is cleverer than that. Provided that you look after it properly, it can be clever enough not to make you feel guilty if you haven't done anything truly damaging yet, but still to guide you away from situations where you are more likely to do something wrong.

This is the second thing to understand about the conscience: it tells you what to avoid.

It gives you useful pain

Thirdly, and only thirdly, the conscience can give you the pain of guilt. When you have ignored the first message telling what to do, and ignored the second message telling you what to avoid, and finally ignored the foreknowledge that doing what you are about to do will give you a guilty conscience, you go ahead and do something wrong, wicked, evil, damaging, something which necessarily takes you further from happiness, then you get the painful prick of a guilty conscience.

Don't say you weren't warned! The pain hurts, of course, by definition! The problem, however, is not your conscience; it is your choice of behaviour that is the problem. When you understand that your conscience only pricks you when you do something which you need to learn to avoid, you will understand that the pain is useful. But even that is not the whole story!

Why the Conscience is Useful

It is not just the pain of a guilty conscience which is useful. That only tells you certain classes of behaviour which are best avoided. The conscience as a whole can do much more for you than just that.

Moving towards joy

We have seen that the prime function of the conscience is to tell you what to do. If you do something else, you feel guilty, but what if you don't? What if you do follow the quiet, positive promptings of your conscience? The answer, rather obviously, is that you will feel something else, but what?

You might feel self-righteous, but that is not a very helpful emotion. More likely, in the very short term, you will not feel anything very much at all. In particular, and it is very important to recognise this, you will not usually feel anything nearly as intense as the feeling of guilt which would have come from the opposite action. (Exceptions to this are possible: you may feel great after doing something truly heroic, but usually the right thing is not very exciting.)

There is something to beware of here. We like to have feelings. We love excitement and intense emotions. We dread the dull, the boring, the unexciting, the routine. A guilty conscience isn't boring, so it has an attraction all of its own. If the conscience as an organ of the human psyche has a weakness, it is this: once it has told you the right thing to do, it doesn't automatically give you nice, intense feelings for positive feedback when you have done the right thing.

In the short term, it can leave you feeling rather flat, especially if nobody else notices and remarks on how good you have been.

What good comes of it, then? Surely not self-righteousness, which is somewhat loathsome in itself. In the short term, as I have said, not very much: the pay-off of a clear conscience is a much longer-term matter. You will discover it gradually, in the form of joy which you will only attain gradually. This is an essential component of happiness. It is impossible to be truly happy without this.

Avoiding the very worst pain

If you follow the positive promptings of your conscience and do what is right consistently, you will find that joy eventually, but what if you don't follow your conscience? What if you consistently do the opposite of what is right? Will it just be a matter of losing some ill-defined good feeling which is a bit far off anyway?

No. Going against your conscience has much worse consequences. While the short-term feeling of a guilty conscience can, even though it is uncomfortable, be in some ways less boring than the knowledge of having done the right thing, in the longer term, the consequences can be dire.

If you do something wrong occasionally, it is often possible to undo part of the damage, and it is always possible to change yourself in such a way that you don't do the same again; you are unlikely to be perfect, and you can be happy without being perfect, even though aiming at perfection can help you to become happy. Occasional wrong-doing is not the point.

Consistent wrong-doing not only hurts your direct victims, it also has ramifications beyond them to the rest of the world. People don't often think this through, but if you dare to think about it, you will realise that almost everything which is unsatisfactory about the way the world works is ultimately traceable to wrong-doing of one sort or another, much of it not even deliberate.

More importantly (to you), consistent wrong-doing on your part will lead to the worst possible type of misery for you. There is no emotional pain worse than that which comes from knowing that a horrible situation is your own fault and that it is too late to do anything about it. This is ultimately the inevitable consequence of disobeying your conscience. It is never too late to change your life, but this kind of pain in the absence of such a change is completely incompatible with happiness.

You can avoid it by following your conscience.

The power of your good example

Doing the right thing usually gets noticed eventually. This can be good for your ego. More importantly, people will often notice the fact that you are obviously happy is related to the fact that you do tend to do the right thing in virtually all circumstances. I must emphasise the word "eventually".

Eventually your happy disposition and the way you choose what to do will probably get noticed, maybe not by very many people, perhaps just one person, but the chances are extremely good that you will have a helpful influence somewhere. This sort of thing grows: you influence a few people, they influence a few more, and so on. It is by this means that the world is improved for everyone, and your contribution to this improvement will help to make you happy.

The real source of happiness

Happiness actually comes from knowing that you have done your best. Whatever evil you suffer, whatever goes wrong in your life, knowing that you have not caused it (or been guilty of failing to prevent it when you could have done) will protect you from unhappiness, provided your rules allow.

Likewise, if your conscience is clear, when good things happen to you, you will not be prevented from enjoying them by guilt feelings.

The only thing you can take with you?

We will discuss the Big Question of death in a later chapter, but now is a good time to give it just a little consideration. Nobody really knows what happens to us when we die, but a few things are clear. Either one completely ceases to exist after death, or one continues in some way. No middle ground is possible.

If there is life after death in some form, it is clear that we don't take much with us, but it seems probable that our conscience goes with us. Better to have a good one, surely?

If there is no life after death, you still have to die. It seems to me that people who have lived a good life find dying easier then those who have not, regardless of whether they believe in life after death. Better to have a good conscience, surely?

How it can go Wrong

Thus far, I have scarcely mentioned the fact that the conscience is not infallible. There are a number of ways in which it can let you down. All of these are to a large extent caused by you.

Lack of exercise

Your conscience can become weaker as a consequence of lack of exercise. What do I mean by this? How can you exercise something so abstract anyway?

You can ignore your conscience. This is most effectively done by acting always on impulse without a moment's thought for the consequences, and filling your life with activity so that you don't notice the characteristic prick of the guilty conscience pointing out the error of your ways. The consequence is that your conscience gets lazy: it just doesn't bother at all with minor matters or with the things you routinely do wrong (or fail to do right); it only bothers to make its presence felt when the issue is especially important or unusual for you. A conscience which has become lazy like this is not completely useless and is not beyond redemption, but is nothing like as helpful to you as one in good working order. Remember that happiness is your goal, and a good working conscience is a useful tool for you in that quest.

You must reflect!

Another way in which your conscience can come to work less well for you than would be best for you is if it gets confused. Your conscience is a part of your psyche, but in a way it can be considered as a device a bit like a computer. It is concerned with the consequences of actions and the consequences of inaction: it has to make very rapid calculations in unprecedented situations so as to judge whether a given course of action, or a failure to act, will have good or bad consequences. To make such calculations, it needs information.

Specifically, it needs information on the past consequences of past actions and past inaction. It will pick up some of this information easily in the course of everyday life, but you can help it a lot, by thinking about what you have done, or not done, and all the consequences. This process, called reflection, helps your conscience calculate potential consequences more accurately.

Moral code

Another thing which can help your conscience in its work is a moral code. I have in mind not only basic things like the "Golden Rule" and the Ten Commandments, but also whole systems of moral philosophy, most of which are grounded in the great religions. There is, however, a subtle danger inherent in such things, and that is the danger of being a "second-hander".

Great thinkers throughout the ages have done their best to address questions of morality and ethics and many have codified their thoughts into rules of behaviour. If you adopt someone else's rules without due thought as to how they should apply to you in your situation, you may never do any real harm, but your conscience will be relaying someone else's message, not your own. Ultimately, you will find that this leaves you less happy than if you had devised your own rules of behaviour, or at least fully understood the reasoning behind the system which you have adopted.

Poisonous ideas

The greatest danger of being a second-hander is to adopt a set of rules of behaviour which are not really ethically based. At worst, this kind of thing can lead to atrocious war-crimes, committed by people who offer as their defence the fact that they were only following orders. Anyone who offers such a defence has had their conscience poisoned by the idea that it is always right to follow the orders of one's commanding officer.

There are other poisonous ideas around, some of which are terrifyingly common. "It's all right as long as you don't get caught." "Everything is relative." "You can't change the system." "Your country needs you (to risk your life trying to kill the citizens of another country)." The last of these may be outdated now, but it was largely responsible for a great deal of killing not many decades ago.

Once a poisonous idea has got into your conscience, it can be very hard to get rid of. I was shocked quite recently (1995) to hear a German person saying of the time of the Nazi régime that individuals were not responsible: fifty years had not been long enough for that poisonous idea to die!

Be very careful about any ideas which affect your judgement of right and wrong. Think very hard about them before you adopt them. Be especially careful about adopting any such ideas pushed by politicians.

How to Make it Work Better

So, how do you go about improving a conscience which is not as efficient as it should be? It is not as difficult to do this as you might think, and the benefits can be tremendous. In fact there are several techniques which are quite easy and effective. (I will deal with some of them in the next few sections.)

Turning the volume up

In many ways your conscience is like a quiet little voice inside you. I don't mean that being sensitive to your conscience is like "hearing voices", but that the prompting of the conscience is in some ways similar. If you concentrate, you can "listen" for it: you can deliberately make yourself more sensitive to this part of yourself.

What is more, if you do this *and* you follow the promptings of your conscience faithfully, it will become easier for you to "hear" what it is "saying"". These are not very good words for something which is silent and internal, but there are no better ones. The point is that concentrating on the messages from the conscience and following them will gradually become easier with practice.

Doing difficult things

Sometimes doing the right thing is hard. The opposite is very often doing nothing, rather than doing something actually wrong. Doing nothing is never particularly difficult and it comes with the perfect-sounding defence: "It wasn't my fault; I didn't do anything."

You need to be ready for the challenge when your conscience prompts you to do something difficult because doing that thing is right and not doing it is wrong. You have to be strong enough (spiritually and emotionally) to do what you know to be right, no matter how hard. If you do do something difficult just because it is right, you will feel a great deal better than you would have done if you had not done it, but even knowing that in advance somehow doesn't make the actual doing any easier. So how can you make the actual doing easier?

I know no better way than arbitrarily to choose to do something which is morally neutral (neither bad nor particularly good in itself) but which is emotionally difficult. When I was embarking on a phase of my career which I knew would involve doing some very difficult things, I also learned to swim; I had never learned as a child and I had a terrible fear of water, but I reasoned that if I could learn to swim, I would also be able to meet other challenges. It helped.

In centuries past, people used to fast in order to strengthen themselves emotionally and spiritually. Nowadays, running marathons and climbing mountains are more popular techniques, but the principle is still the same. Do something difficult (and harmless) just because it is difficult, and you will find it easier to do something difficult just because it is right.

Meditation

This chapter is already full of unpopular old-fashioned words and there are even more to come very soon. If I knew a better word for this, I would use it, but meditation is just another technique you can use to help your conscience do its job better. Because it is such an outdated word, I am going to have to go into a fair amount of detail as to what I mean by it. I have already urged you to set aside some time every day in which to be quiet, and now I am going to suggest how to use part or all of this time, preferably at the end of the day rather than the beginning.

The first requirement is silence. By this, I do not principally mean lack of sound, but lack of distraction. For this, you may also need darkness, which is the visual equivalent of quietness. In this environment of silence, you must next achieve internal quiet. When you first start, you will find all manner of things going on in your head and it takes time for these to calm down, so that you can achieve internal silence.

One of the things you will find preventing you from achieving internal quiet is the voice of your conscience. It will draw to your attention all the recent instances or your having failed to follow it. This is uncomfortable, and it is one of the reasons many people fear silence. Now, however, is the time to learn from the day's mistakes. Remember that to be happy you must be at peace with your conscience. Listen to it; reflect on the day just passed; think about how you can do better tomorrow, and resolve to pay more attention to your conscience, which will work better for you now.

It is only after this time of reflection, and after you have resolved not to repeat today's mistakes that you will find the internal quiet necessary for true meditation. Reflection makes you fully aware of the truth of the recent past, daydreaming can show you the future as you might like to see it, but meditation gives you an awareness of the present moment.

The basis of meditation is being with yourself and aware of yourself as you are in the present moment. It is in meditation that you will discover who you truly are, what your beliefs and fears are, and what you truly care about. You can also learn to face yourself honestly, to recognise those aspects of yourself which you wish to change, and to love and appreciate yourself for the good there is in you. In this you will find happiness.

Meditation can also lead you to a discovery of the reasons why your conscience gives you the signals which it does. If your conscience is being unhelpful for any reason, your understanding will help you to correct it.

Education

Your conscience can be educated. I do not mean to say that following an academic course of any kind will strengthen your conscience, but certain kinds of teaching can help it.

It is very much up to you what kind of education you give your conscience. Its task is to help you to choose right from wrong. It follows from this that

53

reading anything which deals with matters of moral choice is potentially relevant. Likewise, debates with friends about these things can be useful. With both of these things, however, there is the danger which I have already mentioned of being a second-hander.

If you just read or just listen without thinking about what you are reading or listening to and reaching your own conclusions, your conscience is likely to respond to what you have read or heard uncritically, and it is in this way that the poisonous ideas I mentioned before can get in.

So, read, listen, learn, but above all, think.

Confession

Yet another word with unfortunate connotations, "confession" is an ancient, but not totally outdated concept. I am not going to go into the history of the idea within the Christian church. I am just going to recommend one particular useful practice.

The idea is to tell someone you trust about the things in your life that you are not happy with. You need a good listener whom you can trust to keep whatever you say completely secret. It is also very important that this person does not condemn you for anything. That is just about all there is to it.

Try it now and again if you know anyone suitable to do the listening bit. You will probably find that it will help your conscience to work more effectively.

Forgiving yourself

In just the same way that it is important that anyone to whom you confess your failings should not condemn you, although they may agree that some of your behaviour could do with being corrected, so too it is important that you do not condemn yourself.

You are not perfect, and you never will be. It is good to strive for perfection, but you must be able to forgive yourself when you do not attain it. The essence of this forgiveness is to accept that you cannot change the past. The past, even your share in making it, is just something that is what it is, and it cannot be changed. There may be things about the present which are unsatisfactory because of what you did or failed to do in the past, but only the future can be changed.

It is up to you to make the future different and better. You will find this more difficult if you are constantly thinking how you should have handled the past differently. That is not to say that you should ignore the past altogether, far from it. You must face the reality of the past, learn what you can from it, and then get on with making the future better by means of how you handle the present.

This accepting, rather than denying, the past, and accepting your role in it, however despicable, is the essence of forgiving yourself. It will help your conscience to work better, as it will be better aware of how things have worked out before, and therefore how they are likely to work out in the future.

Repentance

The last of these old-fashioned concepts with unpopular names is "repentance". This means "re-thinking", but a more accurate, and certainly more modern, word would be "re-programming". The idea is very simple: any person can change. You just have to think about your life, decide to do things differently, and then do them differently.

One of the most beautiful things about the human race is that every individual within it is capable of repentance. There is always hope. In fact, it seems to me that hope itself is founded on the principle that change is possible. This in turn depends on the idea that people can change themselves. This is the essence of repentance.

Now, how can repentance itself help your conscience to work better? Quite simply, you would not be repenting and reforming your life if it were not for the action of your conscience in the first place. The conscience is encouraged by success. If it can help you to improve one area of your life, it will go on to help you in other areas.

And all the way, it is helping you towards happiness.

Always let your Conscience be your Guide

That is what the cricket said in Walt Disney's cartoon. I want to draw your attention to the word "always" in that little motto. When you have discovered that the conscience is indeed a guide rather than just a source of pain, it is very easy to think of it as being a thing which comes into its own just at decision time.

Actually, your conscience is on duty every waking moment. Split-second by split-second it is there letting you know, if you are sensitive enough to it, the right thing to do at that moment. Even so, sometimes it seems to hesitate. Sometimes it seems to be in doubt.

If in doubt ...

The moments of doubt come when you find yourself in an unprecedented situation, when facing a complex decision, or when it doesn't seem to make much difference what you do. We will deal with the last of these later, in the section about neutral choices, but we can lump the first two together here.

When in doubt, *think*. As I said earlier, the conscience is a bit like a computer which analyses the situation and outputs suggestions as to how to act. If it is faced with a situation for which it has not been programmed, it will not give a useful output. Then you have to think and think about all the things you might do and their probable consequences; then you have to choose what to do deliberately. Often the right answer will come to you after only a moment's thought, although sometimes it will take longer.

It really is that simple, especially given that sometimes your conscience will, in effect, tell you that the right thing to do right now is to think hard about what is the right thing to do. This might sound a bit circular, but it is just what a truly well-trained conscience does do.

Holism

When you are thinking about what is the right thing to do, it is important to take everything into account. Look at the whole situation, not just the local short-term implications of your decision. The wider you can draw the scope of your thinking, the better your decision will be. Integrate into your thinking, if you possibly can, everything you know about the past, present and future of the whole world. Think through the consequences of potential courses of action as far into the future as your imagination will allow.

Then choose one course of action. You may still make the wrong decision, but if you do, you will at least find it easier to forgive yourself, having honestly done your best to make the right choice.

Neutral choices

We cannot leave this chapter on the conscience without mentioning the fact that some choices are morally neutral. When your conscience is generally working well, it can occasionally seem to get stuck over trivial things. You must be able to recognise when something is unimportant.

Even some quite big decisions are morally neutral. For example, if you have decided to buy a house and you have got as far as a short list of potential properties, choosing which particular one to make an offer for will probably be a big decision, but it may be morally neutral.

The important thing is to be aware that some things, perhaps rather few, do not have moral implications. You can be faced with a number of equally right choices. Do not waste effort struggling to make a moral choice when there are no moral implications.

Chapter 7

Self-Control

It is impossible to be happy if you do not have self-control. The reason for this is that if you cannot trust yourself not to do something you would greatly regret, you will never be content with yourself. That is the bad news. The good news is that self-control is always possible.

Don't be Put Off by the Word

"Self-control" is another of these terribly old-fashioned words, sometimes confused with "self-restraint", which is not the same. "Self-control" has connotations of Victorian stiff upper lip morality, complete with the discipline of suppressing emotions. Forget all those connotations: concentrate instead on the question, "If you do not control yourself, who does control you?" A section of this chapter is devoted to that question, but I draw your attention to it now because I want you to understand what I mean by "self-control".

In order to be happy, you must be able to make your own decisions for your own reasons, and to follow them through. Also, you must be able to limit your spontaneity just to the extent that you don't do things you will regret.

Probably, the most important thing is to know why you do what you do. Bear this in mind as you read the rest of this chapter.

The things they say to children

Parents require obedience from their children. The nature of the human being is such that this is necessary. We are born very small, helpless and ignorant. As we grow up, we go through a phase of being able to expose ourselves to various deathly dangers before we have the knowledge and experience to recognise them. Our survival depends on obedience to older people (usually parents) who can recognise the dangers and protect us from them simply by the voice of command. Parents therefore have power over children. This is good and necessary, but it is also potentially dangerous in itself, for three reasons.

Firstly, power corrupts. Parents can easily get into the habit of bullying their children into submission over issues other than the safety of the child. The short dialogue, "Don't do that!" "Why not?" "Because I say so!" is painfully familiar and unanswerable, especially when it is backed up by the implicit threat of force or of withdrawal of affection.

Secondly, powerlessness corrupts. The child, especially when very young, has no real choice but to obey. Consistent lack of choice can lead to the inability to cope with choice when it is possible. Some people grow up so used to being told what to do in all circumstances that when they become adults they have a profound need to be told what to do, and will latch on to more or less any leader who will give them clear orders.

Thirdly, misused power encourages rebellion. It is common for adolescents and young adults to reject not only parental authority, but also all other forms of control, unfortunately including self-control.

Grow up!

When you are an adult, you no longer depend on your parents to make your judgements for you. You are no longer their responsibility. You are your own responsibility. Even if you choose to defer to someone else's judgement and take orders from them, you are still responsible for what you do. Hearing the formerly magic words "because I say so" is no longer a completely sufficient reason for doing anything. The adult form of this is, "That's an order!"

Having said that, I have to point out that obedience does have a place in adult life. It is perfectly legitimate to choose to obey in certain contexts; this is such a big subject that there is a whole section about it later. It always remains true, however, that you are, as an adult, responsible for what you do, even when you are doing what someone else has told you to do.

Consequences of decisions

Whatever you do is actually a consequence of your choice. The choice may be a decision that you will obey orders. More usually, you will make choices on the basis of your own decisions. When you make a decision, the consequences of that decision are obviously your own responsibility. Many people are afraid of responsibility and they try to evade it. Attempts at evasion are always fruitless, but they are so common that we must look at, and dismiss, some of the commonest types of attempt. We have already met the "only obeying orders" excuse, and we will come back to it again later, but there are others.

If you want to avoid the consequences of a decision, you can just postpone the decision until no choices remain. If only one thing is possible, no decision has to be made, so no responsibility can attach to the one remaining possible course of action. Wrong! This method of evading responsibility is simply procrastination. You are just as responsible for your action as you would have been if you had chosen it before the choice evaporated.

"Everyone else does it." Maybe they do, and if they do, that is their responsibility. If you do it too, then you have chosen to, and that is your responsibility.

"If we didn't do it, someone else would" is the arms dealers' excuse, also used by other people in similar contexts. It may be true, but it is not a defence. (An arms dealer who defends his action on the basis that free trade is right and that people should have the right to buy the means of self-defence is on much stronger moral ground. You may disagree with him, but at least he is taking responsibility for his actions.)

Defaulting

If you fail to make a decision when you should, you can be said to have defaulted on the decision. This has consequences. No decision is in fact a decision of sorts: in effect, you have decided not to decide, or at least not to choose.

It follows that you are just as responsible for the consequences of such a default as you would have been if you had made a positive decision. Procrastination, as mentioned earlier, is a particular case of this. The legitimate way to default on a decision is to delegate it, but delegating decision-making does not relieve you of responsibility for the decisions made by the person to whom you delegated them: evading that responsibility is known as "abrogation".

Abrogation of responsibility must be suspected whenever you hear things like, "I don't care: you choose." If you find yourself saying things like that, remember always that you have chosen to commit yourself to someone else's decision, and if you don't like the decision, it is wrong to blame the other person. It remains your responsibility.

If you don't like the idea of taking responsibility for someone else's decisions, make your own decisions. Self-control, however, does not mean never allowing anyone else to make any decisions which might affect you: that would amount to an attempt to control other people, which is not the idea at all.

Delegating decisions, and accepting that the outcome is your responsibility, is consistent with self-control. It is not the same as defaulting on decisions and then claiming that the outcome is not your responsibility, which is equivalent to accepting that you do not have self-control.

If you don't Control yourself, Who Will?

This is the central question. I can only see three possibilities. Either you are consciously in control of yourself, or some other human being(s) control you, or you are controlled by an unconscious or subconscious process within you. The first of these is healthy and necessary for long-term happiness, but very hard to maintain consistently. The others form part of everyone's experience to some extent and from time to time.

Always to be controlled by other people is the normal condition of the soldier or the monk who has promised to obey, but even their promises are deliberate, to some extent conditional, and not wholly inconsistent with self-control, as we will see later. The position of an employee is similar, but not so extreme. It is also quite normal to follow other people's instructions in a variety of everyday circumstances, but this is not the same as being controlled. The danger lies in the risk of being controlled by people who want you to do their will without you deliberately deciding so to do: we will come to them soon.

Being controlled by something within you but which you do not yourself control is essentially pathological. Addictions and other such compulsive behaviours amount to this, but that is not the whole story. When you drift through life without thinking about what you are doing and why, your conscious mind is not in control, you have to some extent lost your self-control, but you are not mentally ill. Something inside you is controlling you, but what is it?

Old voices

What we do can often be strangely affected by the things our elders said to us when we were children. If your parents regularly used to say things to you like "Go on – you can do it" you are much more likely to be successful in life than if they said things like "Don't touch that – you'll only break it". We have a tendency to try to fulfil the prophecies our parents make for us; for the most part we do this quite unconsciously.

It takes a huge conscious effort, and sometimes professional help, to recognise how our lives are affected by the ancient voices echoing from the past. Once recognised, however, these old voices lose much of their power. You do not have to be controlled, or even affected, by things people said to you a long time ago, but to break this control you have to make a personal and conscious effort to achieve real self-control.

New voices

There is a kind of middle ground between being controlled by old voices of which you are barely if at all conscious and being controlled by other people in the present. If someone especially important to you, boss or spouse, for example, impresses some words into your subconscious either by constant repetition or by the emotional overtones with which they are said on just one occasion, this can affect your behaviour without your being fully in control of the effect.

Most people who bring about such an effect do not do so in a conscious effort to manipulate you, even though they do want you to do as they say. Generally speaking, too, in these circumstances, where you can identify the person having an influence on you, and if need be reason with them, your self-control is not in too great a danger.

The danger comes from people who influence you deliberately without giving you much of a chance to answer back. They come in several varieties, and we will deal with them one by one next; you can largely overcome their attempts at controlling you simply by recognising their techniques. Know your enemies and keep control of your own life.

The persuaders

Probably the least dangerous are the persuaders, or "hidden persuaders" as Vance Packard called them. Their technique is advertising.

Now there is nothing intrinsically wrong with advertising. It is a proper part of trading activity, which is itself a fundamentally human thing: we are the only species which engages in voluntary trade and our survival has come to depend upon it. In order to trade, we need to communicate, and it is perfectly reasonable for people who can supply goods in large quantities to use the mass media in order to inform a large number of potential customers that the goods are available.

The problem comes with certain techniques of advertising. The commonest trick to watch out for, and to refuse to be influenced by, is the linking of a powerful positive emotion to the sales message, where that emotion cannot reasonably be expected to be brought about by possession of the goods being advertised. Another is the use of rhythm: just singing the sales message is known to be unreliable as a means of increasing sales, but if the advertiser can induce the prospective customers to repeat the sales message to themselves because it is rhythmically "catchy", many more will buy, and they will do so for irrational reasons. Powerful visual images work in much the same way.

If you decide rationally to do something, and then you do it, this can never have a bad effect on your happiness even if you later realise that you have made a mistake. If you do something for irrational reasons, this can never help you to be happier, even if the actual thing you did turns out satisfactorily. This applies particularly to spending money: if you let the persuaders control you to the extent that you spend money for irrational reasons, your happiness will be impaired even if the purchase itself is good.

Whenever you are about to spend money, ask yourself why: if you have a good rational reason, go ahead, otherwise don't. If you follow this principle, you will not regret it, and you will be able to prevent the persuaders from controlling you, whether you understand their techniques or not.

The other side of the coin is that traders who rely on inducing their customers to buy for irrational reasons tend to destroy their own happiness. Trade is only good when all parties to the trade benefit from it.

The manipulators

There is a whole chapter later in the book about manipulation, who does it and how, and why you cannot improve your chances of happiness either by resorting to it or by yielding to it. For now, I will just point out that there are people who try to manipulate other people for their own (irrational) reasons. Recognise them, avoid them, and don't let them control, or even influence you. Anything they get you to do will be against your long-term interests.

The parasites

There are not many species in which certain individuals live as parasites on other individuals of the same species, but there are human beings who are parasites on their own species. Parasitism never leads to happiness, either for the parasite or for the victim. There will be quite a lot more on this theme later in the book, so what comes here is just an outline of the problem.

For simplicity, imagine the human race divided into two main sections, called "producers" and "parasites", and a smaller third section called "genuinely helpless". The producers are the ones who strive to be self-supporting, working hard to earn their living, by producing goods or services which other people willingly and rationally choose to pay for. Also in the producers' camp are the people who have lived in this way but have now retired to enjoy what they have legitimately earned; so too are students who are honestly working towards becoming self-sufficient producers. The "genuinely helpless" include young children and people so seriously disabled that they are completely incapable of making a significant contribution to the human race. The rest are parasites.

If you deduce from that paragraph that I think you are a parasite, I will be encouraging you later to change your way of life as a necessary precondition of becoming truly happy, but that is not the point of this section. The point here is to recognise that there are people out there using various techniques to encourage you to part with some of your hard-earned wealth so that they can live. The techniques themselves don't matter very much, although I will mention some of them later; the thing is to recognise the type of person, and to be very wary of them.

At all costs, avoid irrational behaviour, which is what most parasites depend upon.

The bullies

Finally, there are the bullies. These people are basically criminal. They are the least sophisticated and most obvious form of parasite. They use force or threat of force to achieve what they want.

Their apparent occupation can be overtly criminal, but such people are actually quite rare, and not as harmful as they seem. There are two reasons why overt criminals are not terribly harmful. Firstly, their force can legitimately be countered by force, preferably by the police: that is what the police are for. Secondly, and less obviously, even a violent criminal can only affect a limited number of victims.

The really dangerous ones are the ones who legitimise their violence by institutionalising it. These people develop police states and military régimes, which have many more victims than any ordinary criminal can affect. These people are much harder to counter especially as violent revolution, which is the obvious solution, tends to lead to the replacement of one tyrant with another. Peaceful protest and civil disobedience on the grand scale seems to work rather better, but the only real solution is for the ordinary citizens to realise that the bullies in power depend on the work and co-operation of the producers in order to survive. The bullies are not self-sufficient, and they do not have to be supported.

The bullies in charge of oppressive political systems rely on conscripts and volunteers for their power. The idea that all potential conscripts could refuse to collaborate is a very dangerous idea, quite enough to get this book banned in some countries, I expect. I am convinced that a conscript into the armed forces of a tyrant is doomed to unhappiness if his duties include the oppression of his own people; I am equally convinced that the same applies to volunteers.

Obedience

One of the recurring themes of this book is the need to make your own decisions and to act on your own beliefs. One of the obvious opposites of this course is the life of obedience, and there are many people who argue that the path of obedience is the way to lasting happiness. I am not going to dismiss this belief lightly, because, subject to some very important limitations, it is a belief which has a lot to be said for it.

There are some long-established traditions of obedience in the world. The three most obvious are the military, some traditional forms of family life, and the monastic tradition. I will be discussing family life at much greater length later in the book and I will also have something to say about military matters too, so for this little chapter I am going to examine the tradition of obedience for monks, not just in the microcosm of the monastery. I will be looking at how the idea of a vow of obedience could affect your life in a number of contexts, and why it can seem to be a good thing.

Can a monk be happy?

The most relevant question, of course, is whether, in the long run, a monk, who takes a vow of obedience and therefore sacrifices his own power of choice, can achieve happiness. Despite everything I have said about freedom, choice and power, it is not actually completely out of the question. It is virtually certain that some people under a vow of obedience have led full and happy lives; it is just about as certain that many others have not, but that is not the issue here. The real question is, if it is possible to be happy having promised always to obey someone else's orders, how is it done?

The monk's secret weapon

The secret is that the vow of obedience (in whatever social context) is a two edged sword. It is a very powerful weapon and it is wielded by the person who has made the vow, and not by the person to whom the vow is made. In other words, if I promise to obey you, you are in my power, and I am not in yours! This amazing fact is true, incidentally, of the volunteer soldier and the mercenary, but not so much of the conscript whose obedience is forced, not given.

How can this be? To understand it, we need to look at obedience in mundane contexts, away from the cloister, and the field of battle.

The "monk" at work

Consider an average day at the office. Your boss makes a stupid decision. You point out to him (politely, of course) the error of his ways, but still he gives you instructions which you know to be to the detriment of the company. What do you do?

If you are committed to obedience, the answer is obvious. You record your objections, point out exactly why you think the boss has made a mistake, and then you say, " ... but you're the boss so I'll do what you say anyway." What happens then?

If he was right all along, you win because of your obedience. If he was wrong, you cannot be blamed for whatever goes wrong.

Tempting, isn't it?

The "monk" at home

You might think that similar tactics might work at home in a family which has an undisputed head of household. The danger is that bad feelings can arise from this, so it is better avoided.

Within the family, a different rule should apply, and that is that obedience and love must be inseparable for any rule of obedience to work successfully. As long ago as the fourth century, John Chrysostom pointed out that Saint Paul's advice to women to obey their husbands only makes sense if the husbands also follow the rule of loving their wives.

In other words, it is safe to obey someone unquestioningly if and only if you can be sure of their love, sure that your obedience will never backfire on you. Incidentally, the same principle underlies the idea of obedience to one's superior in the monastery; so the monk is safe if and only if the abbot can be trusted.

Love, however, does not preclude mistakes. What do you do if you believe that the person whom you normally obey is making a mistake? Love requires you to point this out, as kindly as you can. A truly loving superior will give you a fair hearing.

The "monk" in society

What about life outside the office, family, cloister or regiment? There are laws and rules and regulations applying to virtually everything. On top of that there are conventions of behaviour which help to keep civilisation civilised. What of the person committed to obedience here?

The apparent advantage of unquestioning obedience is that one can never fall foul of the law. You don't get into trouble. This is very attractive.

Alas, not all laws are good. Some exist just to keep you under control. Others exist to make sure that those who control you can have a very comfortable living. There is an analogy here: just as the success of a rule of obedience in the monastery depends on how good the abbot is, and discipline in the home requires a loving head of the family, so in society, obedience is only really good if the laws to be obeyed are just.

We will come back to this principle at much greater length later. For now, let me just say that I am not advocating anarchy, but I have to say that there are bad laws, and unquestioning obedience to them is not conducive to your long-term happiness, even if it does help you to avoid some shorter-term pain.

Is the monk irresponsible?

So, is the monk dodging the issue of responsibility for his own life? Not necessarily. Obedience to someone else may be a means of achieving one's goals. As long as it is a conscious decision to promise to obey someone, and you know why you are doing it, and it does continue to work for you, which it can, then you can make such a promise and still achieve long-term happiness.

However, circumstances might arise when you regret your decision. What do you do then?

Going back on a promise is a serious matter. Your self-respect may depend upon your ability to keep promises, and self-respect is a necessary precondition for happiness. On the other hand, if you discover that you have been tricked or manipulated into making a promise which you should never have made, then you must go back on it in order to rescue both your self-respect and your happiness. Much the same applies in the case of an honest mistake.

What, then, of the vow of obedience? Clearly, it has always to be open to review. One of the saddest things in the monastic tradition is the concept of "final vows": the ceremony in which the young monk or nun makes these binding promises is laden with the emotion which serves to lay a potential future burden of guilt on anyone who later realises that they have made a mistake and wishes to renounce their vows. This use of guilt feelings is the classic means of manipulation and must be resisted.

Yes, by all means promise to obey, and then obey, provided that the promise is not extorted from you and that obedience is a means by which you can achieve your own fulfilment. But there is one thing which must be avoided at all costs, because the alternative can be so terribly destructive. The thing which absolutely must be avoided is *unquestioning* obedience. From this comes the "only obeying orders" excuse offered by war criminals; from this too comes the wrecked lives of people who have been manipulated to their cost. Other evils arise from unquestioning obedience, many of which will become clear later in this book, but at this stage, all that remains is the question, is the monk irresponsible?

The answer to this is up to the individual monk. If he abandons his right to think for himself, gives up the idea of challenging authority when whoever is in authority is clearly wrong, and obeys orders regardless of the consequences for himself and others, then yes, the monk is irresponsible, and in the long run his irresponsibility will destroy his happiness.

But it doesn't have to be like that.

Whether or not you are taking orders from someone else, you can and should always do your own thinking, and it helps to understand things which influence your thinking, such as ...

Devils, Angels and Memes

When I refer to a devil, I do not mean a little chap with cloven hooves, a pointy tail, horns and a trident; that image was always rather a poor way of trying to illustrate a genuine and very old problem. Our ancestors also had the more useful but still weakly-defined concept of an "evil spirit", a concept good enough that it is still much used today. It seems to me that the main weakness of this idea is that it involves creatures with an independent existence whose life-cycle is not observable. In the light of modern knowledge, can we come up with a better description of the old problem?

What problem? Many people have patterns of thought which destroy their happiness. In many cases these thought patterns lead to destructive behaviour, such as violence or vandalism. That behaviour may be what destroys the individual's happiness, and it may also make it more difficult for other people, their victims, to attain their own happiness. That is a well-known and very old problem.

These underlying patterns of thought have been referred to for ages as "evil spirits" or "devils", so I will (in this context) redefine the word "devil" to mean a pattern or system of thought which functions to destroy or obstruct happiness. We can improve on this definition, but it will serve for the context of this chapter.

We now have to ask how these devils survive, how do they get around the world, and how do they increase and multiply?

Neural pathways

Inside your brain there is a huge number of neurons and an unimaginable number of connections between them. When you come across a new idea, or learn to do something new, then new connections come into existence. These can be temporary, fading away after a while. If however, you learn a new skill so thoroughly that it becomes quite automatic, the new connections get reinforced and become virtually permanent.

New skills are learned by practice, and it is much the same with other forms of mental activity. The more you repeat anything, whether it is good or bad, the more stable the corresponding connections in your brain become. In the same way as skills can become "rusty" with lack of practice, so can any pattern of thought fade when it is not exercised, as the corresponding neural connections weaken.

Memes

I think it was the geneticist Richard Dawkins who introduced the concept of a meme as a "unit of cultural transmission". A meme can be something as simple as a tune or even a single word, such as "meme", or as difficult as Schrödinger's equation. More complex things, such as this book or the system of hardware and software known as a computer which I am using to prepare it, involve large numbers of memes.

Now a meme is something which can get around the world. It does this in what Dawkins calls "meme vehicles". The oldest meme vehicles are brains: when the tribe sat around the camp fire thousands of years ago and the old man told stories, memes from his brain got themselves copied, not always precisely, into the brains of his listeners. Nowadays, we have mass media, books and all manner of communications technology, which get new and old memes around the world very efficiently, but word of mouth still works.

Habits

Now it seems to me that a habit, whether good or bad, is a kind of a meme: it is a manifestation of an idea, and it can be transmitted from one person to another. Also, a habit, like a meme, is represented in the brain by a set of neural connections, and the more ingrained the habit, the more permanent the corresponding connections.

The way we build habits is by repeating a pattern of behaviour and associating good feelings with that behaviour. One of the most successful ways of breaking a bad habit is to associate bad feelings with that behaviour: this can be done purely by thought but it is difficult, and particularly so if the good feelings originally associated with the behaviour are very strong. Habits, both good and bad, can also be broken by replacing them with different habits, either good or bad; again, this is difficult if the original habit is associated with very strong feelings.

Addiction and dependency

There is a difference between addiction and psychological dependency. True addiction to a drug (physiological, not psychological dependency) is a medical condition which needs to be properly and professionally treated, but the much more common psychological dependency is in essence a habit which can be broken.

If you have a bad habit, you will find that it helps to know how you got into it, or, more exactly, how it got into you, and for this we need to look again at the idea of a meme. There is a meme going around the world, which I shall call the "booze-meme". It says, "If you drink alcohol, you will feel good." Now you can see it in all its oversimplicity, staring at you from the page. However, countless millions of people are carrying the booze-meme around in their heads without ever having identified it or examined it. Let us examine it, remembering all the time that the heroin-meme, the marijuana-meme, the nicotine-meme, the ecstasy-meme and countless others are very close relatives, and they all get around the world in much the same way.

The booze-meme really is a little devil. Such a simple little thing, it tells a shocking lie, which is shocking because it can be true! How can a lie be true? It depends so much on context. If the booze-meme were honest, it would say something like, "In certain limited circumstances, if you drink a small amount of alcohol, you are quite likely to feel a little better in some respects for a short time." More simply, it could say, "Sometimes, if you drink alcohol, you will feel good temporarily." We only need to strip one word from each end of this perfectly true statement to take it out of context and be left with that nasty little lying devil, the booze-meme.

The booze-meme gets from brain to brain not quite in its naked verbal form as I have presented it: it is so obviously a lie that it wouldn't get far like that! Instead, it gets around by more subtle means of cultural transmission: the image of the happy drunk, the friendly atmosphere of the English village pub, the mystique of the masters of wine, the beauty of the French vineyards, the various flavours of alcoholic drinks, and of course the advertising and merchandising. And the young copy their elders, who did the same.

If there were no truth in the little devil's lie, it wouldn't get far at all. Indeed it gets nowhere with the few people who always feel ill immediately after taking any alcohol at all. It relies for its transmission on the element of truth which it contains. It rides on the back of the expectation of good feelings which are actually a part of it, an expectation which in the long run is doomed to failure, but which works often enough in the short term that the basic lie is perpetuated.

The final thing to understand about the booze-meme, and all its cousins the drug-memes and the gambling-memes, is that when it finds a new home in a new brain, it does not leave the brain from which it has come. It gets itself copied. It reproduces. This is how the devils increase and multiply.

Possession or mental illness?

The devils we have discussed so far may influence your behaviour, but they do not absolutely control it. They tempt you but they do not possess you. Some of the more powerful ones are sometimes actually heard by people as hallucinated voices, and sometimes these voices can seem to take complete control of a person.

This is a symptom of schizophrenia and of some other mental illnesses. It is also the condition which used to be known as "possession by devils". I think it is important to recognise that these are just different names for the same phenomenon, or set of phenomena.

Exorcism or treatment?

Some devils can be evicted by exorcists, others are killed off by psychiatrists; many can be got rid of by either. The important thing is to get rid of them by any effective means, not to argue too much about whose approach to problems of this sort is "correct". Whatever method is used, the unhelpful connections in the brain are disrupted.

What about the angels?

Throughout the ages, people have had visions of brilliant white beings apparently acting as messengers of God. Such visions are fairly rare and, while some people are convinced that these angels are real creatures, others think they are just hallucinations. Either way, I think they can legitimately be referred to as "good spirits" because people who have had such experiences seem always to be happier as a result.

It is not those spectacular angels that I want to discuss here, but some much humbler "good spirits" which go around the world as memes or assemblages of memes. They get themselves copied from brain to brain in much the same way as the little devils mentioned earlier, by the promise of associating good feelings with particular behaviours or beliefs.

The difference is that, whereas the devil-memes are basically liars who deliver just enough of a good feeling to get themselves copied, the angel-memes are fundamentally honest, but, strangely, they have a slightly more difficult time because their pay-off often has to be delayed. All the drugs-meme devils offer an intense and immediate feeling, against which the temperance-meme angel has a very tough job with its honest message that in the long run you would be much better off without the drugs.

Guard Your Mind

You are a meme-vehicle. Your happiness depends upon the collection of memes you choose to carry around. Getting rid of an unwanted passenger, once you have recognised it as a devil, is quite difficult (sometimes exceedingly hard). It is therefore much better to recognise the devils and stop them from getting in, while at the same time encouraging the angels. You can usually tell them apart without too much difficulty. Most of the angels promise long-term benefits for short-term difficulties, whereas the devils are the opposite: they promise short-term benefits and keep very quiet about the long-term problems.

One of the most important things you have to do in order to safeguard your happiness is to stop the devils getting in. The rest of this section is a collection of suggestions as to how you might do this.

Choose your friends

It is not for me to tell you who your friends should be; that must always be up to you, and them. Nonetheless, memes are infectious and friends will always share their memes to a large extent, and it is well worth your while excluding from your life people whose memes are likely to make it harder for you to be happy in the long run.

There are a few warning signs to look out for.

Most obvious is the tendency to pursue immediate pleasure without caring about the long term consequences: if you socialise with people like that, you are likely to have an exciting time which you will regret. People with that tendency have the hedonism-meme which is very infectious and dangerous. Remember that it is possible to have an exciting time doing things you will not later regret; stick to that sort of fun.

Much less obvious is the belief that it is right that people should be sacrificed to "higher causes", or that they have no right to their own property. This is a criminal tendency wrapped up in noble language. There are two dangers in associating with people who have beliefs of this sort: firstly, you could be the next person to be sacrificed, when you are manipulated into parting with what you own for an ill-defined "worthy cause" which actually benefits the manipulator; secondly, and more seriously, you may get infected with one of the most dangerous and virulent memes in the world, thereby becoming a criminal of this sort yourself, and ruining your chances of true happiness.

A person who is forever moaning and complaining is never going to help make you happy. If you really want to, by all means do what you can to help (especially if he has a genuine problem not of his own making), but if he tries to make you feel that you have a duty to look after him, give him a copy of this book and leave him alone to solve his own problems. You will both be much happier when he decides to stop being a parasite.

One final warning sign to look out for in potential friends is a lack of belief in rationality. Avoid gamblers, people who believe in astrology, members of extreme religious cults, people who believe that it is possible to get something for nothing, and people with any sign at all of dishonesty. Many of these people can be quickly recognised when they assert that something is true without being willing to consider contrary evidence: they are afraid of having their beliefs changed by rational argument. Commitment to a falsehood can never help you to be happy, and there are a great many infectious memes around which involve such a commitment.

What do you read?

It is not for me to presume to tell you what books you should read, although you will find a few suggestions at the end of this book. Nor will I play the censor and name specific books to avoid. You must always make these decisions for yourself, as you must always make all decisions for yourself.

When deciding what to read, remember that the issue of who controls your life is always relevant. If you find someone saying that a particular book was so good that they couldn't put it down, be wary of reading it yourself. It may indeed be a very good book, but on the other hand, it might only be addictive without giving any real benefits. Do you really want to be "entertained" to the extent that you lose touch with reality, when your happiness is dependent upon dealing successfully with reality? More to the point, if you find that you can't put a book down when you know you should, then the reading is damaging your prospects of longer-term happiness, even if it is a very good book.

Books consist of large assemblages of memes. Some of these memes are good and useful; others are damaging. It is not too difficult to judge what sort of mix a particular book contains. It is up to you to decide whether you want the memes in a particular book to get into your brain, especially when it can be so hard to evict them. If you suspect that by reading a book you might acquire memes which could influence your behaviour in such a way as to reduce your self-control, avoid the book, no matter who recommends it to you and with what enthusiasm: it just isn't worth it.

I do not mean to suggest that you should never read what is recommended to you. Reading what other people recommend can help you to understand a great deal, including something about the person doing the recommending. It is just that it is important always to be careful about what you choose to read.

Of course, everything I have said in this section about books applies just as well to newspapers, magazines, pamphlets, and so on.

What do you watch?

Everything I said about books also applies to television, plays, films, videos and so on, but even greater care is needed because of the power of the visual image. One short glimpse of a particularly violent or erotic scene, for instance, can remain with you indefinitely. A constant diet of such things can affect your behaviour.

Could this be an argument for censorship? I think not. Censorship depends on the idea that someone else who claims to be an "authority" can properly decide what is safe to let into your brain. If you trust the censor, you are not taking responsibility for yourself and this is not good for your happiness. Also, if the censor misses something which is really bad for you, but you have suspended your own judgement, some very unpleasant memes could get into you. Finally, censors can get political and wish to suppress anything which might undermine their own livelihoods. Better to be your own censor.

Don't reinforce bad pathways

From what I have said in the last few pages, you should be able to recognise any patterns of thought or behaviour you have which tend to reduce your ability to take charge of your own life. The hard part is changing them. (Quite a lot of Chapter 10 is about breaking bad habits and replacing them with better ones, so we will not go into detail about that here.)

At this stage, you should just be able to see what there is in your life which diminishes you as a person, whether it is a habit as innocent as playing patience (or solitaire, as the Americans call it), watching television, reading pulp fiction, or wasting time with so-called friends.

Identifying a problem clearly often gets you a very long way towards solving it, and that principle applies very much in this case. Once you realise that some part of how you spend your time is actually destroying you as a person, you will find it easier to change that part of your life.

What if you don't? If you don't change it, you will repeat it. If you repeat anything, the neural pathways in the brain corresponding to it become stronger. Strengthening, reinforcing those pathways which reduce your self-control cannot help you towards happiness. Don't do it!

Feed your Brain

One of the most sensible bits of advice in the Bible is near the end of the letter to the Philippians where Paul advises his friends to fill their minds with everything good, beautiful, true and inspiring. Why should you follow this advice? Consider the alternatives: either you can deliberately fill your mind with everything evil, ugly, false and depressing, or, alternatively, you could allow more or less anything into it without making any effort at discrimination. Isn't it obvious that neither of these can help you to be happy? So, feed your brain carefully with everything which will ultimately help you towards happiness.

Good books

I have already said something about choosing your reading matter. In that section, I refrained from specific recommendations, but having just mentioned the Bible, I should just say that it is often referred to as "The Good Book" for some quite valid reasons. Admittedly, much of it is somewhat biased history, but there is a great deal to be learned from it too. It is no coincidence that it is still the world's all-time best-seller.

Not being familiar with all the scriptures of the other great religions, I am not completely sure, but it seems to me from what I have studied, that there is a great deal of good in these writings too.

Still avoiding recommending any specific works (because I do believe you have to make your own choices), I will recommend a general type of book. There are sections in many bookshops and libraries called "self-help" or "self-improvement", where you will find a choice of books well worth reading, and where you may even have found this book!

Finally, there are the great classic works of fiction. I do not mean to refer to books which are very popular because of their entertainment value, but those which are valuable because of the insights they provide and because they are thought-provoking.

Reading things of this sort will help you to see how to run your own life. Running your own life, rather than being controlled or manipulated by other people is crucial.

Truth

Why should you feed your brain with truth? The alternatives are to feed it with falsehood or to let it absorb anything without distinguishing truth from falsehood. Without knowing (as far as possible) the true state of everything relevant to any decision, you will not be able to make the best decisions.

If you make bad decisions simply because you have not troubled to feed correct information into your brain, you will not be happy. Strive, therefore, to find out as much about the true nature of everything as you reasonably can. And remember that information taken out of context can be misleading, because some people will try to influence your decisions in a way that is not good for you, and one of their techniques is to provide you with incomplete information.

You will be much happier if you make the best decisions you can, having got the most completely correct information that you can.

Beauty

Why beauty? The alternatives are ugliness and dullness.

Within sight of my window as I write this, there are some trees with the pale green leaves of early spring almost glowing in the late afternoon sunlight. There are also some rather plain houses (dull!) and a demolition site (ugly!). Obviously, the trees do a much better job of enhancing my feeling of happiness.

That, however, is not the point. Remember that this chapter is about self-control: so what is the connection between beauty and self-control? How can filling your mind with beautiful things help you to take charge of your own life? The answer to this question is rather subtle, and I have to admit that I am not sure that it is what the apostle Paul had in mind, but that doesn't really matter.

Clearly, having beauty in your life is good and desirable. You will therefore want to get away from the dull and the ugly. Your subconscious mind tends to influence your behaviour in such a way as to get you into a situation which matches what you habitually visualise. It follows that if you concentrate on that which you want to get away from (ugliness and dullness) you will find it much harder than if you concentrate on what you want to have in your life (beauty).

Therefore, fill your mind with everything beautiful and desirable. It will help you to make and stick to decisions which will help you to get these things into your life, and to keep them there.

By feeding your mind with all these good things, as Paul recommends, you will be building up neural pathways in your brain which correspond to them. Truth, beauty, health, well-being and good ideas will become part of you and part of your way of being.

The activation and reinforcement of these pathways is the very process of feeling good, of feeling the happiness which you will have attained.

Mens sana in corpore sano

It's an old Latin saying, "a healthy mind in a healthy body". You can see it either as an objective, or as an observation.

As an observation, you can see, at one extreme, that it is very hard for mentally ill people to stay physically healthy. It is also true that chronic ill health can lead to depression. Away from these extremes, you can observe that mind and body are so closely related that any disturbance to the one has implications for the other.

The objective is to keep both mind and body healthy. However, sick people can be happy; physical health is not absolutely necessary for happiness, although mental health probably is. What, then, is the relevance of physical health to happiness? There are two things.

The first of these gets us back to the theme of self-control. Controlling yourself includes controlling your body, since it is by means of your body that do the things you want to do. If your body is sick, it will not do everything that you might otherwise expect of it, and this will make it harder for you to do what you have decided you should do. It is for this reason that it makes sense to keep your body as fit as you can without becoming fanatical about it.

Secondly, if you behave in such a way as to damage your body, you will be less able to do what you want to do and what you know you ought to do. This will make it harder for you to be happy. Ultimately, if you make yourself very ill as a consequence of your own actions, achieving happiness could become very difficult.

Look after yourself!

Goals

What you do should depend on what you want. You may be able to control a car, but without knowing where you want to drive it and why, that ability is useless. Likewise, self-control is not very helpful if you don't know where you want to go in life. In fact, if you do not have any specific goals, your self-control will reduce to self-restraint: stuck in the same place, you might almost as well be adrift and out of control for all the good it will do your prospects of long-term happiness.

I said right at the beginning of this chapter that you must be able to make your own decisions for your own reasons. Knowing your goals in life is part of having reasons for the decisions you make.

I will have a great deal more to say later in the book about goals and goal-setting. What follows here is essential but not comprehensive.

The ultimate common goal

Someone once said that in the long run we're all dead. Few people, if any, have no regrets at the end of their lives. Some people, however, do die happy. That, it seems to me, is the ultimate common goal, what everyone should be aiming at: not death itself, which is not a goal, but being sure that, when death does eventually come, you won't be filled with sentences starting, "I wish I had ... "

On the way to this destination, you will, consciously or not, be setting a number of other goals. These are of two basic types, which I will call "achievement goals" and "improvement goals".

Achievement goals

An achievement goal is one which you can be definite about having completely achieved or not. It can be as simple as buying a newspaper, or as complex as building a hospital. Goals like these are either achieved or not achieved. Partly achieved is not achieved.

Going back to the title of this chapter once again, what has this got to do with self-control? Two things: firstly, in order to achieve any such goal, trivial or complex, you must have enough self-control to measure up to that goal; secondly, having such goals in your life is part of how you control yourself.

Knowing what you are aiming at helps you to choose what to do with yourself at every moment. Subconscious awareness of your goals makes this much easier.

Improvement goals

Improvement goals are harder to deal with. It is reasonable enough to aim to be better at something, but how much better? When do you ease off trying to improve one aspect of your life in order to achieve something else or to improve something else? You could, for example, set yourself a goal of getting fitter, but if you don't know where to stop, you could ruin your chances of happiness by becoming a fitness freak, never satisfied with the current level of fitness, and never paying much attention to anything else.

Are improvement goals a bad thing, then? Surely not! It is always better to be better. There are two basic ways of avoiding the pitfalls of improvement goals: firstly, if at all possible, set an achievement goal instead; secondly, keep them under review, asking yourself regularly whether this goal is helping you to be happy.

Sub-goals

Many of the goals you set for yourself, are actually sub-goals. You don't buy a newspaper just in order to have achieved the buying of a newspaper; you buy it in order to read at least part of it, which, hopefully, you are doing either in order to help you to achieve something specific, or in order to help bring about some identifiable improvement in your life. The buying of the newspaper is a sub-goal.

Whatever you are doing at any moment, you should be able to relate it easily to a sub-goal, and, perhaps with a moment's more thought, to a higher goal. If you can't do that, you are not really in control of yourself yet.

All your goals, whether achievement goals or improvement goals should be reviewed regularly. They are all in fact sub-goals. Remember that your ultimate goal is happiness, and, if you find that going for a particular goal is undermining your chances of happiness, ditch it!

Power to Control Everything

When you are fully in control of yourself, the only real limit to your control over other things is that it is impossible to defy certain laws of physics. You may choose, and if you want to be happy, you should choose, not to take control of other people or of things which belong to other people.

If ever you find yourself saying, "I can't do that", then at least one of four things is true. Either it is physically impossible ("I can't lift that steamroller" may be true), or you haven't bothered to learn how ("I can't cook" means "I have not yet learned how to cook") or you know that it would make you unhappy ("I can't break that promise" isn't quite true: it means, "I believe it would be wrong to break that promise") or you are obeying someone else's rules ("I can't park my car there" may not be strictly true.)

To achieve proper control, you must be aware of any limitation to doing what you want to do and decide consciously whether it is right to be so limited. It is, by the way, always right to accept the restrictions which come directly from the fundamental laws of physics; not accepting reality is a sure way of making yourself unhappy.

How are things controlled?

I have just suggested that, whether you should or not, you have the power to control more or less everything. How?

The physical world is very much affected by the human will. Scientists do not yet have a satisfactory theory to account for this, but if you look around you, you can see the evidence for it everywhere. The book you are reading is a consequence of my mental effort and that of countless other people, such as those who designed and built the printing presses, the paper mills and the vehicles used to transport the book to you.

Wherever you look, you will see things which came out of factories or which were painstakingly made by individuals. If you look at more or less anything in a modern home and ask yourself who made it and how, you will find that it is a consequence of someone with the will to turn an idea into reality, to change the physical world by choice.

Co-operation

Individuals, no matter how determined, rarely work alone. More is achieved by co-operation and teamwork than can be done by an individual. Co-operation arises from relationships between people. Part Three of this book is about relationships, so I will say very little about the subject here, except to point out that a great deal of the most useful co-operation between people takes the form of trade.

When I finish this book, I will do a deal with a publisher. The publisher will do other deals with printers, book wholesalers, bookshops, libraries and so on. Ultimately, I hope that you and many others will choose to buy my book. Thus I will have changed a small aspect of the world in that many copies of my words will be there, where they were not before.

All this is a consequence of my self-control working in co-operation with other people's self-control. Without this co-operation which we call trade, if I wanted thousands of copies of my words distributed around the world, I would have to make my own pens, ink and paper, write them all out and deliver them by hand. Would I also have time to grow or kill my own food, as I would have to do if there were no such thing as trade?

Who controls whom?

When people co-operate voluntarily to achieve together something which they could not achieve as individuals, we call it trade or business. There are other ways of getting people to co-operate with you. These all amount to obtaining their obedience. When you have someone's obedience, they have surrendered at least part of their own self-control to yours. You control them.

Involuntary co-operation, otherwise known as slavery, can be used to achieve things which could not be done by individuals working alone. It is said, for example, that the Pyramids of Egypt were built by slave labour. More recently, there was the agriculture of the southern United States, and the Bridge over the River Kwai. So it can be made to work, but it is less efficient than trade, and, more importantly, such achievements do not bring all the benefits to the people in charge that they might hope for.

Leaving aside the matter of parents controlling young children, which is clearly desirable, complete control of one person by another tends not to make either the controller or the controlled any happier. It can be quite thrilling having your orders obeyed unquestioningly, but it is not good for your long-term happiness, knowing that the people obeying you have surrendered their own power of self-control, which was the most precious thing they could ever have had.

Power of that sort always comes from threat of force or from trickery. Using such power can never make you happy. Having such power used against you can make you miserable, but need not necessarily completely destroy your chances of happiness.

If you are getting what you want by means of threat of force (even if you are not personally doing the threatening) or by trickery (even if you are not personally deceiving anyone) you cannot be truly happy. Happiness depends not only on controlling yourself, but also on allowing people to exercise their right to self-control and to benefit from voluntary co-operation with others.

How is co-operation brought about?

Sharing your memes

If you want someone else to do what you want them to, you need to get an idea of what you want into their mind. Ideally, that should be sufficient. If what you have in mind is beneficial both to you and to the person you want to co-operate, then they should see this and co-operate voluntarily; only if you are trying to coerce them are you likely to need to create a negative image of the consequences of not co-operating.

What you are doing is to get your scheme copied from your mind into the mind of the person you are hoping to persuade to co-operate with you. You are trying to transfer memes from your mind to theirs. Memes travel best when they carry with them an idea of how their new host is to benefit by letting them in.

The power of a compelling image

Effective advertising works in this way. Good advertising creates an image in the prospect's mind of how that prospect will benefit from buying the product. Advertising which relies on a negative image of how the prospect will suffer from not buying the product works much less well. This is partly because people subconsciously associate the negative image with the product and shy away from it. Dishonest advertising associates with the product a beautiful image which is not logically related to the benefits that the product can provide.

Probably one of the most effective dishonest advertisements of all time was Lord Kitchener's First World War "Your Country Needs You" poster.

If someone tries to persuade you to do something from which they will benefit by pointing out to you the negative consequences of not co-operating, you can be fairly sure that they are trying to threaten or manipulate you. If they conjure up in your mind delightful thoughts of how much better things will be if you co-operate, but you can't logically associate what they propose with what they suggest might be the benefits, they are probably trying to trick you. If, when you think carefully about someone else's proposal, you can deduce the benefits to them, but not to yourself, they are almost certainly trying to manipulate or trick you.

This kind of technique is much used by politicians. They promise a better world with them in power, but it is often very hard to follow the logic of their arguments. It is, however, always clear that there are definite benefits to the politicians who are the more successful persuaders.

If you want to keep control of yourself, and not be controlled by anyone else, you must be aware of all these techniques so that you can resist them. This is not to say that you should never co-operate with anyone, far from it; civilisation depends upon co-operation, voluntary co-operation, not force, threats or trickery. Nor do I mean to say that you should never seek to persuade others to co-operate with you; seeking and getting voluntary co-operation from other people will help you to achieve your goals, and you can use the power of a compelling image to help you with this, provided that you are honest and non-threatening. If you use threats or trickery yourself, however good your goals, you will make yourself unhappy.

It's what *you* do that counts

Even though you can benefit a great deal from getting other people to co-operate with you, your happiness will depend upon what you do, not upon what anyone else does or fails to do. People may disappoint you, break promises, or cheat on you, and sometimes this will hurt, but it need never destroy your happiness, provided that you have done your part honestly and conscientiously, and also provided that you have not made a rule for yourself which insists on someone else behaving as you require.

What you do is the ultimate cause of the world being changed as you require. If you want your house redecorated, you may redecorate it or you may get someone else to do it or to help you, but just sitting there wishing for new paint won't change anything.

Desire without action only undermines happiness. Do something! Do the right things and you can change the world. That is what self-control is for.

Chapter 8

Honesty and Integrity

We have already noted that in order to be happy, you must follow your conscience, and that your conscience must work with accurate information. It will not tolerate deception or inconsistency of any kind. It requires honesty and integrity, not only within yourself, but also in all your dealings with other people.

Honesty vs. Truth

Honesty does not just mean telling the truth. It is quite possible to mislead someone, even yourself, with nothing but the truth, if the truths you tell are partial or out of context. Yet you know, and everyone else knows, what honesty implies. It means never attempting to mislead anyone, even yourself, by any means, and it means never attempting to obtain anything which you do not deserve.

Courts of law

The apparent purpose of a court of law is to decide whether a crime has been committed by the accused. Sometimes this happens. Quite often, the court finds that the prosecutors have not followed certain defined procedures according to the rules, and the accused is released, never to be tried again for the same crime, regardless of guilt or innocence. Are those responsible really being honest in their quest for justice?

Some courts convict people of "crimes" where no victim can be identified. What has happened to the principle of honesty in such cases?

The traditional oath taken in courts of law is to tell "the truth, the whole truth, and nothing but the truth". Whoever first came up with these words was probably trying to formulate something like a promise to be completely honest, but I think these words are flawed. How can I promise to tell the whole truth, when I am unlikely to know the whole truth about the matter in question? Indeed, if the whole truth were known, the court shouldn't need to sit!

If every witness in a court of law is required to start by making a promise which they can't keep, is it any wonder that contempt of court occurs?

"Economical with the truth"

The now infamous phrase "economical with the truth" originated with a court witness who told no lies but who would have had great difficulty in claiming to be completely honest. Whether his honesty was undermined by the very process of taking the flawed oath is an open question. I should be very surprised if he was truly happy about the way he gave evidence.

Relativity of truth

Many people think of truth as being an absolute, in that every statement is either completely true or completely false. I believe that this is one of Aristotle's axioms, and it is very useful within the realms of mathematics and science, where it is often applicable. In other areas of life, it can be applicable, but an unswerving commitment to this idea is not always appropriate.

In fact, a statement can be true, false, partially true, self-contradictory, meaningless or untestable. Let me give an example of each:

True: Kangaroos are marsupials.

False: Every dog has at least six legs.

Partially true: Grass is green.

Self-contradictory: This is a lie.

Meaningless: The price of an atom of phlogiston is pale pink.

Untestable: Bach would have enjoyed Beethoven's music.

I have entitled this section "relativity of truth", because it is important to realise that partially true statements are more common than any other sort. "Grass is green" is more true in Ireland than in Australia, where grass is often pale brown, but it is not absolutely true anywhere; its degree of truth depends upon its context. A great many statements are like this: the thing to grasp is that one statement may be more true than another without either of them being completely true or completely false.

A higher standard

If truth is relative and depends upon context, what about honesty? Some people may disagree with me, but I am of the opinion that it is essentially impossible to be partially honest. In other words, I believe that partial honesty is basically dishonesty. This is quite different from the matter of partial truth.

A completely honest statement may be only partially true, if, for example, it is a generalisation honestly believed to be generally true. On the other hand, a completely true statement can be misleading when used by someone who is not completely honest. You can probably think of examples of this for yourself ... political speeches, perhaps?

It follows that honesty is a higher standard than truth. The honest person will never deliberately make a false statement (except, perhaps, in order to combat a criminal, and many would not even do that.) The dishonest person will use true statements (as well as false ones) for dishonest purposes.

Honesty will help you to attain happiness. Dishonesty never can. Which would you prefer?

Everyone knows what it means

There are many arguments between people over what is true and what is false. Sadly, many of these are not honest attempts to discover the truth. Much breath and paper and ink is wasted in this way. Some other arguments are between people with opposite views who fail to recognise that each view is partially true and neither view is completely true.

Worst of all, mankind has a bloody history of warfare, oppression and martyrdom over untestable assertions. All religious wars have been of this kind. The real pity is that it is possible to have people on each side who believe that they honestly believe they are right.

An apparently honest person may believe in life after death; an equally honest person may not share that belief. These two may come to blows if neither realises that the truly honest position is to be able to say something like, "I believe in life after death, but I know that it is impossible to test whether or not I am right, so someone believing the opposite can be just as honest as I am."

I said earlier that honesty differs from truth in that you can argue about what is true, but everyone knows what honesty is. This is only partially true! There is a subtle point which many people miss. If you say something, and you are asked, "How do you know?", can you always give an answer, after a moment's thought if need be? If not, do you have the humility to admit that you don't really know? If not, are you truly honest?

Integrity

Like honesty, integrity is quite easily recognised. Happiness and integrity are also closely intertwined. I suppose it might be possible for a person to have complete integrity and yet to be unhappy, but I must admit to never having known one. It must therefore be important, so let's look at it in a bit more detail.

Wholeness

In mathematics, an "integer" is also known as a "whole number". The word "integrity" really means "wholeness". Do people who lack integrity therefore lack wholeness? Have they got bits missing? If so, what are they missing? In what sense are they not whole?

Lack of integrity comes from a failure to deal successfully with some part of the reality of your life. That is what is missing. Some people block out of their awareness whole areas of their lives. Some do this because they choose not to go through the pain of the self-examination which is necessary to get to know themselves. Some others refuse to face certain issues because they would highlight contradictions in their beliefs.

Internal consistency

Your mind cannot successfully support a contradiction; this is because nature itself cannot support a contradiction. Nevertheless, some people have contradictory beliefs. They are inconsistent within themselves. Ironically, they are unaware of these contradictions. If they were aware of them, they would have to change, because the mind cannot bear awareness of a contradiction.

If your beliefs are inconsistent, there are two things you can do. Either you can recognise this, and think your way to a resolution of the contradiction, starting by asking yourself exactly how you arrived at your set of beliefs, or you can block out the awareness of the contradiction and refuse to think about it. If you block it out, you will inevitably block out some of the proper activity of your brain and you will not only lack consistency, but integrity too, because you will be incomplete as a person. This, in turn, will block your happiness.

Unfortunately, this blocking out process is not fully conscious, because if your conscious mind were to become fully aware of a contradiction, it would have to resolve it rather than suppress it. How then, does it happen? What you may find is that there is something in your life which gives you a faint feeling of unease, and so you shy away from it and avoid becoming aware of it, perhaps telling yourself you have more important things to think about, perhaps doing something mindless instead.

That feeling of unease is your clue. If you don't really feel comfortable thinking about some aspect of your beliefs or the way you live your life, then, if you really want to be happy, that is exactly what you must think about. Resolve any contradictions you have, thereby achieving internal consistency; this will free you up to achieve integrity, and then you will inevitably show ...

External consistency

We are not very much concerned in this book with what other people think of you, but it is relevant here. When you are consistent within yourself and have that wholeness known as integrity, people will notice your consistency. What is more, you will become aware that they tend to trust you, because they become aware that you are not likely to give them any nasty surprises by inconsistent behaviour.

Reliability

You will become known for your reliability. This is a two-edged sword. If you are reliable, people will tend to want to rely on you, very often because they can't rely on themselves. Relationships with other people are dealt with at much greater length in Part Three, so I won't go into much detail here, but it is worth mentioning a little danger here.

If you make rational decisions about what responsibilities you want to take on and show yourself to be reliable in these matters, this will be good for your happiness. On the other hand, if you allow people to manipulate you into taking on responsibilities which are not really in your own interests, simply because you are reliable, this will tend to undermine your happiness.

You have to be able to recognise when other people are trying to unload their own responsibilities onto you, and be blunt about pointing this out and refusing them if necessary. In the short term, this may be uncomfortable, not least for the people whose responsibilities you are refusing to adopt, but in the longer run, it will be better for all concerned.

Sine qua non

"Sine qua non" is a Latin phrase, literally meaning "without which not". Dishonesty is one of the universal barriers I mentioned at the start of this book. Honesty and integrity together are a *sine qua non* of happiness.

Chapter 9

Confidence

Happy people are confident people, and confident people are quite often happy. You will need confidence in order to be happy; it is not sufficient on its own, but it is necessary. Mostly, you need self-confidence, but you also need some degree of confidence in the rest of the world too. In particular, you need to be aware that there is quite a large degree of predictability and controllability in the material world, but we will go into that in Part Four.

This part of the book is about being happy with yourself, so we are mostly concerned here with self-confidence, but what, exactly, do we mean by that?

Etymology and Definition

The root of the word "confidence" is the Latin word "fides" meaning faith. "Confidence" literally means "faith with" something or someone, but we usually say "faith in", rather than "faith with". Actually, if you say you have faith in someone, you mean that you believe that they will keep faith with you, that they will be reliable.

As I said earlier, we are concerned at this stage more with self-confidence than anything else, so what does that entail?

Self-knowledge is a prerequisite

It is not wise to put your faith in someone you do not know. It may be reasonable to trust a stranger in certain small ways; in fact, life would be virtually impossible if we could not trust people to behave reasonably most of the time, but that is not quite the same thing. Sometimes you may need to trust your life to someone else's hands, such as when you travel by public transport, or undergo major surgery, but that is not quite the same thing either.

If you are going to trust someone else absolutely and in all circumstances, to have absolute faith in them, you had better know them very well indeed. Can you trust yourself? You should be able to after you have assimilated this book, but remember the chapter on self-knowledge!

You must know yourself before you can have faith in yourself. Self-knowledge is a prerequisite for self-confidence, and self-confidence is a prerequisite for happiness. You just cannot be happy if you are afraid to trust yourself.

Faith

I will have more to say about faith later in the book, not only later in this chapter, but also in chapters on material wealth and money, and of course when

I come to talk about religion. For now, I just want to point out that there is more to faith than trust, and that therefore there is more to self-confidence than trusting yourself.

Moving mountains

It is by means of faith (and I do not just mean religious faith) that you will change things. Even the smallest change you make in your life requires you to believe that it is possible. You would never even eat or change your clothes if you did not believe it was possible. This is faith on a very small scale, and I mention it so that you are aware that you do have at least some self-confidence.

The proverbial moving of mountains requires the same sort of faith, just on a larger scale. To do anything of any consequence, you need to believe that it can be done and that you can do it.

Just trusting yourself

When you do trust yourself both to judge things correctly and to get things done, as I hope you will after you have read this book, you will be safe from people who depend upon your gullibility and on your lack of self-confidence.

You will not be taken in by self-proclaimed "authorities". This includes many religious sects, one of whose first requirements is that you give up the ability to make your own judgements. It also includes many agents of government, and bureaucrats in large organisations of all sorts. When you get instructions from such people, always ask their reasons, and if they boil down to "I know best and you have no right to think for yourself or to question my wisdom", reject them; if you don't, it is very likely that you will regret it.

This is not to say that you should never trust someone else, but when you do, it will be because you have made the rational judgement that, in the particular circumstances, their judgement or ability is probably superior to yours. If they still let you down or trick you, you will at least know that you made the best judgement you could, and you are less likely to regret it.

You will also be safer from other people's incompetence, a form of evil which is rather commoner than malevolence or deliberate wrong-doing.

Self-image

Your self-confidence depends upon your self-image, how you see yourself. There are two aspects to this: your belief in your ability, and your sense of self-worth. To an extent, your sense of self-worth is dependent upon your belief in your ability, because it is hard to say "I deserve ... " when you have earned nothing, as might be the case if you have had no confidence in your ability.

However, your self-image is more likely to have been formed irrationally than rationally, and this can lead to all sorts of problems, which I hope I can help you to overcome.

Why you feel inadequate

As we saw in Chapter 1, a great many self-image problems start in childhood. Your parents very probably spent a good deal of time saying things to you like,

"No, you can't", " ... because I say so", "Let me do that for you", "Don't touch that – you'll only break it", and so on, thereby reinforcing your sense of inadequacy. It is even possible that you might still be being undermined by things said to you by other children when you were young. Even nick-names can go on being damaging long after they have stopped being used.

When, as an adult, you get something wrong, all these old "You're useless" voices come back and echo around your mind and, if listened to, can become self-fulfilling prophecies. It can be hard to realise that now it is *you* telling yourself you're incompetent and worthless. What you actually have are memes which need to be replaced, but how do you replace them?

Tricking yourself

The answer may be astonishingly simple. Just tell yourself the opposite! At this stage, it doesn't really matter whether you believe it, but go on telling yourself things like "You can do it", "You're great", "You're worth it" and so on. It doesn't matter too much what particular words of encouragement you use, except that it is better to avoid the word "not" because the part of your brain you will be affecting isn't really very clever and, from a sentence like "You're not useless", it might only pick up the single word "useless", which is not what you want it to do.

It is up to you how you tell yourself what a worthwhile and competent person you are. I have heard of people who stand in front of a mirror for half an hour a day shouting encouragement at themselves, but I think this is a little extreme. By all means do that if it suits you, but it can be just as effective to repeat your encouragement silently to yourself within your mind. Best of all is probably the barely audible whisper, but most important is that you use a technique you are comfortable with, because the process must feel good.

It is vital to keep on and on at it. Constant repetition is the key to setting up and reinforcing new neural pathways corresponding to these new memes, which you need to disrupt the old memes. Repetition of the new ones will also give less mental space for repetition of the bad old memes, whose corresponding neural pathways will consequently wither.

It isn't a trick after all!

Are you telling yourself things which you do not believe? Are you, perhaps, telling yourself lies? Is this trickery? Can it be justified?

The old idea that you are incompetent and worthless is very unlikely to be justifiable on reasonable grounds. Secondly, even if a rational assessment led to the conclusion that you are incompetent and worthless, this is not the final word, because you can change.

One of the mechanisms for bringing about change in your life is this trick of telling yourself that you are competent and valuable. It is not really a trick because these statements cause themselves to become more true. When you tell yourself you are competent, you will become more competent, your self-confidence will improve and you will become more competent still.

Justifiable self-confidence

As you become more self-confident, you will become more competent. Your self-confidence will therefore be more justifiable. Your work will also become more valuable, and your feeling of self-worth will improve along with this, always provided, of course, that you are earning your living honestly. If you are not earning your living honestly, your improved self-confidence will make it easier for you to change your career so as to earn an honest living, and thereby give yourself a sense of self-worth which you can justify.

The positive feedback loop

By now, you should be able to see how the whole process works. You give yourself a sense of self-confidence which may at first be hard to justify on past performance. This is justified by your improved performance. This improved performance enhances your feelings of self-worth. This in turn gives you added self-confidence which helps you to improve still further.

As you get more competent and self-confident, you tell yourself how well you are doing, and then you can get better and better. The only limits to your improvement are the pinnacles of human achievement or any lower limits which you choose, or to which you are genuinely constrained by physical circumstances.

What other people think is not a relevant consideration here, unless you so choose. Be wary of so choosing, however. If you choose to be limited in your achievements by concerns over what other people will think, then either you are being manipulated by someone, or your sense of self-worth needs further improvement, or both. In any such case, your chances of happiness will be impaired if you make it dependent on what someone else thinks, a matter which is not directly in your control.

You can be sure that when you start on this feedback loop wherein your confidence builds your competence and your competence builds your confidence, there should be no stopping you.

Faith is Causal

People who make changes in the world, whether small or great, have to believe that the changes are possible. The alternative to this kind of faith is fatalism or determinism, the simple belief that what will be will be and that we are powerless to affect anything. A quick glance at the modern world will show that fatalism is an error: all the artefacts in the world are the consequences of people's belief that things can be changed and things can be done.

How do things get done?

In order to get anything done, you must first believe that there is more than one possible future. This is a consequence of believing that you have the power of choice. The alternative futures which face you include ones in which you will have done whatever it is you are considering doing, and those in which you will not have. Your decision to do something (and then the doing of it) carry you forward into one set of possible futures, and not into the other.

Collapsing possibilities

As each moment arrives, a large number of possible futures collapse into a single actual present, which becomes the unchangeable past. You and I influence this process by the exercise of the unique human power called the will. It is by exercising the power of your will to make choices that you affect the way in which all the possible futures collapse onto a single present moment.

The choices you make, whether consciously or not, come from your system of beliefs. The faith you have in yourself, or in anyone else for that matter, has a direct influence on the future. That is to say that of all the possible futures at any given moment, the one which becomes the present and then the past is chosen by people on the basis of what they believe to be desirable and possible.

How to choose your world

Year by year, hour by hour and second by second, you are making choices or failing to make decisions. Exactly how you do this depends upon your vision of the future and what you believe to be possible. What this means is that the future you will have depends upon your faith in it.

If you hold constantly in your mind a beautiful vision of the future, backed up by faith in it, the choices you make will automatically lead you towards it, or something like it.

If it Can be Done, You Can Do it

As the author Napoleon Hill says, what the mind can conceive and believe, the mind can achieve.

If you can imagine something being done, it follows that you believe it must be possible for someone to get it done. If you believe it is possible for someone, there is probably no reason why that someone could not be you.

If you believe that something should be done, and can be done by someone, but can't be done by you, then the most likely explanation is your lack of confidence. If you are really physically incapable of the task, not just fearful of it, then you will need to elicit the co-operation of other people to get it done. If you don't think you can do that, then you are certainly lacking in confidence, and that can be overcome!

Dream big dreams

Building your confidence and building your happiness are very closely tied together, but it is no good being confident without any idea as to purpose. Sitting there thinking, "I could do anything", but not being specific as to what you want to do, gets you nowhere.

As a child, you may have been told off for daydreaming, and this may make it harder for you to daydream properly as an adult. You may have to silence some old voices in order to be comfortable with it, but regular and frequent daydreaming will help you to achieve happiness, provided that you follow a few simple guidelines

Firstly, only dream about what is good and right, and what you believe ought to happen. Dream about the way the world should be and your part in improving it, never allowing any destructive thought to enter.

Secondly, do not let yourself be limited by any feeling of inadequacy, incompetence or worthlessness. Aim high, thinking of how life would be in a truly ideal world. Utopia is OK!

Thirdly, if you find yourself thinking of what someone else has but you haven't, imagine yourself having what they have if you like, but don't dream of them being without, because that is a destructive thought, which will not help you to be happy.

Last, and by no means least, enjoy it! This is how the world ought to be, and how you are going to help make it. That is good, it is fun, and it is worth revelling in. Furthermore, the enjoying of this process will help your subconscious mind to work to bring about what you are imagining.

In the words of the song, "You gotta have a dream: if you don't have a dream, how you gonna have a dream come true?"

Believe them

Having your dreams is necessary, but it is not sufficient. To have your dreams come true, the next thing you must do is to believe in them.

At first, this is not easy. You know that daydreams are imaginary, and that what is in the imagination is not real (in the sense of being physically tangible). How, then can you get yourself to believe in your daydreams?

The key to this is to realise that your imagination is conjuring up images of the possible. Difficult, maybe, but possible. What the rest of your mind has to do is to verify that the dream is desirable in every sense, and to work out a way of bringing it to reality. The imagination can also help with this bit: it may see ways of doing things which the intellect hasn't managed to work out.

Now you have a dream and you can see how to make it come true. What next?

Do the necessary

Dreams and plans are completely worthless without action, and the action must be purposeful. All your wakeful life, you are either doing something which helps you towards realising your dreams, or you are not. Activity which does not help you in this way is no good. Inactivity likewise. The two things to avoid are action without purpose, and purpose without action.

Do the necessary! This includes keeping a careful watch on what you are doing, and checking it against your dreams. You must keep dreaming your dreams, but not to the exclusion of doing what you have to do about bringing them to fruition.

Tenacity

Tenacity means sticking at it. Keep going. Hold on to your ideals. At times you will feel that you are getting nowhere, because your progress is so slow, but sticking at it will keep you going in the right direction.

Having said that, remember that it is your dreams of how life should be that are worth sticking to, not necessarily a particular method which you might have chosen a while ago. You do not need to stick to something that you have found to be ineffective! Misplaced tenacity can amount to pig-headedness or even bigotry. Success depends upon being willing to try a new method to achieve your aims if you find that your current method isn't working.

Keep to your dreams. Work for them. Keep thinking and dreaming about how better to bring about what you want. Don't just sit there, but keep up the action. That is how you will change things, and change them for the better. In your own very personal sense, this is wealth creation, and it is very large part of the process of creating happiness.

Start Small and Build Up

The main disadvantage with dreaming big dreams is that they can seem out of reach. In the short term, of course, they are out of reach; otherwise, we would call them plans rather than dreams.

There is a Chinese proverb which says that a journey of a thousand miles starts with a single step. You must not be put off taking that first step on account of the millions of steps to follow, because you have to start from where you are, no matter where it is that you want to go. The more steps you take, the closer you get to your destination.

Taking steps

Each step you take on the "journey of a thousand miles" brings you new knowledge, a new skill, or maybe a new material possession. These are all things which you own, which are within your sphere of control. At the very least, each step brings you a new memory, something to add to your store of experience, which you can use later in the journey.

Have you ever gone on a long walk over unfamiliar territory to a place you have never visited before? When you do this, you have in your imagination an idea of what your destination might look like, but at the start of the journey you cannot see it with your physical eyes. Likewise, you probably know from a map, or from directions you have been given, that there are various landmarks you will pass *en route.*

As each landmark comes within sight, you feel that it is within reach: there are not too many more steps to take to reach that point. In life's journey, there are similar times, when you feel that, although you haven't attained a particular sub-goal yet, it is at least within reach, in that you can see exactly how to get there.

As you attain each sub-goal, or reach each landmark, you add this to your collection of things done, achieved or owned. Then you go on to the next one. At each stage, you concentrate on the next few steps to be taken, where you can see your way, and eventually, your final destination comes within sight, and you can reach it.

Self-congratulation

One step in a journey of a thousand miles may not feel like very much but it is important not to get discouraged by the smallness of the step. You need, therefore, to make the step feel good. You do this by self-congratulation.

How you congratulate yourself is up to you. It can be enough just to say to yourself, "Well done! Keep it up!" The important thing is to let yourself feel good about achieving something, no matter how small. In fact, making yourself feel good about really small achievements can be very helpful. Every little step on that long journey is worth celebrating because it brings you closer to your dream.

By celebrating, I do not mean throwing an expensive party and sharing the great news with all your friends. There are times for this, but your small achievements are a private matter, and your celebration should be internal. Just tell yourself that you are doing the right things, and enjoy the fact that what you are doing is right.

If something is right, it will feel good anyway. All I am saying is that you must enjoy the good feeling! This will help you to continue doing the right things. Your confidence will grow, you will grow as a person, and your dreams will come within reach.

One goal leads to another

When all goes well, you will reach your goal and your dreams will come true, but what then? I said earlier that the only limits should be the pinnacles of human achievement, but some people have created new such pinnacles. Many people do things which have never been done before. You could join them!

When your dreams have come true, that is not the end of the story. You can dream new and bigger dreams, above and beyond what has gone before. Then go for it. Much of your joy in life will come from the journey rather than from the achievement itself. When you have completed your journey of a thousand miles, you can start another if you want to.

Coping with setbacks

What if all does not go well? Then you are part of the human race! None of us has everything go right in every respect all of the time.

You can learn a great deal from Thomas Edison. One of his great dreams was the electric light, but he did not just sit down one day, design it, make one, and switch it on. That would have been a great achievement, but what he actually did was even greater. Before he came up with an electric light which worked, he built over a thousand prototypes which did not, and carefully documented every failure! When asked about this, he said that there had been no failures, but that he now knew a thousand ways not to make an electric light.

It was Edison's self-confidence and tenacity which brought him to the invention of the electric light which he had dreamed of, and that has changed the world. When you have setbacks, as you will, remember Edison's prototypes, and how his attitude to them changed the world. He too was a human being, just like you.

BEING HAPPY

Whether you model your behaviour on that of Thomas Edison, or any other great achiever, or whether you have your own ideas of how you want to do things, one of the most useful skills you can learn is ...

Chapter 10

How to Change Yourself

Reading the last few chapters, you may have come to realise that, in order to be happy, you must be able to change. Changing is hard. There are many reasons for this, some of which will become clear in this last chapter of this part of the book, but we will be more concerned with how to do it rather than why it takes effort.

It may be difficult at times, but it is possible, and, if a change is desirable, then the effort will be worth it. If there are barriers to happiness in your life, you must change, no matter how hard it might seem. The rewards will make all the effort worthwhile.

That's enough exhortation, let's get on with the real business of how you can get yourself to bring about change in your life.

First, Forgive Yourself

There are things in your past which you regret. (If there aren't, why are you reading this book?) Even though your regrets tell you that you should change, having them can make it harder for you to change. This is a strange feature of human nature which is not very easy to understand, but you can deal with it. What you have to do is to forgive yourself for everything which is past.

Destructive anger

It can be hard to forgive. If you can see that someone has done something wrong, and you can see the damage done, it is often right to be angry. If the person who has done wrong is you, then you can be angry at yourself.

Being angry at yourself is of limited usefulness. It can be helpful insofar as it gives you motivation to change (that, after all, is what anger is for) but anger at yourself can easily go too far and become destructive.

When you are so angry at yourself that you spend all your time telling yourself how evil, wicked, lazy, incompetent and worthless you are, you won't give yourself a chance to make things better. This is when anger becomes destructive. What actually happens then is that your subconscious mind keeps hearing all these negative statements, and then makes sure that they remain true, or even become more true. Your behaviour deteriorates.

Nobody is perfect

What you need to do instead, is to accept that you are not perfect, as nobody is perfect. All the good in the world is done by imperfect people, and you can be one of those doing the right things, no matter how wrongly you have done things in the past.

You will still not be perfect. You will still do some things which you will regret. Everybody does. The key is to accept that this is natural. This does not mean that you can become complacent and continue with your old bad habits, or allow yourself complete latitude in all matters of good and evil.

What it does mean is that, having done something wrong, you can take the consequences, which will always include some misery for you, resolve not to make that particular mistake again, and get on with the future. Don't go on for ever punishing yourself for some ancient imperfection!

Giving yourself another chance

Getting on with the future means giving yourself another chance. You may have done things wrong in the past, but that does not mean that you have to do them wrong again. You might, but you don't have to. If you do, then accept that you still aren't perfect, forgive yourself again, make a new resolution, and give yourself another chance, and another, and another, and another, ...

Repentance

In Chapter 6 (on the conscience) we came across the idea of repentance. As I pointed out there, repentance is a very old-fashioned word, which just means re-thinking. In the way it is usually used, it means rather more than just "having a re-think". It has connotations of religious conversion, Roman Catholic confessional boxes, and medieval penances, some of which connotations are not useful. Nevertheless, it is so important for happiness that we will go over the whole subject again, this time in greater detail.

When things are not going right, and especially when you find yourself feeling guilty, repentance may be what you need. I think this is best described as reprogramming the mind.

When a piece of computer software is not working properly, and the computer needs to be re-programmed, the re-programming has to be preceded by a careful analysis of what went wrong and why, so as to be sure of overcoming the problem. It is the same with the mind. If you are going to re-program your mind, the major re-think which we call repentance, has to be done carefully. It starts with a process traditionally known as "reflection".

What have you done?

Reflection is necessary for happiness. What it means is looking at your life, what you have done, how you are living, how you are feeling and so on. It is necessary for happiness for two reasons: firstly, even if you have no barriers to happiness, you will not feel the joy you deserve for living well, unless you consciously see and enjoy the good things; secondly, if you have some barrier to happiness, you will not be able to get rid of it without looking at it.

It is the second of these reasons which mostly concerns us here, particularly when the barrier is the problem of guilt, although virtually everything here can be applied to other barriers. The process of reflecting on the causes of guilt feelings is uncomfortable, but, if you are going to rid yourself of these painful feelings, you have to go through this pain: this is necessary to achieve happiness in the long term. Any alternative is like taking paracetamol when you really need surgery.

If you are feeling guilty, you must ask yourself why. This starts with looking at everything you have done recently. If you have the excellent habit of daily reflection, you may not need to look much further back than what you have done (or failed to do) today. You will probably find that something you have done recently, or some recent omission, will be clearly associated in your mind with the feeling of guilt.

If you can't find anything recent, then you need to go further and further back into your past to find the root of the guilt feelings. In some cases, you might need professional help with this.

Most likely, though, you will find something in the last few hours or few weeks, something which you have done or failed to do, with which guilt feelings are clearly associated. This may or may not be the true cause of the problem. You haven't finished yet! There is more analysis to do before you get to the re-programming.

Any bad consequences?

Having found some aspect of your behaviour which carries guilt feelings with it, you must look at that behaviour carefully, with one question in mind. The question is, "What were the consequences?"

There can be any number of possible causes for your feelings of guilt, any number of actions or omissions on your part, and all manner of possible consequences, so obviously, I can't go into every conceivable permutation here, but the whole lot can be divided into three broad classes. The observation which enables us to do this is that every crime has a victim and there is no such thing as a victimless crime.

The question is therefore: "Who is the victim?" The three classes of answer we are concerned with become clear when we look harder at the consequences of whatever it was that was causing the feelings of guilt. Go looking for the victim!

Sometimes you can see clearly how your wrong-doing or omission has hurt somebody, maybe you. If someone is physically or materially worse off, then you have found the victim, and this part of the process is complete. If it is only someone else's feelings which have been hurt, then we might have found the victim or we might have a more subtle case, which will be easier to understand after we have looked at what is going on when no victim can be found.

If you cannot find the victim of your apparent crime, the chances are very good that the crime is quite different from what you think, and that you are the victim. When you are the victim of someone else's manipulation, you can find yourself feeling guilty when you have done nothing more than break the rules which they have set up for you in order to serve their own ends.

This brings us back to the case of hurt feelings. Only you can judge, when you seem to have hurt someone else's feelings, whether you have really done something objectively wrong, or whether you are being manipulated by the person whose feelings you think you might have hurt.

Now we have identified the crime, your action or omission, and we have identified the victim, you or someone else. The next stage in the analysis is the question ...

What should you do next time?

If you are your own victim, that is you have done or omitted something and you are worse off as a consequence, this is a straightforward case of natural justice. You are taking the consequences of your own decisions and defaults. Obviously, if you want different consequences, it is up to you to make different decisions and follow them through with different actions.

If someone else really is the victim, much the same applies, but there is a bit more to it. Next time, do things differently so as not to do the damage. That much is obvious, but you can still be left with the guilt feelings associated with the past. Making amends as best you can does help but it is not a complete solution. Your guilt feelings in these circumstances are friends: they tell you to do things differently when you need to, and when it is certain that you will do things differently in the future, they can go away.

If you are the victim of someone else's manipulation, what you need most is the courage of your own convictions. If you think that what you are doing is really right, but someone else has been trying to make you feel guilty about it, just do what you know to be right, and let the would-be manipulators take the consequences. Natural justice will follow its course and the real criminals will suffer for their crimes. You do not need actively to do anything different: you just need to change your interpretation of what is going on.

Is anything stopping you?

Your analysis is now nearly complete. You know how your guilt feelings started. You know who the victim is. You know what to do differently next time, even if it is just looking at things differently. The only remaining question is, "What is stopping you?"

Your answer should be, "Nothing!" Most likely, though, a more honest answer would be lack of will, or maybe lack of faith.

It may be that you believe that something is actually preventing you from doing what you believe to be right. This is an error. Anything which is truly impossible can never be right, and trying to do the truly impossible is a waste of effort, which is always wrong, and can never make you happy. (Admittedly, you may sometimes have to struggle against almost overwhelming odds, and you may sometimes not succeed in your efforts, but that is different; in this case, you are doing what you believe to be right, it is just that your efforts are not bringing about everything that you are trying for, and you almost certainly took that as a conscious risk to start with.) If you just believe that it is impossible for you to follow your conscience, you are lacking in faith, or, rather, you have a negative faith, which you need to change.

Re-programming the mind

Whether you need to do things differently knowing that nothing is stopping you, or you recognise that you are short on willpower or faith, or you can now see that you only need to interpret things differently, your next job is to re-program your mind.

This is the kind of re-think which is known as repentance, the life-changing, world-changing change of mind. When you do this thoroughly, you can leave the whole past behind and start again afresh. Some people call this being "born again", but that phrase has so many unhelpful connotations that I think it is best avoided, and repentance of this sort is not the exclusive preserve of the fundamentalist Christians who describe themselves as born again.

Very often it is not necessary to drop the whole past and start completely afresh, even though it is always possible. Usually, it is best to keep most things and confine your repentance to a small area of your life which is giving you trouble.

Either way, you have to get your mind to behave differently, because it is from the behaviour of your mind that all your behaviour and your interpretation of it stems. Getting your mind to behave differently is what a great deal of this book, and all of the rest of this chapter is about. Read on!

Eliminate the Negative

Because we usually see change as something which happens to us against our will, we see it as unpleasant. Changes we bring about in our own lives are much easier and hugely more satisfying than those imposed upon us from outside, but we don't often see that, and part of us inside just objects to change anyway.

What you will find, especially when you first start to make real changes, is that your mind throws up all sorts of stumbling blocks. Some of these appear as conscious "I can't" thoughts, others just as negative feelings about change, and still others as a lack of willpower. You will have to identify and eliminate these negative thoughts and feelings.

You will also have to eliminate from your life, or at least greatly reduce your contact with, all the negative external influences on you which make it harder for you to change.

Recognising everything of this sort which needs to be eliminated from your life is up to you. All I will do here is point out a few typical barriers to change and show how to deal with them.

Letting go of guilt

Guilt feelings can be useful but they can also get in your way. It is ironic that the guilt feeling, like any sort of pain, is a signal to you that you need to change something in your life, but it makes the change harder, because it is such a negative and demotivating feeling. There is a way to deal with this.

Firstly, you identify whether the guilt is earned or unearned. As we saw earlier, when you identify the source of the guilt, it should become clear whether you have done something genuinely wrong or whether you are suffering unearned guilt feelings because of someone else manipulating you.

If it is the latter, you can just let the guilt feeling go. You may find that, as it goes, its place is taken immediately by anger. Anger itself is a negative feeling and can be demotivating if you can't see how to direct it, or if you feel that directing it at its cause is fruitless: there is no point in being angry at someone who has already shown that they care so little about your feelings that they will use them to manipulate you! Anger is an emotion which exists to give you the motivation to change; in this case, it should give you the motivation to change how you perceive those who have been manipulating you, and thereby become free of their influence.

If your guilt is genuinely due to you, you can still let go of it, subject to one essential condition. That condition is repentance. The guilt is there as a natural part of you, giving you the motivation to change so as to be happier, but it only works as it should if you recognise it, accept it, decide how you need to change, resolve to change in that way, and then let go of the guilt. That last stage is vital. The actual change will be impeded if you are still lugging around your burden of guilt after it has fulfilled its purpose. Drop it!

Identifying bad influences

Are there people in your life still living in a way you have just realised is objectively wrong? If you have just discovered, for example, that you have been making your living dishonestly and that you need to change this in order to become happy, the chances are very high that many of your "friends" and colleagues are living just as dishonestly, but with more effective blinkers.

It is not your task to rip off other people's blinkers so that they can see the evil they are doing and get their own lives better in order. (That is one of the purposes of this book, so I suppose you could always buy more copies and give them to people whose happiness you care about, but that is not the issue here.) Your task, having thrown your own blinkers away, is to make sure that other people living dishonest lives do not keep their influence over you.

Have the courage of your convictions and do not be influenced by the old and futile defences of evil, such as ... "Everybody does it", "If we didn't, someone else would", "Idealism just isn't practical", "They won't miss it", "Just one more", and so on. These are easy to recognise. Identifying the people who think along such lines can be a bit harder because often they are too subtle to use such obvious rationalisations of their evil, and very often they are not even aware of the harm they are doing because, unlike you, they have never dared to think through the consequences of how they are living their lives.

Having identified the people, though, you must get their influence out of your life. Ostracism is the only effective defence against people like that.

I have used the example of dishonesty because it is often hard to recognise, but there are other destructive lifestyles too. Maybe you should take a second look at your drinking partners and ask whether their influence on your life is good. What about your other friends?

Identifying bad habits

I just mentioned drinking again. There is also gambling, pornography, and all sorts of other ways of numbing the mind, such as excessive television or a fanatical interest in sport. I have mentioned all these things before, so why am I bringing them up again?

Your next job is to eliminate your bad habits. We will come very soon to the methods you can use to get rid of them, but how do you recognise them in the first place?

If you just ask yourself what your bad habits are, you may not get the whole answer. It is much better to ask yourself what all the things you do regularly are, and write down the answers. Then look at the list, asking yourself for each item on it, whether that habit can hinder your quest for happiness in any way. Any such habit is a bad habit, even if it is harmless in itself, but just makes other changes for the better more difficult to bring about.

Obliterate your Bad Habits

Perhaps the hardest but most useful kind of change you can bring about in your life is to eliminate your bad habits. Of course, you may be one of those especially virtuous people who has no bad habits, in which case, you can skip this section, but most of us have some kind of habitual behaviour we would rather do without, whether it is smoking, drinking, gambling, or something less harmful.

The "occasions of sin"

Here is another old-fashioned concept, which is useful in the modern world, despite its horrid old name, "occasion of sin". It is, I think, best understood by way of example.

Let us suppose that one of the bad habits you want to eliminate from your life is a small line you have in gambling. On your way to work and back every day, you walk past the shop where they sell the lottery scratch cards. Maybe you know that unearned wealth never brings happiness so the jackpot would not be really useful. Maybe you understand that the odds are so heavily stacked against you that almost any remotely realistic investment in your own business would stand a much better chance of making you a millionaire. Maybe you even understand that you do it just for the short-lived thrill of the rare occasions when you get back twice or even five times your stake, and that that short-lived thrill does nothing for your level of happiness.

Nonetheless, the temptation is still there. Just one more? Could it be the jackpot this time? The good feeling of winning might not last, but it would be good wouldn't it?

What do you do about all this? It is not the whole answer, but one of the most helpful things you can do is to recognise that that shop is an "occasion of sin". It is one of the negatives you need to eliminate from your life in order to help yourself to change. In this case, you have to change your route to work, perhaps just by crossing the road.

Mind the gap

When you do manage to stop a behaviour which has been a bad habit, there is a terrible temptation to slip back into it. It is as if one piece had been removed from a jigsaw puzzle. There is a gap, and it has to be filled, and the shape of the hole is exactly the shape of the habit which has been removed from it: this is what fits most easily! The only way to resist a return to the old habit is to develop a new behaviour which, as it were, plugs up the hole so that the bad old habit can't get in. This is why ex-smokers often get fat when they replace their smoking habit with an extra eating habit.

Sensible things to do

The last thing you want is for a bad old habit to be replaced with a worse new habit, and therefore it would seem logical to find something sensible to do with the time and energy you used to spend so badly. This is a fine idea, and great if you can get it to work. The difficulty is that most bad habits give an instant reward, whereas the sensible things which you might choose to do instead give little or no instant reward, so you are left feeling frustrated in the short term, and very tempted to return to your bad old ways.

Silly things to do

Why choose something sensible? It may seem very worthy, but this is no good if it just doesn't work. Since the objective is to get rid of something nasty, it is fair enough to replace it with something harmless but frivolous. Anything which generates a laugh is a good idea, since a laugh is the quickest and one of the best rewards. Do you want examples? Think them up for yourself: remember that the best way to happiness is always to solve your own problems, rather than to follow other people's ideas without thinking; and anything you think up for yourself will be valuable to you in a special way, a way which will help you to break the old habit, which was probably not one of your own invention!

Smash the old jigsaw

The gap in the jigsaw puzzle is most easily replaced by the piece which you removed from it. This ceases to be true if you smash up the whole puzzle. If you make changes to all the things that surrounded the bad old habit, it will be easier to resist a return to the way things were. You may need to change your circle of friends, or maybe even your job or the place where you live.

Building new patterns

Of course, it is no good just destroying the bad old habit or even the bad old habit and its environment. Unless you build anew, the old stuff will tend to grow back into the gap. The old neural pathways are there in the brain and can easily be reactivated unless they are, as it were, recycled. You have to build new habits to replace old habits, and if you have had to change your environment to help you to break an old habit, you will have to work hard at your new environment so as to help you to build new and better habits.

Reward and reinforcement

We will come back to the subject of building habits soon, but it is as well to mention here the fact that a new habit needs a short-term benefit to help it to develop. It is all very well telling yourself that you will be glad of your new habit in a few decades time, but this just won't help you much.

What really will help is some kind of instant gratification which you can link in some way to the new habit. This is, after all, how the bad old habits got themselves established. on the basis of short term benefit with no regard to the long term cost. How Jo you give yourself instant gratification? Strange as it may seem, it can be sufficient just to take a moment to look at what you have done and tell yourself how well you are doing; you don't have to do this out loud, but it can help. This kind of reward, or anything else you choose for yourself, helps you to reinforce the new habit, and gives you something which will help you to repeat it; and repetition is the key to building any new neural pathway, whether it is for a habit or for a skill.

Do What You Fear

If there is something you know you ought to do, or would very much like to do (and there shouldn't be any difference!), but you are afraid to do it, what do you do? Very often the answer is to do it anyway, despite your fears.

That answer on its own, however, is too trite. We need to look at the whole issue of fear a bit more closely. If you do do what you fear, you will never be able to see life in quite the same way again. You will have reprogrammed your mind, in such a way as to change yourself. Provided that you make intelligent choices, the change will be for the better.

Real perils

By making intelligent choices, I mean that it is unlikely to be useful to choose to do something physically dangerous, just because it is dangerous. Some people do do this, and they get a thrill each time they survive an unprecedented peril, but the thrill doesn't last: like drug addicts, they want more and bigger thrills until they get to the one they don't survive. If you don't survive the danger you have faced, it is still true that you will never be able to see life in quite the same way again, but that is not what we are aiming at!

Bravery

It can be right to do something which you know to be actually dangerous, if you are taking a calculated risk, intending to achieve something good which you judge to be worth the risk. This is what we know as bravery. It is not to be confused with foolhardiness, which is a refusal to be honest with yourself about what the dangers are.

To a limited extent, this idea of bravery can include doing dangerous things apparently just because they are dangerous. If your objective is to build that particular kind of self-confidence known as courage, in order to use it later to achieve something else which you want to achieve, then you are still taking a calculated risk for a definite purpose, even though it might look to other people as if you are just hooked on the thrills, and you must always be aware of the danger of becoming hooked like that.

Whenever you do something brave, and survive it, you will become stronger in spirit. You will be better able to achieve what you want.

Irrational fears

If you are afraid to do what you believe to be right, the first thing is to look squarely at your fear, and ask yourself what it is exactly that you are afraid of. You might, at first, be afraid to do even this, but you only have to remember that looking at your fears does nothing other than improve your self-knowledge, and, as we have seen, self-knowledge can't harm you.

As I said earlier, fear of physical injury, illness or death is natural, so, if you can see exactly how doing what you fear could quite probably lead to such dangers, then your fear is rational and to be respected. Note the crucial words "quite probably" in that sentence: you must judge these probabilities as rationally and logically as you can. Risk assessment is quite difficult, and it is not what this book is about, but you must understand that it is not rational to be afraid of very remote physical dangers. Everyone has to have at least a little bit of courage for everyday life. Crossing the road does not require much of what we call bravery, even though it probably represents the greatest physical danger faced by most people in the civilised world.

If you cannot honestly explain to yourself or to someone else exactly how doing what you fear will quite probably lead to you getting hurt, then your fear is irrational.

I have not mentioned fear of emotional pain, because it is not really relevant in this context. We are talking about doing what you know to be right. If you overcome any sort of fear in order to do the right thing, you will feel so good afterwards that any emotional pain which you might have feared will hold no sway.

Smashing the bogey

When you do something you fear and find that it did not hurt after all, or that the discomfort was hugely outweighed by the good feelings which came from the knowledge of having done the right thing, the little meme inside you which used to say, "Don't do that, it might hurt" will be shown up as a complete fraud.

A meme of that sort cannot survive when you know it is telling lies, it just will not get the repetition necessary to support the neural pathways it needs. Putting the same thing in more old-fashioned language, that little devil will have been exorcised. You have smashed the bogey of irrational fear, and then ...

New freedoms

... you are free! You are free of a nasty little trap which was stopping you from doing everything you always wanted to. You are free to enjoy life without worrying about nameless fears. Most importantly, you have discovered that doing the right thing always feels good, even if you were afraid to do it beforehand, and you are free to enjoy that feeling with a clear conscience.

Enjoying that clear-conscience feeling of having done the right thing (despite your fears) is right, and good, and the very foundation of happiness. Revelling in it will help you to repeat the pattern of doing the right thing, building up the best possible habit in life, and changing yourself in the very best possible way, into the happy person you ought to be.

Building New Habits

Happiness is heavily dependent upon your habits. Bad habits will make you unhappy, and good habits will help you to be happy. This is, in fact as good a definition of good habits and bad habits as you will find. Building good new habits will therefore help you very much on your way to happiness, but this involves ...

Necessary work

No good habit is ever developed simply by deciding that it would be a good idea. You have to work at it. The first stage of this work is thinking. What do you want to do? I can't answer this for you, but you probably know by now what you want to do for yourself, and what new good habits you want to develop.

The next really hard bit is starting! You have to remove any barriers there are to your potential new habit, and this may involve some one-off changes. Bringing those about may involve some work, but this may not be as hard in itself as starting with the new habit. You may just have to force yourself at first.

Repetition is vital

Once having started, the next thing is repetition. This is physiologically necessary. You have to keep repeating your new behaviour in order to lay down and reinforce the neural pathways which have to be there in order to keep the habit going. This is always true for any habit (good or bad) and any knowledge or skill. The old saying is that practice makes perfect, and there is a great deal of truth in it. In the case of a habit, practice makes possible: if you don't practise, it just cannot be a habit!

Self-congratulation

At first, it may seem that practising takes a huge effort of will, and so it might, but there is a trick to make it a little easier, and that is to congratulate yourself each time you enact your new behaviour. Just saying "Congratulations" to yourself in a formal kind of way is not likely to be effective; it would ring hollow, and could act as a turn-off. No, the idea is just to let yourself feel good about having done something good; that really can help.

Enjoy the consequences

Part of the feeling good about your new behaviour can and should come directly from seeing the good consequences of what you are doing differently. Building new good habits usually involves choosing a behaviour which has a short-term cost for a long-term benefit, so you might think that you cannot see the good consequences. It is because there is some truth in this that the self-congratulation method has value, but it is not entirely true to say that you can't see the good consequences in the short term: you can imagine them. This is not a pretence; it is an application of the idea of creative visualisation, and it is one which will help you to become a better person, and happier with yourself, as you develop new and better behaviours.

PART THREE

Being Happy With Other People

Very few people choose to live the solitary life of a hermit. Solitary confinement is often thought of as a particularly harsh punishment. Happiness may not be entirely dependent upon having good relationships with other people, but we are social animals, and relationships are fundamental to our nature.

If you are truly happy with yourself, you will find relationships with other people much easier. Also, if your relationships are healthy, your own general sense of well-being will be enhanced, and this is good for your happiness.

It also helps to be aware that there are people who try, consciously or not, to undermine other people's happiness for purposes of their own. Recognising this kind of enemy will help you to defend yourself and maintain your happiness regardless.

Being happy with others, whether they are enemies or friends, depends upon understanding others.

"One thing in life is more certain than taxes and just as certain as death: the sooner you make new friends, the sooner you'll have old ones."

Eric Berne

Chapter 11

Understanding Others

In the same way as being happy with yourself requires self-knowledge, being happy with other people requires knowledge and understanding of them. Some of your understanding of other people will come from your self-knowledge: you can assume that other people are in many ways similar to you, but you must remember that everyone is an individual. You will, therefore, always have only ...

Incomplete Understanding

... so if you ever find yourself thinking, or, even worse, saying, that you understand someone completely, correct yourself. You cannot know anyone better than you know yourself, and we have already seen that you have to put some effort into achieving a useful level of self-knowledge. Yet sometimes someone will say to someone else, ...

"I can read you like a book"

Has anyone ever said that to you? How did it feel? It is a put-down. It is never completely true. It is said in order to belittle the hearer. It usually just creates resentment, because that saying is just a very weak and transparent tool of manipulation, which, in practice, often does more to undermine the speaker than the hearer.

So, you can't really read anyone "like a book", but what kind of understanding can you have? This comes in four broad categories, for reasons which may have to do with the structure of the brain.

The left hemisphere of the brain (usually) handles language, logic, mathematics, and pretty much everything we refer to as "thinking". The other hemisphere deals with art, images, dreams, and pretty much everything we refer to as "feeling". Generally, the former is slower and more precise, whereas the latter acts extremely fast but is not so careful about details.

Understanding thoughts

The first type of understanding comes from thinking about someone else's thoughts. This is what you are doing now, reading my book. If the left hemisphere of my brain has done its work well, my words should be clear. If yours does its work well, you will understand me. The same sort of thing goes on whenever people communicate honestly and straightforwardly by means of language.

Something very similar, and in the same general category, occurs when you stop and ask yourself what someone else is thinking, even when they don't want to tell you. Thinking about someone else's thoughts, whether they want you to or not, will help you towards this category of understanding.

Understanding feelings

I will call the second category I want to consider "understanding feelings". Do not confuse this with empathy, which I will come to shortly, where you use your feelings to understand someone else's, even to share them. What I want to consider here is the intellectual analysis of what you think someone else is feeling.

You can get a very particular kind of understanding of someone by trying to analyse their feelings. There are a number of basic emotions, such as joy, fear, anger and pain, and often it is possible to deduce the causes of whatever mix of these someone is evidently feeling.

This type of understanding is valuable, whether or not the person being understood actually likes the idea.

Intuition

The third category, using your right hemisphere to understand someone else's left, comes from that power which is sometimes called "intuition" or "insight", and sometimes "jumping to conclusions".

It is a power which you use unconsciously, but which can be enhanced by the use of conscious thought. What usually happens when your intuition works well is that you suddenly recognise an underlying pattern and see the corresponding outcome. In the circumstances we are considering here, you suddenly grasp someone else's pattern of thought, and understand it by insight.

That can be great when it works well, but the right hemisphere of your brain is not very painstaking: it can easily miss things and make huge mistakes. This is where conscious post-processing of the intuition comes into its own. When your intuition seems to give you an insight into something, follow this up with conscious thought, asking yourself why you reached the conclusion you did.

Usually you will obtain an even deeper insight into the situation or person you are trying to understand because you will have both an intuitive and an intellectual grasp of what is going on. Occasionally, you will see some detail which you missed before, and thereby manage to avoid being tricked by someone or needlessly condemning someone about whom you could easily have been wrong.

Empathy

The fourth category of understanding comes when your feelings tell you about someone else's feelings. If you weep with those who weep and laugh with those who laugh, not through any sort of pretence but because you are truly sharing their feelings, you have that unique form of understanding known as empathy.

Sharing someone else's feelings is quite a different experience from having an intellectual grasp of the types of feeling they are experiencing, but the two can go hand in hand. You will not destroy empathy by thinking about it, unless there is some kind of deception going on, in which case it is as well to recognise it and root it out before it does any damage.

Empathising with someone can be quite a strain if they are suffering, but it can also be one of the most rewarding ways of becoming close to someone. You must make your own judgements as to how far you let yourself go in empathy and with whom.

There are a few scroungers in this world who can tell their hard luck stories with such passion that they would bring tears to the eyes of Scrooge himself. Beware of people like this who use the idea that empathy is good in order to induce feelings in you which they can then exploit for their own ends. Such people are not your friends.

Overdoing it

Where does understanding end and prying begin? People like to be understood, but they like their privacy too! You cannot have a complete and universally applicable answer to this question; you just have to judge where to stop. If in doubt, ask yourself how much you want to understand and why. You will know when you are just prying and when the benefits of understanding are clear.

It's Worth Doing Badly

As I implied earlier, an understanding of anyone else is necessarily incomplete. This does not mean that it is not worth trying. It is often said that if a job is worth doing, it is worth doing well, but when it is impossible to do a job really thoroughly well, it can also be worth doing incompletely or even badly. To a great extent, this is true of understanding other people: you can never achieve it completely, but it is still worth quite a lot of effort!

How, then, are you to cope with the idea that you are trying to do something which can never be perfect?

Humility

This question brings us back to one of the themes of this book, honesty. Humility, despite its connotations of grovelling and self-denigration, should just mean honesty, particularly honesty with yourself about just what you have achieved, and what you haven't. In this case of understanding someone else, you need to be honest with yourself about just how much you do not understand. You also need to estimate, as best you can, just how well you understand what you do.

It can be hard to admit to yourself that something into which you have put a good deal of effort is imperfect, but that is where the virtue of humility comes in. If you are truly honest with yourself, you will know how well you have done, and you will not be troubled by the fact that you have not achieved the impossible. Rather, you will be content that you have done and are doing your best, and that everyone is better off for the understanding which you have gained.

Keep trying

A lady in her sixties, who had been happily married for over forty years, once remarked to me that her husband was still capable of surprising her. She was not unhappy about this, but nor had she ever given up trying to understand him. Indeed, she had a deeper understanding of him than many people ever achieve in respect of another individual.

If you are building a relationship with another person, keep trying! The process is never complete, but the more you keep at it, the closer you can get.

Other people in general

Much the same applies to people in general. As an amateur, or even a professional, psychologist or sociologist, you will never know everything, but that does not mean that you should not even try to understand the human mind or society in general. Quite the contrary!

Do not be disheartened by the fact that people and society will always retain some element of mystery, and be capable of surprising you, but keep working at understanding as best you can. Deeper understanding of people will help you to deal more successfully with them, and the more successfully you deal with other people, the happier you are likely to be.

Listening

Understanding another person starts with listening. There is much more to listening than just hearing words and comprehending their meaning. It is a skill which comes naturally to some people, but which can be learned by anyone. What does it involve?

Be quiet

To listen effectively, you must be quiet. If you are talking yourself, you cannot properly take in what is being said to you, but that is not all there is to being quiet. If you are talking *to* yourself, you aren't listening properly either: internal quiet is just as important as keeping your mouth shut.

In order to be quiet internally, you must have at least a minimum level of internal peace. You will not have this if you are in dispute with yourself! In other words, you will get on much better with listening to other people, on which happiness with other people depends, after you have mastered Part Two of this book, and are happy with yourself.

Even that is not enough, however. It is very tempting, during a conversation, to think about what you are going to say next more than you are thinking about what the other person is saying. If you develop the habit of listening first, thinking second and speaking third, you may not always have an instant reply, but people will quickly learn that what you say is worth waiting for.

Pay attention

There is more to paying attention to someone than just being quiet. You could be so quiet internally as to switch off mentally. This is not listening; this is being bored!

If you concentrate on what someone says, and try to understand all the reasons why they are saying it, you are very unlikely to get bored. If you do get bored, the chances are that they don't really want to communicate, they just want an audience. You can handle this if you recognise it.

If someone really does want to communicate, rather than just to be heard, then what they are trying to communicate is almost certainly worth hearing: in that case, paying attention and using all your listening skills will almost certainly pay dividends.

Most importantly, think about what is being said to you. Understand it, analyse it, and consider the implications.

Use your imagination

When someone is telling you a story, you will understand it much better if you apply your imagination to what you are hearing. Rather than just listening to the words, imagine what it was like for the hero of the story, most likely the person talking to you. You will gain greater insight into what they are saying by trying to see the whole situation from their point of view.

This includes trying to imagine what they felt. In other words, empathy is a listening skill, and one which can be used deliberately.

Reflect

The most basic technique taught to people who are learning to be counsellors is called "reflection". This does not mean the kind of self-examination I referred to in Part Two, but to the idea that people become aware that they are being listened to if the listener repeats back to them an accurate paraphrase of what they just said. Including some comment about feelings, provided that it is accurate, helps with this.

If, therefore, you want it to be known that you have been listening, reflect back what you have heard. Very often this will prompt someone to open up more and be clearer about what they really wanted to say. If, however, you do this in a systematic but unnatural kind of way, you are quite likely to annoy: the art is to respond in some natural way which shows that you have really been listening both with your mind and with your heart. Reflection is, as I said, a *basic* technique for this, not the only possibility.

Imagination

I have already said that you can use your imagination to help you to a deeper understanding of what someone is saying to you, but you can use it for more than just that.

Use as a tool of understanding

Used carefully and deliberately, your imagination can help you to understand other people. It will not give you a complete understanding, nor even a completely reliable one. As we have seen, your understanding of other people will never be complete or perfect, but you can make useful progress not just by intellectual effort, but also with your imagination. How is this done?

Dream deliberately

What you have to do is to use conscious control of the process of daydreaming, followed by conscious analysis of what your imagination has come up with.

When trying to understand a single individual, you can either imagine being that person, and living out a part of their life, or you can imagine watching that person as they go about their daily doings, or, better, both. Having done that, you will have a collection of images in your mind, the thoughtful consideration of which will lead you to insights into the nature of that person.

In a similar way, you can understand groups of people, or society as a whole, better by dreaming about what it would be like to live amongst such people in a variety of hypothetical circumstances. Again, follow this up by thinking about the images your imagination has come up with.

Don't be too confident

Always remember, when using the imagination in this way, that it is not a reliable tool of cognition. What it tells you can be useful, but not necessarily completely accurate. The imagination does not follow the rules of logic very well, is not very good at spotting contradictions, and is very weak at spotting false assumptions.

Therefore, do not be too confident of any insight given to you by your imagination, until after you have thought carefully about it. The follow-up with conscious thought will help weed out the weaknesses in what the imagination has come up with, whilst retaining the useful insights.

Putting Yourself in Their Shoes

The most effective way of understanding someone else is to put yourself in their shoes, that is to try to see the world from their point of view. This involves thinking, imagining and feeling. The most difficult part may be taking into account the fact that there are things which you know and things which you have experienced which they have not; when you know something, it can be very hard to imagine what the world must look like to someone who does not have your knowledge.

Integrate all the techniques above

When you are trying to understand someone by trying to see everything from their point of view, you will get on best if you put together everything mentioned so far. You use your imagination and conscious thought, simultaneously if you can, to guess by intuition what they would think, think what they would feel, think about their thoughts and empathise with their feelings. Then stop and think about what you think you might have discovered about them.

If you are still confused about them, if what they say or do seems inconsistent with your understanding, remember that what you observe them saying or doing is real, and anything which you think you might understand but which conflicts with that reality is incorrect. You have made a mistake somewhere. You may have been deceived by what someone else has told you, or just failed to take something into account yourself, but you must always remember that wherever there is a contradiction, there is a mistake of some sort.

Perhaps the most important apparent contradiction to be aware of is in the case where your efforts to understand someone lead you to the point where you say to yourself something like, "I just can't believe that someone who seems so nice could really be that evil." You had better believe it! There is no such thing as a contradiction in reality, and you cannot change the way things are simply by refusing to believe the truth when you don't like the truth. Nor will your happiness survive if you allow yourself to behave as if you believe a lie.

Feel!

Weep with those who weep, and laugh with those who laugh ... but do not pretend. Allow yourself genuinely to feel other people's joy and pain if you really want to understand them. Empathy may not come easily with someone about whom you care little, but when you care deeply about someone, you will find that empathy is virtually inevitable.

It follows that it is easier to understand someone you really care about. Also, if you really want to understand someone, for any reason, you must learn to care about what they feel. This can, of course be painful, even damaging, and it is perfectly reasonable for reasons of self-preservation to cut yourself off from someone else's feelings, even if you do care about them, but, if you do this, do not kid yourself that you have more than an intellectual grasp of what they are feeling.

There is no need for you to disturb your own sanity by becoming too deeply enmeshed in someone else's emotional problems, as you can do if you empathise fully with someone who is profoundly disturbed. There is no point in destroying your own happiness in this way. Making someone else's psychological problems your own helps no-one.

By all means empathise with sane friends whom you care about, as everyone is likely to benefit, but if you think someone is in need of psychiatric care, help them to get it from a professional.

Being understood

The final step in understanding someone is to understand the effect on them of your understanding. If you can imagine what it must be like for them to be understood, you will understand them even better. Most honest people in most ordinary circumstances like to be understood by those around them, especially their family and friends. It is the exceptions to this general rule which are enlightening.

Criminals do not generally like other people to have a clear understanding of the way they live their lives. In the same way, and for essentially the same reasons, people with parasitical ways of life fear complete understanding, not only by others, but also on their own part: they hate to have to admit to themselves, let alone to anyone else, that their lives are dishonest. (For such people, the way to happiness is hard, but the radical changes they need to make in their lives are possible, and you may be able to help them on the way by helping them to understand themselves: at first, they may not thank you, but in the long run, everyone will be better off.)

The golden rule

Finally in this section, we come to the matter of privacy. The "golden rule" of the Christian faith is that you should do to others what you would wish them to do to you. In other faiths there is the subtly weaker idea that you should not do to others what you would not wish them to do to you. Neither of these rules precludes you pursuing your own interests, but both rule out doing so at other people's expense. So what has this to do with privacy?

Privacy is the concept which defines the difference between the kind of mutual understanding which helps everyone, and prying. If someone is trying to understand you for your own benefit, you will usually be pleased. If it is for their own or other people's benefit, but at no cost to you, you are unlikely to mind. If it has no benefit to you, and they are finding out things about you which they might be able to use in any way to your cost, you are entitled not to like it. At this point, they have overstepped the bounds of privacy.

Do not do this to other people, no matter how noble you think your objective is. People are entitled to their privacy. The only exception to this is that no-one has a right to the secrets of objectively criminal activity: people who live by force or fraud are criminals in this sense; people who infringe regulations, but who have no objectively identifiable victims, may not be.

Fiction

It is possible to waste of great deal of time on fiction but fiction does have its uses. Fiction, whether written or performed, can help you to understand other people, and sometimes yourself. This is how I would distinguish good fiction from bad: good fiction can help you to a better understanding of reality, whereas bad fiction merely distracts you from it.

Aid to imagination

Fiction of any sort requires you to engage your imagination. Spectacular cinema films require much less from the imagination than the written word, with television, radio and stage plays somewhere in between. I do accept that some things are much better presented on screen than in print, but if your imagination needs exercise, reading will give it more to do.

Understanding unfamiliar situations

Fiction can help you to understand unfamiliar situations. How useful this is depends on your need to understand situations similar to those presented in the story. Sometimes you may come across circumstances in real life which remind you of analogous circumstances in a fictional world: remembering how the fictional characters handled the situation and what became of them in consequence may help you to see your best course of action.

Understanding the fictional characters themselves, especially when the author tells you their thoughts or feelings, may also help you to understand real people who are quite different from you. You will then be better equipped to handle situations involving unfamiliar people.

Sharing fiction

When you have read a book which gives you a better understanding of something, you may wish to communicate your newfound understanding to a friend. If your understanding is less than perfect, or you don't think you could explain it very well, you suggest that your friend read the same book. If the friend follows your suggestion, and understands the book and why it is important to you, you will have achieved some valuable communication.

Now, watch for that happening the other way around! If a friend urges you to read a particular book, or to watch a film or play or such like, try to understand why. You are quite likely to discover something about the friend, something they wanted you to understand, and which, for some reason, they couldn't put into words.

Other People's Needs

There is more to understanding other people than comprehending their thoughts and feelings. No-one's life is truly complete: everyone has desires, wants and needs. Your happiness will depend in part on your approach to other people's needs, and your ability to deal with the existence of those needs. Sometimes it is right to supply other people's needs, and sometimes not, but, either way, it is important to understand them.

Know your own needs

Understanding other people's needs generally starts with understanding your own. This is a kind of self-knowledge, which comes principally from introspection, as we have seen.

When you understand your own needs, you can handle them. You will always have some sort of needs of your own, but if you are happy with yourself, you will not be overwhelmed by your own needs: you will have them basically under control, because you will know that you are working towards satisfying them. This is a precondition of being able successfully to handle other people's needs. It is unrealistic to expect yourself to do anything about, or even properly to understand, anyone else's needs unless your own are under control.

When you are trying to understand someone else's needs, it can help to remember how things were for you at some past time when you had a need which you no longer have: this can be particularly useful in helping you to understand the needs of children or adolescents. Likewise, you can use your imagination rather than your memory to get an idea of what needs you may have in the future: this could likewise help you to understand the needs of older people.

Other people are different

When using your understanding of yourself and your needs in order to try to understand others, beware of projection: people are not identical to one another, and their needs are not identical to your own, even though there may be some similarities.

Your perception of a person's needs may not be the same as their own. Neither your perception nor theirs is likely to be complete. If you ask someone what they need, you will often find that, never having really thought about it, they do not really know, and sometimes you will find that they are quite sure, but also obviously wrong. You might be just as sure, and just as wrong. Discerning real needs in this field of potential confusion and misperception is difficult.

But not that different!

People do differ from one another, but they also have many things in common. It follows that projection is not necessarily wholly wrong; when you recognise that that is what you are doing, and recognise the limitations of the technique, it can help you to understand other people and their needs.

The same is true of generalisation. All generalisations are faulty, even this one, but many are still useful, and some sweeping generalisations about the needs of human beings can help here.

Universal needs

In order to survive at all, a human's first needs are for food, shelter and clothing, in that order of priority. Without food, you die fairly quickly. In most parts of the world at certain times of year, you die if you do not have proper shelter. It may be possible to survive without clothing, given proper food and shelter, but in most circumstances you will need it, if only as part of the necessary means of acquiring food and shelter, and providing portable shelter in the process. (In any case, clothing is a universal human need, and the lack of it takes priority over all other needs apart from food and shelter.)

Those things are your physical needs for survival, but in order to survive as a human being, you also need sufficient self-respect to want to live. For all other animals, this is automatic: suicide is a uniquely human phenomenon. A person with no self-respect at all dies, not always by deliberate suicide, more often from excessive drinking or drugs.

We do not survive alone. We acquire at least some of our food, shelter, and clothing from other people. For healthy adults, the natural way of doing this is by trade: the alternatives are theft, cheating and scrounging. Whether we acquire the things we need honestly or not, we depend upon relationships with other people for them.

In order for these relationships to be successful, we must have something to trade. This is the contribution we make to society by means of productive work. The whole human race and everything we value depends upon productive work, and people trading what they produce for other things which they value. Some people opt out of this, contributing nothing of real value, but surviving on those who do, to the detriment of their own and everybody else's happiness.

The need to contribute, to work productively, is fundamentally human and it is universal. Everyone has this need, and those who deny it undermine their own self-respect, thus turning towards escapism rather than realism, and finally towards death rather than life.

What about the genuinely helpless, the very young, the very old, and the seriously disabled? These are cared for by healthy adults, some of whom give their time out of love, and others of whom are paid for their trouble by charities or by the state. Although there are a great many parasites in the so-called caring professions, many of these carers are honest people who are effectively trading: their productive work is in caring for the helpless, and their own livelihoods are provided for by other productive people who wish to have otherwise helpless people receive the support they need.

Individual needs

There is also the need for an individual to be an individual, that is to be different from the rest of the human race. This is a prerequisite for self-respect. Extreme individuality is seen as abnormal, and people also have a need to conform to the norms of the society in which they live. One of the difficulties of adolescence is in coming to terms with this seeming contradiction: most adolescents strive to conform to their peer group at first, and subsequently struggle to assert their individuality.

Because of our individuality, we each have personal, individual goals. To understand an individual, you need to know what their personal goals are, as well as to acknowledge that they share the same universal needs as the rest of the human race. Sometimes it is clear what someone's goals are, but if you are in doubt, you can ask, although asking does not always work.

If you have particularly ambitious aims in life, people's incredulous reactions to hearing about them can undermine your ability to believe that they are attainable, and thus your ability to achieve them. People who understand about this tend not to discuss their goals. More usually, you will find, if you ask what someone's goals are, they won't understand the question. If you follow it up by asking what they want, they may tell you what they don't want, but fail to offer any really clear idea of what they want instead.

When you have discovered what someone wants or appears to want, have you discovered their individual needs? Maybe not! Wants are not the same as needs.

Your understanding of people will never be perfect, but when you do your best to understand their real needs, you will be in a better position to supply them, and supplying other people's needs is fundamental to being happy in your relationships. It is also fundamental to getting what you want for yourself, and for this you should understand that, in almost all circumstances, you will do better to supply other people's needs before you expect them to do anything for you.

Chapter 12

You Give Before You Get

If you are going to be happy in your dealings with other people, you must not cause decent and honest people to wish to avoid dealing with you. I will be arguing in this chapter that you will find people easier to deal with if they find that you are valuable to them before they have to have any concern with your wants or needs. This is true whether the people concerned are decent and honest or not. How to cope with those who aren't is another matter, but you will still find them easier if you start by following the principles outlined here.

Supplying needs

If you have followed the previous chapter about understanding people, you should be able to see what another person's needs are in many circumstances. When you see that a person has some need, you are likely also to see how that need can be met. This is true whether it is a simple matter like holding a door open for someone or whether it is something more complex; if you can see what the problem is, you are a long way towards solving it.

The essence of contribution

When you do anything at all for someone else, whether you expect an immediate reward or not, you are contributing to making the world a better place. This is satisfying even if the beneficiary of your efforts is ungrateful. If they are ungrateful, at least you know you have done something good and you can enjoy it; you have learned something about the ungrateful person, and you may not do much for them again, but you can feel good about what you have done.

If you go through life doing the best you can for other people, except for those who seem to be trying to take advantage of your good nature, you will make the world a better place for all of us to live in, yourself included. Above all, you will feel good about yourself.

Why do I make an exception for those who are trying to take advantage of you? Remember that there are people who contribute nothing of any real value, but rely on the efforts of others for their survival. If you support these people, you will do nothing to help yourself or anyone else (even them!) to be happy. Helping people to live parasitical lives is not contribution.

Basic business thinking

Everyone has something to contribute, and everyone has needs which they cannot supply entirely by their own efforts. As a species, we survive by trading.

Civilisation is dependent upon business: tyranny has worked in the past, but even tyrants depend upon their citizens trading amongst themselves to make enough wealth for the tyrants to plunder.

You work to produce something of value. In exchange, you get money, either from your customer or from your employer, who is only your customer anyway. You then take your money and exchange it for something which you value more, which was produced by someone else. There are exceptions to this general rule. If, for example, you are a full-time housewife and mother, being supported by your husband, you are not paid money for your work. Nonetheless, your work is genuinely productive and you are making a contribution. There is a sense in which you are trading with your husband. Nobody actually involved in these transactions loses anything, provided that there is no fraud. If everybody is honest, everybody wins.

Contradictory needs

Sometimes it may seem that your needs are in conflict with someone else's. At other times, you might find yourself apparently having to choose between two or more other people's needs which are apparently in conflict with one another. Such apparent conflicts are often illusory: when you examine them carefully, the seeming conflict disappears.

The first possibility is that one party is a producer, and the other a parasite. Supply the needs of the producer, and encourage the parasite to change their ways.

A second apparent conflict arises from competition in business. Always get the best value you possibly can from your money, taking as much information into account as you reasonably can. It is never your duty to shore up a failing business by giving it money it does not deserve; in the long run it is better for all concerned to let it fail, and the sooner the better. There can be painful short-term costs for those involved, but if everyone is determined to compete productively as best they can, there will be longer-term benefits.

I must also mention the subject of jealousy here. There are actually two very different forms of jealousy, which I call "proper jealousy" and "envy". With the first of these, you may see that someone else has a better car, house or whatever than you do, and find yourself wishing that you had one like that too: this is natural and inevitable, and there is nothing much wrong with it. If, instead, you wish that they didn't have what they have, that is envy and it is evil. If you think that there is no difference between these two, then you are probably assuming that the only way to get a house or car like the other fellow's is to deprive him of it, and you are thinking like a parasite, and not like a producer. A desire to keep what you already legitimately own is also a form of proper jealousy and it is not evil.

Between producers, there is no real conflict of interest. The conflicts arise when people try to get what they do not earn.

The great balancing act

When you are serving other people's needs, you should not be destroying yourself.

Consider two opposite types of character. At one extreme, a person who looks only to their own immediate needs, with no consideration whatsoever of what harm they might cause others, is not a healthy human being, and is very unlikely to be happy. At the other extreme, a person who destroys himself in what he calls the "service of others", is actually likely to be exploited and very likely to end up unhappy too.

Some of the most sensible things ever said by anyone in the entire history of the world were said by Jesus of Nazareth. What he had to say on this subject was, "Love your neighbour as yourself." This is actually a middle way between those two extremes and does not involve harming anyone. The path to happiness lies along this middle way.

The Danger of Asking First

When you do something for someone else before they have ever done anything for you, they will often feel that they owe you, and they are likely to want to do more for you than you have done for them. Many good, mutually supportive relationships get started like this, but what if it is the other way around? What if you ask for help or support first?

The exact answer depends upon many things, such as the character of the person you ask, how appropriately you express your gratitude, how quickly you are able to return the favour, and so on. Generally speaking, however, you will be happier in your relationships if you are not usually the one to ask favours first.

Don't be a burden

If you get into the habit of getting as much out of people as you can and avoiding giving much (if anything) in return, you will be a burden on society. You will not be happy with this, for several reasons.

First and foremost, you will be denying yourself the lasting satisfaction which comes from contribution, by going for the shorter term thrill of getting something for nothing. In fact, you will not even be getting something for nothing, because there is a cost to you, and the cost is the quality of the relationships with other people which you might otherwise have had.

This brings us to the second point. If you are widely perceived as having chosen to be a burden on society, you are likely to be unpopular, and unpopularity makes for unhappiness.

Finally, if you refuse to contribute, you will feel worthless. You won't be able to avoid this feeling, although you might try to escape from it into drink, drugs, gambling, promiscuity, crime or some other source of short-term thrills. The only solution is to start thinking of other people's needs, and supplying them.

This feeling of worthlessness can also strike people who are disabled or elderly and infirm, especially if they used to be able to achieve a much higher level of contribution. If you are in this position, please do not worry. Firstly, those of us who are able-bodied do not mind looking after you if you really need it. Secondly, if you are determined, you will find some way of improving your sense of self-worth; some real-life examples spring to mind: a blind clergyman, a computer consultant in a wheelchair, and a caterer with an artificial leg. These few examples come from my own acquaintances, and they represent determination in the face of real difficulties, more inspiring to me even than the achievements of such disabled greats as Beethoven or Stephen Hawking. Some people have successfully started new careers when past retirement age, most notably Colonel Sanders of Kentucky Fried Chicken fame, but if you are elderly and you think you are necessarily dependent upon other people, you can still contribute by being as considerate of your carers as you can.

Have your own needs under control

Leaving aside the matter of physical disability, you should, for the sake of your own happiness and for the benefit of your relationships with other people, be self-supporting.

We have already dealt with the physical aspects of this. You are unlikely to grow all your own food, make all your own clothes and build your own house, so you probably have to get and use money for most of these things. In order to be happy, you have to get this money honestly. This is what I mean by being self-supporting in respect of your physical needs.

As I pointed out earlier, money is not always involved; if, for example, you are a full-time housewife and mother, you are trading with your husband: between you, you agree which of you will do what to achieve what you jointly want, and then you each work in different roles, each working for the benefit of both. Thus the principle remains the same: although money doesn't enter into the trade, you are nevertheless working honestly for your living, and thus being just as self-supporting in respect of your physical needs as if you had a paid job.

Apart from these physical needs, you also have psychological needs. If your relationships with other people are to be successful, it is important that you are essentially self-supporting psychologically. If you are religious, you may find that your spiritual life helps you with this. It is not that you should be self-supporting to the exclusion of God, if you believe in God, just that you should not be dependent upon the support of other (human mortal) people for your psychological stability.

You do have a need for healthy relationships with other people, but if you find that your relationships are dominated by your need for psychological support, then you must address this problem, get your needs under control, and become more able to give as well as take, and indeed to be able to give (where required) before you take.

Investment in Relationships

When you invest money, you expect to wait a while and then get back more than you invested. Sometimes it doesn't quite work out in the way that you hoped, but if you are both careful and patient, it generally does.

It is much the same in human relationships: if you give before you expect to get, and you are patient, you will usually be repaid with interest. If you are generally and genuinely helpful without looking for any immediate return of favours, most other people will be happy to do even more for you when the occasion arises. Even when you get no return, you can still be happy about the good things that you have done.

Payment in advance?

To use a similar commercial analogy, when you pay in advance for something, you can usually expect a better deal than if you buy on credit, and if you borrow money to buy something, you will usually pay more for it in the end.

Likewise in human relationships: do your bit first, before placing any demands, and it will cost you less in the long run.

Build up credit

When you borrow money in the commercial world, you are expected to pay it back with interest in a certain time. If you do so, you will be allowed to borrow more next time. If you are late in repaying your loan, it will cost you more and borrowing next time will be harder.

Again, similar things apply in human relationships. If your first dealing with a new acquaintance involves them doing something for you, the relationship can still be successful, provided that you are immediately and always willing to repay the favour with interest. Your new relationship can thrive on the basis of any reasonable kind of give and take, but if you take and take without giving, your relationships will rapidly wither.

Beware!

I should at this stage just warn you about a rare but dangerous kind of person. There are just a few around who use the principles I have outlined in this section for a particularly nasty kind of manipulation.

They start by doing something for you, but their objective is not genuine contribution in the hope of building a healthy relationship. Their objective is to get as much out of you as they possibly can, giving back just enough to keep you feeling in some way indebted to them.

You can recognise such people principally by the characteristic that they survive on relationships of this sort rather than on truly productive work and trading. Many of them are politicians or leaders of religious cults. The most successful and dangerous of them are dictators or very wealthy religious leaders. Some hold seemingly prestigious jobs in public life, where they dispense taxpayers' money to certain needy people, many of whom would not have been so needy were it not for the heavy burden of taxation. Such people are never truly happy.

Your best defence against such people is to recognise them, and never ever accept any favours from them.

Patience and Gentleness

Returning to the subject of healthy relationships, I want to point out that they are generally characterised by patience and gentleness. The opposites are aggression and violence, which obviously have no place in a good relationship. Let us consider patience first.

These things take time

Good relationships are not built instantaneously. It is true that occasionally you will meet someone with whom you have such a natural affinity that you feel very close to them immediately, and you may even experience the extreme form of this, which is known as "love at first sight", but that is not the same as having established a relationship, although it can make the process of establishing a good relationship faster and easier.

This whole chapter is called "You give before you get", and the question to ask here is, "How much before?" Alas there is no universal answer, because it is up to the person to whom you have given to respond, in their own way and in their own time.

In a commercial trading relationship, you agree in advance who is to give what to whom and when: this is fair, honest and conducive to happiness. In a social relationship, there is no such specific agreement, so it is unfair to have any such specific expectations.

Patience with yourself

If, in the past, your relationships with other people have been unsatisfactory, it will take you time to learn to establish better ones. It will take even longer to mend damaged old relationships. When you are learning new principles for relationships with people, you are actually changing yourself. The decision to change may be instantaneous, but establishing new behaviour patterns, which is what you will be doing, takes time.

For the improvement to be successful, you must be patient with yourself. The alternative would be for you to get angry with yourself for something which is inevitable; you would then be carrying around an inner conflict, which could only serve to interfere with the relationships you are trying to build.

Patience with your friends

It takes time for your relationships with other people to improve. Your friends will respond to your improved behaviour towards them, but only if you let them do so in their own good time; if it becomes apparent that you are expecting and waiting for some particular sort of response, you will undermine the whole process.

When your friends do start to change their behaviour towards you as a result of your improved behaviour towards them, you may well be delighted with the result. It is worth waiting for. Be patient, and don't have any specific expectations.

Patience with the situation

I said earlier that it will take you time to learn to establish better relationships than you might have had in the past. It will take at least as long for people around you to realise that good relationships with you are possible, especially if this has been your weak point hitherto. If you are consistent in your improved behaviour towards others, people who know you will gradually come to realise that you have changed, and new acquaintances will just accept the new you.

None of this will be as quick as you might like, although you may notice some improvement virtually immediately. You must be patient with the situation. It is not a situation which you can't change, because you are changing it, but the change takes time, and it will take longer if you are obviously impatient with it. (Just imagine someone ranting and raving and complaining about how nobody accepts how likeable they are. Don't be that person: it is not the way to win friends!)

If the situation you find yourself in is completely intolerable because of bad relationships you have had in the past, moving to a new area where nobody knows you might help, but this is not a decision to be taken lightly. If you are thinking about it, practise your new behaviour patterns in your old community first. There are two reasons for this: firstly, it is better to arrive in your new community already having had some practice in the techniques of building good relationships, and secondly, you might find that things improve so much in your present community that you don't want to move away after all.

Gentleness is patience!

I entitled this whole section "Patience and Gentleness" but I have said very little about gentleness, concentrating wholly on patience. If someone is truly patient, they will also be gentle. Lack of gentleness is a symptom of lack of patience. It is also a symptom of lack of happiness.

More importantly, lack of gentleness is a cause of lack of happiness, both for the victim and for the perpetrator. Perpetrator of what? Well, how do you conclude that someone is not gentle? Lack of gentleness shows itself either as physical violence, or as other things done or said with the intention of hurting. Deliberately hurting someone, physically or otherwise, cannot help anyone to be happy, except when it is a proper defensive response to a physically violent criminal.

Gentleness, which is necessary for happiness, is a symptom of patience, which is also necessary for happiness. Patience can mean suffering, but suffering does not necessarily mean unhappiness. When you know that a situation is improving, and you have to accept that this takes time, and that for the time being certain things are uncomfortable, this is no reason to be unhappy. Concentrate on the improvement, and the causes of the improvement, be patient, and be happy that things are improving.

Pay-off

We have been concentrating on the idea that you give before you get. You give social pleasantries, the courtesy of remembering what people have told you about themselves and what they care about (especially their names!), you give emotional support, and physical help. What do you get back?

Self-respect

Your most immediate pay-off is completely internal to you, and does not require any response from anyone else at all. Knowing that you are doing the right thing in your relationships with other people immediately gives you grounds for self-respect. You cannot be happy without self-respect.

Being liked

If you follow all the advice about relationships with people, respecting them, caring about them, caring for them when necessary, and maintaining your own self-respect, you will be liked. This is inevitable.

Being liked is not an absolute precondition of happiness, although the two things do tend to go together. You must not expect to be liked by everyone, and it is not wise to make your own happiness dependent upon being liked by a particular individual who might not respond to you as you wish. This would be to make a rule for yourself which would create an unnecessary individual barrier to your own happiness.

You should also be very careful not to let your happiness be dependent upon being liked by someone who suggests that you should not be happy unless they approve of you. This is a manipulative technique used by some very nasty people, including, for example, the late David Koresh, the man who led members of the Branch Dravidian sect eventually to their terrible deaths at Waco, Texas. It is more commonly used by ageing parents who wish to maintain control of their mature children.

Being loved

If people like you, they will enjoy your company. If they love you, they will do their best to make your life more fulfilled. Being loved, and being able to accept being loved, will bring joy into your life like nothing else can. I will say no more about this now, because the whole of the next chapter is on this subject, but it is part of the pay-off.

Being a good influence

When you go through life doing the best you can to make other people's lives better, you will make your part of the world a better place for the people who live in it. After a while, your example will inspire others to the same kind of patient kindness and generosity, and they will be happier too. This inspiration spreads wherever it is not undermined by viciousness, short-termism or parasitism.

As it spreads, the world becomes a better place for all of us to live in. Your influence can help with this, and you can feel happy about it.

Wisdom

Why do I mention wisdom? How can wisdom be a pay-off from giving before you get? The answer is simply that, as you study people's needs and observe the consequences of your doing your best to help them with them, you come to a much deeper understanding of people and the way that the interactions between them constitute the way in which the world works. You will never attain such wisdom by looking only at your own desires.

Can someone be unwise but happy? I think not. Wise but unhappy? Maybe, but it is not common. Wisdom is therefore correlated with happiness. Go for it, starting with the effort to understand other people.

Chapter 13

How to be Lovable

Babies and young children naturally inspire loving feelings in adults, especially in their parents, but not all adults are lovable. If you are a lovable person, the chances are good that you will be loved, which will be good for your self-esteem and happiness. You will not be loved if you are not lovable, because, contrary to what you might often hear said, love is actually deserved and earned, and very rarely freely and unconditionally given. When you are an adult, your need for love is not enough to guarantee your getting it!

To be lovable, you must first know how to love, and you must know the all-important difference between loving someone and "being in love".

"Love" is such an overused word that it really does have a number of different meanings in different contexts, and different people use it to mean different things. I choose to define it as making the effort to make someone else happier, but I also acknowledge the currency of another relevant usage, and that is "in love". "In love" also has two basic contexts: "falling in love with" and "being in love with", expressions which have much more to do with feelings than with action. I will leave aside for the time being "making love" and such qualified specifics as "brotherly love", "Christian love", "love of country" and so on.

Loving

To love someone is to make the effort to help them to be happier. You can do this by choice regardless of how you feel about them. You can do it without damaging yourself or your prospects of happiness: there need be no sacrifices in that sense. In fact, there can be no such sacrifices, because if you are damaged in the process, this very fact will undermine the intended enhancement of the other person's happiness.

Discerning

To help someone else towards happiness, you will need to discern their barriers to happiness, help them past those barriers and then help them on to their own fulfilment, for which you will also need discernment. People who are already happy can still be helped on to greater happiness, but only if you have the proper understanding.

I am not suggesting that you approach every relationship with the attitude that you are there to identify problems and solve them, sweeping away every barrier in everyone's lives. Understanding and gentleness go together. Ultimately, people can only solve their own problems, but if you understand someone well, you can support and encourage. You do not even have to do this explicitly: basic, straightforward friendship and helpfulness go a long way towards helping people to cope with life and to enjoy it.

It is most important to discern when you are genuinely contributing to someone's happiness, as opposed to being on your own "I'm helpful" ego-trip, or being manipulated by someone who is using your inclination to be helpful for their own ends without any care as to the cost to you.

Giving

There is always a cost. You cannot do anything for anyone else without there being some cost, but the cost should always be less than the benefit. If you really care for someone, you will do what you can for them, accepting that it is costly to you, but you do this not to your own destruction, but largely for your own benefit, actually in the expectation of the good feelings you will get as a result of making your contribution.

Self-destruction in the service of someone else may sound noble, but it is inconsistent with happiness. The idea of laying down your life for your friend, said to be the highest form of love, surely means risking your life for someone you love, should the occasion to do so be forced upon you. That would be love indeed, whereas deliberate self-destruction is just wrong.

It would also be wrong to allow yourself to be destroyed by someone who argues that it is your duty to serve them to the exclusion of your own self-realisation and happiness. Not only would you become unhappy as a result of falling for this kind of manipulation, but so too would the manipulator.

Being deliberate, not spontaneous

Spontaneity is often thought to be an essential component of a loving relationship. It can be relevant, but it also contains dangers. To be spontaneous usually means to act without thinking. Action without thought rarely leads to happiness in practice.

There are two reasons to beware of spontaneity. Firstly, anyone trying to manipulate or exploit you will encourage you to act quickly or immediately, and will almost never encourage you to take time to think through the implications of what they are encouraging you to do. Secondly, even in a healthy relationship, it is possible to make mistakes and to hurt people without meaning to, but this happens much less where deliberation wins over spontaneity.

Tenacity

It is not enough just to be kind to someone on a few occasions. To be truly loving, you must be consistent, constant and reliable. That is to say, you must practise the virtue of sticking at it, or tenacity.

You might eventually reach the point of deciding that your happiness and theirs would be better served by giving up your efforts at kindness, but you should reach this decision (if you ever do) on the basis of what you truly believe to be best for all concerned, not on the basis of lack of tenacity. That decision, not to be taken lightly, could still be a loving decision.

While you are concentrating on someone's needs, it is important not to let your own needs intrude. Do not burden the person you love with your troubles, unless and until they show clear signs of really wanting you to. This can be hard sometimes, but your tenacious concentration on other people's needs will actually help you to deal with your own.

What Paul said

Probably the most famous piece of writing on the subject of love is in chapter 13 of St. Paul's first letter to the Corinthian church. (You will find it near the back of any Bible: it is the passage starting, "Love is patient; love is kind ... "; in some translations, the word used is "charity", but this doesn't matter.) It was written a long time ago, but there is a good deal of sense in it.

If I just suggested that you read it, you might do so, and you might benefit from it, but we can do better than that! Try reading it (aloud if you can do so without embarrassment), but not exactly as it is printed; instead, substitute the words "I am" for the words "Love is". As you do so, you will probably find yourself making some true statements and some false ones. It doesn't very much matter which is which at this stage; the thing to learn is that the better you get at the art of loving people, the more of those statements will become true.

Falling in Love

Falling in love, as opposed to loving, has everything to do with feelings, and very little to do with thought or action. It is a sexual response, albeit not necessarily a directly erotic one, in that it is the feeling characteristic of a young adult couple. You will only feel it for someone whom you would like to become your mate.

There is a widely held belief, encouraged by Hollywood, that for each young man, there is just one young woman in the world who is the *right one* and *vice versa*. When you meet the *right one*, you will fall in love, get married and live happily ever after. If you fall out of love, you obviously made a mistake, it wasn't the *right one* after all, so the only possibilities are to stay in an unhappy marriage or to divorce that partner and have another go at finding the *right one*.

Much misery has been caused by that belief system. It is quite a successful meme, because it is attractive, carrying around with it a promise of lifetime happiness, and because it contains an element of truth, which renders the whole thing plausible.

That melting feeling

It is undoubtedly true that there is a particularly intense emotional feeling, which can be triggered off by a member of the opposite sex. (If you are homosexual or bisexual, it might be a member of your own sex, but I am not discussing homosexual relationships here.)

Only a tiny minority of the opposite sex will trigger this feeling, which is doubtless the origin of the idea that there is just one *right one* for you, but how do you recognise it?

It's like a sneeze

Like happiness itself, the feeling of falling in love has much in common with a sneeze. You can't successfully fake it. When you experience it, it is absolutely unmistakable. Aside from that, it is nearly impossible to describe satisfactorily.

When you do experience it, you will find yourself in the grip of a powerful combination of joy and desire. You will be emotionally extremely vulnerable, and apt to behave irrationally.

Not sufficient in itself

The worst mistake to make at this stage is to believe that you have now found the *right one* and that it is therefore inevitable that you will get married and live happily ever after.

The feeling of falling in love is not sufficient to guarantee that anything else will follow at all, especially not everlasting happiness. The feeling only does two things: it tells you that you find the individual extremely attractive (but you knew that anyway) and it gives you the motivation to do whatever is necessary to nurture and to maintain the relationship.

Motivator

As a motivator, the feeling of falling in love is almost without parallel. This is probably because it is a manifestation in the human being of the drive to reproduction shared by all living organisms. It is the beautiful face of the sex drive! Properly handled, it will help you to behave truly lovingly towards your partner, and maybe even towards the rest of the world as well.

It will, if properly maintained, even after the initial intensity of the feeling wears off, help you to be a good spouse and parent.

Being on the receiving end

We have talked about falling in love, but what about when someone else falls in love with you? There are two basic possibilities here: either you are horrified, or you are delighted. The grey area in between is usually short-lived, as your own feelings are very likely to polarise one way or the other fairly soon after it becomes clear that someone has fallen in love with you.

You will be horrified if undying love for you is declared by someone with whom you couldn't bear to spend a single evening, let alone the rest of your days. It will be made worse if they seem to think that because they have fallen in love with you, it is inevitable that you should feel the same. Send them away. They will be hurt, but that is not your fault. You need have no guilt feelings about someone else's error of philosophy, which is what they will really be suffering from.

You will be delighted if undying love for you is declared by someone with whom you have already fallen in love yourself, or whom you find irresistible, when you realise how great they think you are. Then you are in love with one another. This is blissful, but it is up to you both to keep it going.

Being in Love

When you have fallen in love with someone, it is very hard to believe that the intense feeling is in any way temporary.

If your love is not returned, it feels as though the most terrible emotional pain will last forever. It doesn't. You will never forget your first love, but, in time, you will recover. Even more shockingly, you are likely to discover eventually that you can feel the same about someone else. This can be deeply shocking, and extremely hard to believe, but it is an observed fact of reality that this does indeed happen to people, and they very often end up emotionally and spiritually stronger having gone through the crisis and pain of rejection.

In this section, however, I want to look in a little more detail at relationships in which the feelings of falling in love are shared.

When it's mutual

When two people fall in love with one another, they share a particularly strong emotional bond, a great deal of joy, and a desire for sexual fulfilment with one another.

When a young couple are in love, it is usually obvious both to themselves and to others around them. Although it is sometimes possible for them to keep the intensity of their relationship secret, it is often clear just from the way they look at one another.

Don't presume it will last

When you are in love, it feels as though this most intense joy of your life will last for ever. It won't. No matter how good the relationship, the intensity of joy will wear off. If the relationship lasts well, and it is quite likely that you can make it do so, you might occasionally have little high points of delight in your partner, which are reminiscent of the joys of your early love.

Although the intensity of the initial feelings of love will not last, happy marriages do exist, and there is no reason why you shouldn't have one. The trick is not to presume that, just because the two of you are in love with one another, that the relationship will last of its own accord. You must also avoid falling into the error of thinking that, because some of the feelings wear off, the relationship is doomed.

A relationship which starts with you falling in love can quite likely be a source of continuing joy and happiness for the rest of your life, but only if you ...

Make it last

Remember that what you want to last is the relationship itself, not the initial feelings characteristic of the beginning of the relationship.

If you fail to maintain the relationship in good repair, you will end up with a most miserable situation. Broken marriages, whether formally constituted as such or not, are the source of much of the pain and unhappiness that there is in the world. Most of this pain can be avoided. Some could be avoided by greater caution before marriage, and we will come to that in greater detail in the next chapter, and most of the rest could be avoided by effort.

Work at it

The maintenance of any sort of relationship takes some amount of work. If you do not work at a relationship which you want to last, it is your happiness which will suffer, as well as perhaps your partner's. Even if you think things would be better if your partner put more work into it, it is still your responsibility to do your bit.

Maintenance by loving and being loved

The work you put into a loving relationship is the love itself. The beauty of a loving relationship is that, while you are working for the happiness of your beloved, you are also working for your own happiness.

This remains true, to some extent, even if the beloved does not work for your happiness. In a really good relationship, both partners work for each other's happiness and end up achieving their own too.

For best results, do your bit, and allow your partner to do theirs. Allow! Do not try to force! Any pressure of any sort you use to try to get your partner to make some effort will undermine your own happiness as well as theirs. Equally, when they do work at it, enjoy being loved, be honestly grateful, allow yourself to be loved, and be happy, knowing all the while that the person you love is happy too.

Being Lovable

I said at the start of this chapter that to be lovable, you must first know how to love. I hope that I have now outlined the idea of love well enough that you understand what is involved, but let us have a very brief recap.

To be lovable as an adult, you must know how to love. To love is to work for someone else's happiness. That involves understanding them and their needs, and being able to supply at least some of those needs, without being a burden yourself. Understanding comes from your study of human nature, including your own, and from acquaintanceship built up by the common process of social interaction. Not being a burden means that you must have your own needs under control but still be capable of allowing other people to care for you if they so wish.

The principle of expectation of good feelings

The best salesmen, and some of the worst, understand that the only real reason why anyone buys anything is because of the expectation of good feelings. What is less widely understood is that this is the only reason why anyone does anything! Whatever we do is done either to avoid pain of some sort, or to achieve pleasure of some sort. Sometimes it doesn't look like that, because we sometimes accept short-term costs in order to achieve long-term benefits and we sometimes look for short-term benefits ignoring the long-term costs, but it is the benefits which motivate, and the motivating benefit is always a matter of anticipated feelings.

What has all this got to do with being lovable? The answer is simple. If people find themselves expecting to feel good feelings as a result of interaction with you, they will find you lovable. There are people who bring this expectation to every acquaintanceship; they find everyone lovable, at least at first, but even they can go off certain individuals.

Your task is to induce that expectation in other people in general. You will not do it anything like as well if you try to do it only for people whom you particularly want to like you! Be generally likeable and lovable, and put up with the fact that you will have the adulation of some people whose respect and liking you would happily be without.

How do you inspire this expectation of good feelings? It must never be a false expectation. If the expectation is founded upon a deception of any sort, you will undermine your own happiness, and the whole effort will be wasted. It follows that you must bring about genuine good feelings in people, so that they will reasonably expect you to do so again.

Causing good feelings

If, in your dealings with people, you genuinely care for them, remember their names, what they say to you, what they care about, their troubles and their joys, and if on subsequent meetings, you show that you did take in all that was said last time, people will feel good about talking to you. Doing all this is not easy, especially if you have your own troubles to worry about, and if you are burning to talk about them. I am not saying that it is easy. It does take effort, but it is much easier if you have your own needs under control first.

If you genuinely care about people, you will also do what you can to help solve any problems which show up during your interactions with an individual. Solving a problem does not necessarily mean eliminating it! Helping someone to cope with their own problems just by listening and empathising can do a great deal to create good feelings, and, consequently the expectation of good feelings.

But you don't want to spend all your time on other people's troubles, do you? If they have their own needs well under control, and maybe even if they don't, you can still have a lot of fun! Good feelings are to be had from all sorts of entertainment, and sharing entertainment with someone can be a good way of building rapport and the expectation of good feelings. This does not mean that you have to spend many of your hard-earned pennies taking people to shows in order to win their favour. All it means is that it is good, right and proper, to enjoy the good experiences of life, and to share them with other people.

Best of all, share laughter. You do not need to learn the contents of a joke-book and pour out second-hand humour, although even that can be fun sometimes. Just sharpen up your own sense of humour, and get people laughing, not to the exclusion of dealing successfully with reality, but as part of it. You can learn, if you want to, techniques for extracting a giggle from almost any non-traumatic situation.

Being consistent

You can undermine the expectation of good feelings by inconsistency. If people never know what to expect from you, because you are moody, occasionally irritable for no apparent reason, or just plain cantankerous, they will not feel at ease with you. If they do not feel at ease with you, they will not find you lovable.

But not boringly consistent

Although you should avoid upsetting people by being unpredictable, there is a lot to be said for coming up with pleasant surprises from time to time. Others will keep their general expectation of good feelings associated with you if all the surprises they get are good.

This, however, takes planning on your part! If you are to be sure of pleasing people with something they are not expecting, it is generally better if you think hard about it in advance. This is because surprises are inherently dangerous to any relationship, and lack of forethought can lead to an intended pleasant surprise being upsetting instead.

When you know someone really well, and the relationship is thoroughly well-established, then you have, in effect, already done a fair bit of thinking in advance, although you may not have done it consciously. Then you can afford true spontaneity. If you do get it wrong, forgiveness for the mistake is easier in the context of a well-established relationship.

Be rewarding

Other people put some effort into their relationships with you. Do not let them feel that this effort is wasted. Unless you specifically want to withdraw from a particular relationship for some reason, always try to reward people's efforts in their relationships with you. From the simplest smile in returning a greeting, to making the lifelong efforts of care involved in marriage, always try to return at least as much as you have received, if not more.

If you do this, two things will follow. Firstly, you will feel good about yourself, because of the way you are improving other people's lives, simply by being good to them. Secondly, you will be more popular, likeable and lovable, which will, in turn, boost your self-esteem. Both of these things will help you further towards happiness.

A third thing might follow, which is less desirable, but which is fairly easy to handle. While most people will respond positively, and generously, to your attitude, you may find one or two who do not play fair in this game of give-and-take. If you find yourself being drained by a relationship, and you can't improve matters by talking about it, dump it, no matter who argues that you have a duty to keep putting yourself into it. We will come back to this in Chapter 20, but now let's return to the subject of the best of relationships.

Chapter 14

Love and Marriage

In the words of a once famous song, "Love and marriage go together like a horse and carriage ... you can't have one without the other." Well, of course, you can. A horse is a usable form of transport, and horseless carriages have been with us for a hundred years, and they now work rather better than the type which used to need horses.

It is still true, however (even though it is an idea which has been challenged in recent decades) that love and marriage do go well together, provided that the partners know what is meant by "love", what marriage entails, and provided that both are prepared to work at it.

The Irresistible Combination

When two people are in love, and they love each other, their desire to live together is likely to override virtually every other consideration in their lives. There are powerful reasons for this. Biological, cultural and individual personal expectations all work together to drive the couple together. These forces are all triggered when two people feel the same about one another and act lovingly towards each other. Let us look at this irresistible combination in more detail.

For the combination to be irresistible, all of these three components must be present.

Love + "in love" + mutuality

The first vital component of the irresistible combination is love! You must love one another. Remember my definition. Although a marriage can survive with only one partner putting in that effort, you are both likely to be happier if you keep on making the effort to help each other to be happier. Ironically, if you are the only one putting in the effort, you are the one who is likely to be happier. Making the effort to help someone else to be happy is good for you. If they are making the effort to help you to be happy, it will be good for them, as well as for you. Pointing this fact out to an unloving partner does not work, however.

Being "in love", as explained in the previous chapter, is a temporary feeling, but nonetheless a good one! When you are in love and the feeling is mutual, you will be well-motivated to build the foundations of a good and long-lasting marriage. Successful marriage is possible without this feeling ever having been present, but it is more difficult, especially if one of the partners should ever fall in love with someone else. If you have been married for some time, and the feeling of being "in love" has worn off, your marriage will be good if you are still behaving lovingly, and you will still be sustained by the memory of the intensity of the feelings of your youth.

Mutuality is also a very important factor in a relationship. If you have strong feelings for someone, and they are not returned, the relationship is unlikely to have a successful future, although that is not out of the question, but first you have to concentrate on what your beloved wants, setting aside the needs which arise from your own feelings for the time being. But any relationship in which the parties have similar positive feelings for one another is likely to have a good future, provided that both continue to put some effort into it, and even if the future is at a less intimate level than marriage.

Why it's precious

This threefold combination of mutuality, feelings and love, is the most precious thing you are likely to experience, but why? Let's look at the so-called hierarchy of needs.

At the most basic level, you need food, clothing and shelter, without which you will die. It is easier for a couple to share in the provision of these things than it is for an individual to acquire them alone. Also at the physiological level, you have a natural desire for sex and procreation. Marriage is the best context for this.

You need to be sure that you can keep what you own, and that you will be able to keep what you will earn in the future. On the face of it, sharing your life with someone else might seem to work against that need, but if you are working together for each other, you will have greater security in this respect. Let me give two rather obvious illustrations of this by way of explanation. Firstly, if two of you share just one house, you are about half as likely to be burgled than if you had one house each, and the probability is reduced yet further by the increased chance of that house being occupied at any given moment. Secondly, in most civilised countries, even the tax parasites take less from a married couple than they would from two individuals.

You need to feel that you are a valued member of social group. The smallest such group is the couple. A couple is likely to become a family, which is the next bigger group. If you are putting in the necessary effort of love, you will be valued within such a group. As a good spouse (and maybe parent), you are also better equipped to be a valued member of many other larger social groups, even though you will be less well fitted to certain others.

Being a valued member of a family, or just a couple, will also boost your self-esteem, and your self-esteem is crucial to your happiness.

Finally, having the backing of your partner, and perhaps the love of the rest of your family, will help you to feel the strength necessary to achieve everything else you want to achieve in life.

So, if you have such a valuable relationship, do not just take it for granted that it will last simply because it is so good. It is so precious that it is worth putting in a great deal of effort to maintain it.

Shared determination to maintain

If you have a relationship based on the threefold combination which we have been discussing, you will naturally be determined to maintain it. If the relationship is going to continue to thrive indefinitely, it is better if your partner shares your determination to maintain it.

There is a subtle little difficulty here, however. You can actually damage a relationship of this sort by directly suggesting that its survival is dependent on your partner's continuing determined effort to maintain it! It is up to you to decide how to be sure that your partner understands that shared determination to work at maintaining a relationship is important, but I would recommend the sharing and discussing of fiction. The reasons for the success or failure of a fictional relationship can be discussed non-threateningly.

What you have to do is to put your effort in, safe in the knowledge that you will be the most valuable person in your partner's life, as a result of this. If your partner completely fails to contribute anything of value to the relationship, you may eventually wish to give up the effort. This is unlikely to occur because, if you are doing your bit, your partner will most likely quite naturally wish to do their bit.

If you do eventually find yourself wishing to give up, that is not necessarily the end of the road, but it is certainly time to look for help: that is what marriage guidance counsellors are for. They are cheaper and much more useful than divorce lawyers.

When not to maintain a love-relationship

In Chapter 20, we will return to the subject of failed relationships in greater detail. For now, I just want to mention a few cases in which you might wish to maintain a relationship which would be better terminated for the sake of your happiness and everyone else's. I will deal with them in increasing order of commonness, starting with the rarest, and perhaps the most difficult.

It is said that it makes evolutionary sense for pretty young girls and rich old men to get together, hence the "sugar-daddy" syndrome. There may be very little wrong with this where the pretty young girl concerned is actually an adult woman. When she really is a girl, one gets rather close to the risk of statutory rape, or, even worse, paedophilia. If you are a grown man, and you find yourself attracted to a young girl, get out, and get out quick. If you really love her, you will just have to wait until she has grown up: this may be hard, but it is a case of making the effort to improve her chances of happiness; that is to say, it is the truly loving thing to do!

Secondly, there is the all-too-common case of the asymmetric relationship. The usual case is boy meets girl, boy falls in love, girl tells him to get lost. The same thing with the sexes reversed is also common. If the case is hopeless, and many are, give up gracefully before things get really unpleasant, which they easily can; you may even get on better later if you respect your beloved's right to say "No" and mean it. How can this case fit into the section of the book on the irresistible combination? What can easily happen is that, feeling as you do, you find it so hard to believe that your feelings are not reciprocated, that you believe for a while that your relationship is symmetrical, when in fact it never was. This hurts, but the only solution is to get out. There may even be a danger that your "beloved" was just taking advantage of your feelings: in such a case it is even more important to get out and get out quickly and permanently, not only for the sake of your own sanity and happiness, but also because such people need to learn that they cannot achieve their own happiness that way.

Commonest of all, sadly, is the adulterous relationship. If you are married, you will have promised, amongst other things, to be faithful to your partner, which is to say that you will not embark upon any relationship which competes with your marriage relationship. To do so would be to break your promise. If you break a promise, any promise, you will undermine your own happiness, as well as that of anyone else who was relying on you to keep your word. If you find yourself embarking upon a relationship which you judge is even moderately likely to make it hard for you to keep your promises, get out, and get out quick.

Promises, Promises

What promises are we talking about? The promises individual couples make to each other when they agree to live together permanently do vary, and it is not strictly necessary for there to be a wedding at which these promises are formally exchanged for the couple to be effectively married.

Some people say that definite promises are unnecessary, provided that each partner understands that they must continue to be valuable to the other partner in order for the union to be successful, and that if they continue to put the necessary work in, then they will get more and more valuable indefinitely, thereby guaranteeing that the relationship will last. Such people also argue that, as soon as partner A ceases to be valuable to partner B in any clearly definable sense, then partner B is perfectly entitled to abandon partner A. If both partners agree to this, it is their choice, their responsibility and eventually their problem. Their minds may be closed to the idea that sickness and old age are to be expected.

Whatever such opinions are held by some individuals, the fact remains that marriage, in the sense of the formal exchange of promises, is still very popular, and for good reasons. Although there are plenty of unhappy marriages, it is not hard to find truly happily married couples.

Let's look in detail at some of the promises commonly exchanged at weddings. These things do vary, but we'll go through a set which is in common use.

Have and hold

Everyone needs a cuddle occasionally. When you promise "to have and to hold" your partner, you are promising to be available to them in a sexual sense. This is the origin of the old idea of conjugal rights. The promise should not mean that a woman grants to her man unlimited use of her as an object whereby to gratify his sexual appetite – the newer idea of rape within marriage is just as valid! A man who loves and cherishes his wife will never force himself on her, which brings us to the next promise.

Love and cherish

I have already defined the verb "to love" as meaning "to make the effort to help someone else to be happy". This definition is just as valid within marriage as anywhere, but what about "cherish".

"Cherish" is a funny old word, etymologically related to words like "care" and "charity". It has connotations of nurturing and of gentleness. I don't think we need add anything to my earlier definition of "love". If you love your partner, you will cherish them, whatever you understand the word to mean.

Comfort, honour and protect

All these three follow too. Loving generally includes comforting, honouring and protecting, but just what are you promising to do here?

"Comforting" means "being strong with". It is natural to feel weak sometimes, especially when struck by illness or bereavement, but also occasionally for no readily identifiable reason. You promise to support your partner when they are feeling weak. They will feel better able to cope, and you will feel happier. If you weren't married, in the sense of not having made a formal promise to comfort, you might think, when your partner is feeling weak, that now is the time to leave: the result would probably be unhappiness for both partners.

Some people try to bolster their own inadequate self-esteem by being rude to or about their partners. If you honour your partner, you don't do that. If you do do it, you will hurt them and make yourself even more unhappy. Don't!

Protection shouldn't be that much of an issue in a civilised society. Nonetheless, the promise to protect does work for your happiness. If your partner were threatened and you did not make any sort of protective effort, how would you live with yourself? Promise to protect, then, and if the occasion should arise, keep your promise!

Forsaking all others, be faithful

Adultery is always a bad idea. Always? I think so. I have yet to come across someone who is obviously truly happy with having broken the promise to be sexually faithful to a spouse. It can be a different matter when a relationship has completely broken down and ceased to exist for reasons other than sexual infidelity: after such a breakdown, it is possible for a former partner to find happiness in a new relationship, although this is relatively unusual.

Remember that sexual infidelity does not necessarily entail actual sexual intercourse. You can make yourself unhappy by means of any relationship, the intimacy of which you conceal from your partner, or which offends your partner when not concealed. A bit of flirting, which you may believe, or wish to believe, is innocent, is adulterous if it causes hurt.

If it does hurt your partner, or you think it might hurt your partner, it will make you unhappy, even if you enjoy it in the shorter term.

For better/worse, richer/poorer, in sickness and in health

Life is full of ups and downs. The essence of marriage is the agreement to stick together through all the ups and downs. Any change of circumstances, for better or for worse, in any part of life can put a strain on a relationship.

If you have been kept together for years largely by your shared struggle with shortage of money, and then one of you manages to earn enough that this is no longer a problem, how easy will you find it to learn that new strategies are now needed in the effort to help each other to be happy? If your shared joy has come from mountain climbing, how will you cope when one of you is confined to a wheelchair with a degenerative disease?

There are no general answers to these questions, but there is a general principle, and that is the principle that love leads to happiness. If you put in the effort needed to help your partner to cope with the changed circumstances, whatever they are, you will be helping yourself further on the road towards happiness.

Till death

I think it was Benjamin Franklin who said that the only two certain things in life were death and taxes. He may have been wrong about taxes, but eventually you will have to face death, and so will your partner. In some ways the one who dies first has it easier. The second will not have the support of their partner at the end.

If you leave your partner, and your partner then dies before you do, you will have the knowledge that they reached the end of life without the company that you had promised. This knowledge will not help you to be happy. Better to support your partner right to the end, even if it is hard, which it may very well be.

Maintenance can mean Work

If you are married, you will need to maintain your marriage by working at it. If you don't put any effort in, the relationship will deteriorate, and the marriage may eventually break up. Putting in the effort is, quite simply, loving. As I said earlier, you will find this easier, having a greater incentive, if you started off being in love.

There is no magic

Being in love, however, is not magic, no matter how wonderful it feels. You are both human beings, with something of a tendency to be disappointing to yourselves and to each other on occasion. There will be times when you will need to forgive, and times when you will need to be forgiven.

You will not be perfect, but it is within your power to be exceptionally good. Again, there is no magic ingredient to help you here. What might help is the knowledge that, as you put in the effort to help your partner to be happier, you will be making yourself happier as a direct result.

Contribution

The effort you make in your marriage is your contribution to it, your contribution to that small society known as the couple. Contribution is what makes you feel valuable in society as a whole, and the same is true within the couple. By loving, that is to say by making your contribution, you will be improving your own sense of self-worth, and thereby helping yourself to be happier. Remember that lack of self-worth due to failure to contribute is one of the universal barriers to happiness.

Values

When you are a contributor to your marriage, your partner will value you. This means that your partner will strive to keep you. In the same way, before you were married, you and your partner strove to win each other. This striving to gain and to keep is how we can identify what we value.

When we no longer value something, we no longer strive to keep it. This can apply just as much to relationships as to material objects. Why should your partner strive to keep the marriage intact? Isn't this the same question as asking why they should strive to keep *you*? Either way, the answer has to be that you must be valuable, and consequently valued. Contribution is the only cause of such valuing.

Ever deeper understanding

As your marriage goes on, you will acquire an ever deeper understanding of your partner. This is more or less inevitable, but it is a process which you can help along by putting some effort into it. Why should you do so?

The better you understand your partner, the more effective will be the contribution you make to the marriage, and consequently the more valuable you will be to your partner. Knowing that you are valued by your partner will improve your own sense of self-worth, which will be good for your own happiness.

It takes a lifetime

The work of understanding another person is never-ending. To do a good job of understanding another individual takes decades, the whole of your adult life, if you are lucky. Even then, your partner might still take you by surprise occasionally! So, is something which takes so long to do incompletely worth doing at all? Yes! There is no better source of joy than a happy marriage.

Keep Giving

To make your marriage work, you must keep working at it, keep contributing, and keep on giving. This is true even if your partner doesn't do their part. This is a very old-fashioned idea of marriage, isn't it? Current thinking is more along the lines of "easy in"/"easy out", with the "quicky divorce" regarded as entirely normal.

Why should I recommend continuing to contribute to a relationship which is giving you nothing back? I am not absolutely against the idea of abandoning a marriage if it has gone wrong in certain ways, as you will see in a later section on failed relationships in general, but the whole idea of marriage is that it should be permanent, so let's look at the advantages of sticking with a marriage which is not going as well as originally hoped.

The payoff can be slow

It is a simple fact of human nature that, if you do something for someone else, they will wish to return the favour. The return is not always immediate, and you may need to wait quite some time for it.

Your objective in working for your partner's increased happiness should not be to try to get this sort of returned-favour type of payoff. If that is your objective, you will undermine the whole thing. It only works really well when you work for your partner's happiness simply because of the joy that that brings to you directly. Nonetheless, if you do understand your partner well and do manage to make a genuine contribution to their happiness, it is virtually inevitable that you will eventually get that kind of payoff, although it might take a very long time! Or ...

It might take forever

It is just possible that you might spend your life-time being a brilliant husband or wife for a totally unappreciative spouse, perhaps one who just assumes that the joys of marriage do indeed come without any effort. You will observe that such a person is not truly happy, and will not be until they discover the virtue of contribution, and it is just possible that they might never make that discovery.

But the alternative is worse

This is when you get tempted to leave. If you do leave, you will take with you the knowledge that you could have tried harder and longer, that you are no longer making a contribution, and that your spouse now has a much poorer chance of discovering from your example how to be happy. Having this knowledge is likely to to be harder for you than staying with the struggle.

Remember your promises

Furthermore, you will know that you have failed to keep those promises which you made so solemnly. The promises were not conditional upon a particular response from your partner, although you may decide that, if they have never kept their side of the bargain at all, there is no reason why you should keep yours.

Only you can decide whether you can bear to live with yourself knowing that you have defaulted on the most serious promises you ever made. It will be less difficult if you are satisfied that your partner was never intending to make a genuine contribution in the first place, but was only trying to exploit your good nature. Even so, it will hurt.

Chapter 15

Families

Commonly, of course, a couple becomes a family after a while. In this chapter, we will be discussing not just the nuclear family of mother, father and a few children, but family relations in general, and the idea of the extended family.

Happy Families?

Various images of idyllic family life are currently popular. The one which the advertisers love presents mother, father, two children, and usually one pet, living a happy life in a moderate-sized modern house in a leafy suburb. Then there is the romantic little country village where everyone seems to be at least distantly related to everyone else, and everybody helps everybody else out with everything. You can even transport the community from the little village to the terraced houses of an industrial town, without disturbing the concept much!

But are these images valid? Where do they come from? More importantly, to what extent can they be realised in practice? Is the idea of a happy family valid?

Families can be happy

The short answer is yes. Happy families are possible and they do exist. The idealised images are just that, they are idealised versions of something which really does exist.

First, let me make clear what I mean by a happy family. It seems to me that a happy family is one in which the relationships between the members of the family do not impede the chances of any individual member of the family achieving happiness. This does not mean that every member of the family is constantly joyful, or even that every member is profoundly happy, just that the family relationships are not destructive.

It is virtually impossible for a relationship, especially a family relationship, to be neutral in this respect, so a relationship which is not destructive is likely to be constructive. In other words, a happy family is one in which the members make positive efforts for each other's happiness. If you recall my definition of "love", you will realise that, in a happy family, people love each other.

Putting that the other way around, families in which people love each other are happy families. Such families do exist.

Families can be very unhappy

At some level, we all know that family life can, in principle, be happy. If you come from an unhappy family, you probably feel that you have missed out on something very precious, even if you are not sure what it is that you have

141

missed out on. It is because we know that happy families can be very happy that we feel so bad about unhappy families.

An unhappy family is one in which the members do not work for each other's happiness. Consequently, the members themselves are very likely to be unhappy. Exceptions are possible. Within a family in which the majority of the relationships are bad, there may be an individual who does manage to love the others; this individual is likely to be much happier than the others. There may also be two or more people within an extended but unhappy family, who get on well enough with one another that they do work for each other's happiness, and thereby make themselves happier.

If you are a member of a fundamentally unhappy family, you will find it tough, but you don't have to be unhappy yourself. If you decide that you will act lovingly to the other members of your family, even though you feel you detest them and they seem to despise you, you will be on the road to making yourself happier. This is a matter of choice, albeit a very hard one, working for the happiness of people who seem to want to destroy you is not easy, but the only alternatives are to do nothing, which will not help you to be happier, or to leave.

Leaving an unhappy family may be the right thing to do. We will come back to this idea in Chapter 20. For now, let us assume that you are staying where you are, and look at how to approach family life, whether your family is basically happy or not.

Constructive pessimism

I like the idea of constructive pessimism. The constructive pessimist says, "I don't expect anything good to happen, so all my surprises are pleasant ones." Being constructive, he then does his best to bring about a good result.

This is the spirit in which to approach family life. Never expect other members of your family to love you, to do anything specifically for your benefit. Love them: do what you can to help them to be happy. This may include bringing up your children to be helpful, which may, in turn involve asking them to undertake certain specific tasks around the home, for example. This is not the same as expecting them to act lovingly towards you.

You may encourage other members of the family to be loving towards each other, but do not ask them to be loving towards you. Show the best example of love that you can, but expect nothing in return. You will get surprises, and many of them will be pleasant. More importantly, you will be happier with the result than if you had gone for the alternative.

The alternative ... destructive optimism?

The obvious alternative might be called destructive optimism. In this scenario, you argue that it is the duty of other members of the family to love you. You demand that they work for your happiness. Maybe you also do what you see as being your duty, but it doesn't help, and you can't see why not.

The reason it doesn't work is that by demanding other people's love, you create resentment in them, thereby making it very difficult for them to love you. This undermines their chances of happiness, as well as your own.

To make a demand of any sort, and to justify that demand on the basis of family loyalty, is a manipulative ploy. If you try it, you will destroy your own happiness, and undermine everyone else's. It is so important to understand this subject that the whole of Chapter 19 is about manipulation.

The Smallest Community

If you are to be happy with other people, you must be able to fit into a community. Communities are of various sizes, and your family is the smallest community in which you are likely to be involved. When you know how to handle the small community of the family, you will do better with larger communities too.

What is a community?

A community is any group of people who share something. This is a very broad definition, and deliberately so. At the highest level, the whole human race is one community, because we all share the planet, and we all share human life. The idea of community is usually more useful when considering a relatively small subset of the human race.

To take a few examples, we use phrases like "the medical community", "the business community", and "the farming community", to denote groups of people with certain shared interests, without any regard to where, or how widely scattered they are. More commonly, we refer to the people living in a small geographical region as a community, but the principle is the same. All these groups of people share something. What they share is the defining feature of the community.

If you are good at sharing things in a way appropriate to your community, you will be a successful member of that community. Let's look at how that works in a few tiny communities.

Husband and wife

The very smallest and most close-knit community is the married couple, who share virtually everything. This is a very simple idea, and the better you are at sharing everything with your partner, the happier your marriage is likely to be. As soon as you start keeping things just for yourself, or having secrets from your partner, you start to damage the relationship and to undermine your happiness.

Nuclear family

Father, mother and their dependent children share a great deal, but not everything. The children have to learn the idea of private property and privacy. Wise parents therefore make clear what things in the home the children have free access to, and what they do not. They also allow individual children to own things, which the parents and any other children can only use by permission of the owning child. If you can afford it, you will allow each child to have their own room; as far as is practicable, you will respect the privacy of that room, and expect any other children to do likewise.

You will still be sharing your food and your shelter, the two most fundamental physical needs. You will also share a fair proportion of your money, your social life, and all the advantages and disadvantages of living in the area in which you live.

Most importantly, if you have children, you will love them, and in a traditional nuclear family, your partner will also love them. This shared love is what binds the family together. You are working together for your children's happiness, and this effort will, in itself, make you happier. Furthermore, it is likely that eventually your children will love you too, but don't rely on this; be a constructive pessimist instead.

Extended family

Love within the family can extend beyond the limited confines of the basic nuclear family of mother, father and dependent children. In families where the tradition of love is well-established, uncles, aunts, grandparents and cousins all do what they can to make the family as a whole and the individuals which make it up happier.

What do all these people share, which defines the community in which they live? Their genes! We all have a natural interest in seeing our genes propagated and in maintaining the health of any relative who is close enough to share a good proportion of our genes.

But the extended family also propagates our kind of culture. In other words, we support our extended family because they share many of our memes. As long as you care about the system of beliefs you were brought up with, you will want to be good to your close relatives who share those beliefs.

Family comes first

One such belief, which is a persistent meme in its own right, is the idea that family comes first. This can be a healthy and useful meme to carry in your personal meme pool, provided that you only let it influence your behaviour to a limited extent. By all means let it inspire you to family loyalty when acting lovingly towards a member of your family makes you happier, but do not let it be used as a weapon against you and do not use it as such yourself.

If you use the "family comes first" slogan to define what you see as someone else's duty to you, then you will make yourself unhappy, whether or not the so-called duty is carried out. The same is true to a lesser extent if you use the duty argument to try to bring about any sort of behaviour. Finally, if a member of your family tries to use the idea of duty to persuade you to do something which you do not want to, just point out to them that manipulation of that kind doesn't help anyone to be happy.

Never Manipulate

The theme of manipulation keeps recurring, and I mention it here because it is commonplace within families. The emotional ties between family members are such that it is very easy to exploit them, so easy, in fact, that you might find yourself doing any of the things discussed in this section without even being fully aware that that is what you are doing.

Don't induce bad feelings

If someone in your family does something you don't like, by all means ask them to stop. Don't try to get your own back by trying to make them feel guilty about having upset you: you will upset yourself more if you do. Don't get so angry that you induce fear: that won't make you feel better in the long run. Don't try the vengeful tactic of doing something which you know is annoying or upsetting: you are likely to make things escalate and get worse for everyone.

All these moves are unpleasant ways of reacting to someone who you think has done you wrong, but some people use them pre-emptively so as to gain or regain power. Don't do that either: any power you get that way you will have got by cheating, and it won't do anything to make you happier. You cannot make yourself happy by making someone else unhappy.

Beware of "you should"

If you have children, you will have to teach them right from wrong, and you will therefore have to use words like "you should" or "you ought to" from time to time, hopefully backed up with a rational answer to the inevitable question "Why". Properly and responsibly used, these words will help you to control your children and help them to grow into happy, moral adults.

Your children are vulnerable and dependent upon you, and they will therefore do virtually anything you require of them, if it is backed up by a convincing moral imperative. Some parents misuse this power to suppress their children's natural desires in order to make their own lives easier, or so they think. In the long run, it is not worth it.

Whenever you use the word "should", you are, in effect, making someone else's moral judgement for them. This might be a fair and proper thing to do if you are really doing it genuinely for someone for whom you are responsible. If you say "you should" in such a way as to suggest that there is a moral issue at stake where there is none, or if you say it to someone who should be able to make their own moral judgements, you are probably trying to manipulate someone, and it won't do you any good.

Beware of the voices you instil

Again, if you have children, you will almost certainly find yourself saying to them the very same words that your parents said to you when you were a child. (Memes can be passed from generation to generation in this way, almost like genes.) This may or may not be a good thing, depending on what the words are, and the way in which they are used.

It can be difficult, but try to catch yourself before the words come out, and then think about whether it is really right for this meme to pass on to another generation. You may decide that, because you really love your children and you want them to be happy, you won't say the things your parents said to you, or maybe you will decide that you will.

In short, do not repeat anything you have heard, without first thinking about it. If you fail to think, you might even become a tool of someone else's manipulation. Would you have repeated the words "Heil Hitler" without having thought deeply about their meaning?

"I love you therefore you owe me"

Nobody is so crass as to use the "I love you therefore you owe me" argument in exactly those words. It is too transparent. You might still be tempted to use it more subtly, however, and maybe so subtly that you don't even notice it yourself.

If ever you find yourself thinking that someone in your family ought to so something for you because of all you have done for them, you are falling into the "I love you therefore you owe me" manipulation trap. I say you are falling into it, because it will hurt you even more than anyone else.

If you catch yourself thinking along those lines, remind yourself that it is up to the others what they do for you, and when, if anything, and if ever. By all means ask for what you want, but don't ever argue that they owe you: it will only make for disharmony. And, for heaven's sake, don't just sit there getting angry that they haven't guessed what you want, nobody owes you that, ever!

X would have wanted ...

Whenever someone says "Grandfather would have wanted ... " (Grandfather being dead and buried), they mean, "I don't wish to be straightforward about this, but I want ... " You can stop them in their tracks by pointing this out. You can stop yourself in your tracks, if ever you feel tempted to use this trick, by reminding yourself that it always creates resentment in the person against whom it is used, and never makes the person using it happy either.

Lead by Example

If you love your family, you will want your relatives to be happy, and you will make the necessary efforts to help them with this. There is no better way than to lead by example. Be happy, and let people copy the way you live your life so as to be happy.

Follow this book and others will follow you

When you follow the advice in this book, you will, I hope, find that you are much happier than ever before. This will show. People will wonder why, and ask what has changed. You could encourage them to buy their own copy of this book, but you will probably also wish to talk about the basic principles of honesty and love.

People do want to be happy, and spreading happiness is most worthwhile. You will not find it hard, having attained happiness yourself, to help others along the road you have followed. This should be easier within the family than with relative strangers.

Spreading happiness

Happiness is not a limited commodity to be hoarded; it can be created in virtually unlimited supplies. You can make yours even greater by helping other people to create theirs.

Amongst the people you are closest to, like your family, you can just talk about it. You do not have to say, "I am happy because ... ". Just talk, when others are ready to listen, about your beliefs, your values, and what you understand about the world.

Perhaps with other people, those who are not so close to you, you might, when the occasion seems to require it, quote a few words from this book, if they mean a lot to you, and if you think the person you're talking to doesn't understand them. If they seem puzzled, you could say, "Haven't you read 'How to be Happy'?" This might lead you to a deeper conversation, or to someone else reading this book, and, I hope, benefiting from it.

Imparting this understanding of how to be happy is, I believe, the very best way of spreading happiness. If I didn't believe that, I wouldn't have written this book!

Small children have to be told

Children come into the world with a capacity for everything, but no knowledge. They have to learn that violence, lying, cheating and stealing exist, and that they don't make anyone happy. They have to learn that happiness and unhappiness are both possible, and that one or the other will follow from the choices they make. They even have to learn that choices are possible.

Learning all this by trial and error would take a lifetime, and a lot of that lifetime would be miserable. Some people, whose parents didn't help them with these basics, do live such miserable lives, finding out the hard way that violence, dishonesty and manipulation lead to unhappiness and that unearned wealth brings no joy.

We can help our children to much happier lives by teaching them ethics, not just on the basis of well-tried formulas, like the Ten Commandments, but on the basis of principles which actually help people to be happier. When you know in yourself that happiness comes from morality, and that misery comes from immorality, you will find it quite easy to explain this to children. You will only have any difficulty in this area if you still believe that you can gain anything yourself by dishonest means.

All ages imitate

Although you will be copied by children whatever you do, you will only be copied by adults when they see that what you do works. When you have absorbed this book, and made whatever changes are necessary in your life, you will be happy, and it will be obvious to people that you are happy. People will want to copy this.

People may wish to copy you, but they will not necessarily know what it is they should be copying, since many of the secrets of happiness are internal. It is the reasons for your behaviour which guarantee your happiness rather than the behaviour itself. It is only people close to you, your family and friends, who are likely to understand you at the necessary depth to benefit from copying you.

It is up to you to work out how to help people who wish to copy your happiness. It is important that they understand the basic principles, and that they do not try to cheat on the process by simply copying some external behaviour, but you will have to handle this need for understanding on an individual case-by-case basis. There are no general rules.

Letting Go

Returning to the subject of families, let us look at what is probably the very hardest part of family life. If you have children, they will eventually grow up and leave home. If you love your children, you must let them go when they are ready, and they will decide when that is.

They have their own lives

You have been working all these years for your children's happiness. They have their own lives and they will only be happy if they are free as adults to live their lives in the way they believe to be right. Letting them do this goes against all your nurturing and protecting instincts, but it is what you have been building up to all these years. The transition from helpless infant to independent adult is so gradual that it is hard for parents to believe that their children are ever adults, but adults they are, and the defining moment comes when they decide (not you) that they are ready to live under a different roof.

Of course you want to keep them

Over the years you will have taken great delight in your children. They can be a joy to have around. If your relationship with them is healthy, the time you spend with them can always be a source of joy. Of course you don't want them to go. You like having them around. Especially if you have been a good and conscientious parent, a lot of the meaning in your life is wrapped up in the time you spend with your children.

But you must remember that joy is different from happiness. Joy is often a passing emotion, whereas happiness is fundamental to the core of your being. To retain your happiness, you sometimes have to forgo a bit of shorter-term joy.

The great parental paradox

If you try to persuade your children to stay with you longer than they really want to, you are likely to succeed, but you will create resentment. You are likely to succeed because of the strength of your parental influence. You will create resentment because you are using your influence not for the long-term benefit of your offspring, but for your own short-term feelings. The net result will be bad for the happiness of all concerned, and your children are unlikely to want to visit you very often afterwards.

If you let your children leave home when they want to, but let them understand that they will be welcome to visit you whenever they wish, the chances are good that your relationship with them will improve, that they will visit you, and even come to you for advice and help when they want it. Thus your parental role will continue, and everyone will continue basically happy, despite the initial pain of separation for you.

There is, therefore, this paradox. If you try to hang on to your children when they grow up, you will lose them; if you let go of them, you will keep them.

Never cling to anyone

Something similar is true in all relationships. People are put off by clinging. If it is clear to someone that your relationship with them is so important to you that you can't let go, they are likely to want to get away. If you are strong and happy in yourself, always willing to welcome them into your life but equally ready to let them go and do their own thing when they want, your relationships will be good, both in the family and outside it.

Chapter 16

Villages, Towns and Cities

Outside your family and your immediate circle of friends, your next most important set of relationships should be with your colleagues at work, but I want to postpone that subject until after we have considered the neighbours! Even if you do not work, you still have neighbours, unless you live somewhere very isolated indeed.

If you are going to be happy with people in general, it is as well to make sure that the relationships you have with the people in your local community are good relationships. Many of these are likely to be relatively superficial, but you might find some good, true, close friendships amongst the people you meet in your local community.

What is your local community? It is the people with whom you share the area in which you live. This could be anything from a tiny hamlet to a vast city, and socially successful behaviour does vary a bit according to the size of the community. Let's start with the smallest.

Village Life

If you live in a village, there are few enough people that it is possible in principle to be at least slightly acquainted with every one of them. More significantly, it is possible for each one of them to be at least slightly acquainted with you. If there are too many people for you to know all of them at least by sight, then you certainly live in a town, rather than a village.

Your village will be a pleasant place to live if all the people in it try to make it a pleasant place to live. Probably not all of them will, but if enough people put in the effort, it will work. You will have noticed that one of the main themes of this book is the matter of contribution. This is because you must make some effort to be valuable to other people in order to have the self-respect you need in order to be happy. But how do you contribute to village life?

If you work at making your village pleasant for the other inhabitants, two things will follow. Firstly, you will enjoy it more yourself. Secondly, you will be more popular. If you do really well, a third thing might follow, and that is that some other people, who hadn't previously bothered, might now start to do their bit. The net result will be that everyone will be happier. But where do you start?

Politeness and the façade

The first thing is not to be offensive. Even if you actively dislike a fellow village resident, it is as well to be polite to them. Be polite, in fact, to everyone.

There is nothing to be gained anywhere by any other attitude, but in a small community it is especially true that politeness makes everyone's life easier.

You may feel that there is a certain falseness in this, but it should not be so. Remember that you are sharing your village with these people, and everyone can pull together to make the place happier to live in. One of the ways you do this is to spread this habit of avoiding giving offence.

It is hardest when you have a real problem which you are struggling with. If you are worrying or feeling sad about something, or your physical health is not at its best, it can be difficult not to let superficial relationships suffer too. If you have a headache, it can be harder to be pleasant to someone you bump into in the village shop, but it is worth the effort. In many places, it is conventional to say you're fine when they ask how you are, but there is no harm in telling the truth, as long as you don't go on about your ills to the point of being a burden.

Never hurt

We are more mobile than earlier generations. People move house much more frequently than they did centuries ago, and it is quite unexceptional to move from one area to another some distance away. We tend, therefore, not to think of our neighbours as permanent features of our lives. You might be tempted, therefore, not to care about those relationships, and, if a neighbour offends you somehow, to respond hurtfully. Even worse, you might just strike the first blow, metaphorically of course, possibly without thinking.

The consequences of this are worse in a village than in a larger community for several reasons. Firstly, if you do something gratuitously unpleasant, word will get around, and you will become known as an unpleasant person, prejudicing your chances of friendship with people. Secondly, you are likely to meet the person with whom you have had your little difficulty much more often than you would in a larger place. Thirdly, villages are places where people do still tend to reside for very long periods, and this might well include you, so you won't want to have the place tainted by any relationships which you have yourself poisoned.

Therefore, even if someone seems to be determined to make you lose your cool, keep the façade of politeness intact, and address whatever problem seems to be the cause of the difficulty calmly, quietly, gently, considerately, and without ever being offensive.

Say hello

When you first move to a village, make a point of greeting everyone you meet. It will very soon become clear what the local conventions are. In some places, just a smile and a nod as you pass are the norm; in others, you will seem rude if you do not stop to converse about some trivia. Copy the local conventions.

If these involve conversations longer than you expect to have time for, allow more time whenever you can: only when you have established the idea in other people's minds that you do fit in, will you be able to afford, when it is true, to cut short any attempt at chat, by saying what a rush you are in this morning. If you seem to be permanently in too much of a hurry to pass at least a little of the time of day with the people you share your village with, you will be seen as someone who does not want to fit in. And it will be true!

Remember that the purpose of these conversations is not to exchange information about what you are overtly discussing. The purpose of them is to establish and maintain the sense of community, which is a large part of what makes the village worth inhabiting in the first place.

Join in

Your village is very likely to have some sort of shared activity. Whatever it is, try joining in. You might think that you have no interest in hockey, but if there is a local hockey team, go and watch at least once. You might end up making new friends.

If there is a local church, try going to it, even if you have no interest in religion. You are likely to meet some of the best people in the community.

If the place seems to have nothing, try starting something! Whatever you are interested in, the chances are that there are at least a few others in the village with a shared interest. All you have to do is find a room you can hire (or use your own house), put up a few posters around the village inviting people, include drinks if you can, and get people to come to the inaugural meeting of whatever club it is that you were thinking the village ought to have.

Trust your neighbours

One of the ways in which a village differs from a city is that crime is rarer. People are more inclined to be honest in their dealings with their neighbours if they are close enough to meet regularly, and if anonymity is basically impossible. If a villager is seen committing a crime of any sort, the chances are very high that they will be recognised, and this acts as a powerful disincentive to law-breaking.

Wanting to keep what we rightfully own is a fundamental human instinct. Living in a low crime area will help you to be happy because your fundamental human right to keep what you own is less likely to be violated. Being able to trust your neighbours is good for your sense of well-being.

It is another simple fact of human nature that trust builds trust and mistrust builds mistrust. You should therefore make an active effort to build the atmosphere of trust which can help to make a village such a pleasant place to live. You can do this by always being ready to lend things to your neighbours, and always being ready to welcome them into your home.

It may be less wise to trust them with confidential information. You will have to judge each individual as you find them, but gossip is such a feature of small communities that you should not be surprised when things are discussed quite openly which would be regarded as too personal in a larger community. What you thought of as a confidence might be regarded just as a normal part of a conversation, perhaps especially if it carries the injunction not to tell anyone. You might feel hurt by this, but it is often not malicious; if you really want to talk about something *and* keep it private, be very careful who you talk to, anywhere!

How to Enjoy a Small Town

A small town has some of the advantages of a village and some of those of a city, as well as some of the disadvantages of each. The key to happiness here is to concentrate on the positive aspects of the place and not to let yourself be annoyed by its limitations. Accept the place for what it is, except in so far as you can change it by your own influence.

You are unlikely to be able to introduce many of the better features of a great city, such as cathedrals, big museums, art galleries, opera houses, universities, and major hospitals, since they are not in the nature of a small town. You might, however, be able to introduce some of the better features of a village, at least into your life in the town, even if you don't have a great deal of influence on the lives of most of the other people living there. How do you do this?

Treat it like a village

Your life in a small town will be more pleasant if you treat it to some extent like a village. The two ways in which you can do this are by being basically friendly, and by joining in local activities.

Politeness and inoffensiveness will stand you in good stead anywhere, but in most towns, it is not considered normal to greet every person you meet. Instead, be ready always to exchange a few inconsequential words with another inhabitant if the occasion arises, and do not shy away from chance conversation. The town may contain a few eccentrics whose mission in life seems to be to spend as long as possible telling all their troubles to anyone who doesn't refuse point blank to listen. You will soon learn who these people are and how to avoid them without hurting them too much, but be ready to chat to anyone else, if they want.

It is a very good idea to make a point of getting to know your immediate neighbours. Remember that you share a common interest in the corner of the town you live in, as well as in the town itself. Do not force unwelcome attentions on people who do not wish to be friendly, but at least acknowledge their existence with a smile and a wave as you pass. When you get a chance, talk to your neighbours about what you suspect might interest them. If next door's car is obviously loved, but the garden is scruffy, talk about cars, even if your own passion is gardening, and vice versa.

Every town has some sort of local club, society or church: join in with something which interests you. Many towns have an annual event of some sort: go to it. If anyone in the town invites you to a party or suggests you attend a meeting, go and join in. Join in whatever you ethically can, and can find the time for. When the local amateur dramatic group puts on a play, or the town orchestra does a concert, be there, no matter how amateur you expect the performance to be. Even better, be part of the show, if you can. The more time you make for things in the local community, the happier you will be in your town.

Shop locally

As far as possible, use the local shops. The ones in the city down the road may offer more choice, better prices, or a better designed shopping mall, but your local shops are the heart of the commercial life of your town. Without you, they die, and the heart of the town dies. Get to know your shopkeepers. They may not have exactly what you want in stock, but they can probably get it if you ask.

If there is a good local restaurant, go to it when you can afford to, rather than to one further away. Likewise, if you want to see the new blockbuster film, wait until it comes to your local cinema, rather than travel miles and spend your money outside your local town. If your town has a theatre, go to as many plays there as you can.

If you spend what money you can within your local town, and encourage other people to do so too, you will help the town to be a better place, better for you and for everyone else who lives there. Everyone wins, and you will feel happier about it than if you regard your town just as somewhere to sleep, while you both earn and spend your money elsewhere.

Who knows whom?

You will never be acquainted with everyone in the town, but after a while you will have a few hundred acquaintances, in addition to a smaller number of real friends. Each of the people you know also knows a few hundred other people. There are only a few thousand people in the town. It follows that you are very likely to have a common acquaintance with anyone you meet, that is to say that whoever you talk to probably knows someone who knows you, and you might well meet them again in a different context.

Would you like an illustration of this? I once lost my temper with an ignorant shop assistant in a small town I lived in. I didn't know her, but a week later, I was told off for my rudeness by her daughter's boyfriend's brother's girlfriend's sister, whom I did know quite well.

There is therefore not much more anonymity in a small town than there is in a village. If the town contains so many thousands of people that anonymity is a real possibility, then, to all intents and purposes, you live in a city, even if it calls itself a town.

Surviving in a Big City

The human race has only recently invented cities of the size we now have. We have not evolved far enough for them to feel entirely natural. Many of our instincts are better suited to life in the jungle, or at least in the countryside. To survive successfully and happily in a big city you must concentrate on the culture which makes it possible, rather than on your animal nature, which makes it difficult.

You can't know everyone

If you live long enough in a small town, you will eventually recognise virtually all the faces, even if you only know a small proportion of the names and characters which go with them. In a city, this is impossible. You will never get to recognise everyone, not only because there are too many of them, but also because they come and go too frequently. In a really big city, there are more new residents every day than you could expect to meet in a year, and more in a month than you could ever know in a lifetime.

The loneliness problem

As you walk through the streets of a city, there will usually be other people there, but even when the streets are thronged with people, you can still be very lonely. You might even be frightened.

The presence of other people will not help you to be less lonely, and it may not even help you to be less frightened. What will help with both of these things is social relationships with other people, but if you have just come to the city, and you know no-one, where and how do you start?

Find a small community

Within every large city, there are numbers of small communities. Unlike other places, these tend not to be so well-defined geographically. A community is, as I said earlier, any collection of people who have something in common. In any city, there is bound to be a community of some sort which you can join.

Buy and read the local paper. Look out for events which might interest you, and go to them. Try going to your local church, mosque or synagogue. Join a club, any club! Find (or start) the local city branch of the national society for your hobby.

Talking to total strangers in a city is not usually regarded as normal behaviour, but talking to total strangers within the context of a known common interest, such as membership of the same club, society or church, is a good idea. They are probably there because they want to talk to someone too.

If you have come to the city because you have a new job there, you may find that you have the beginnings of a social life laid on. Many companies have social events you can join in with, and you will probably also be able to make friends at work, and become part of their social life too.

Loneliness does not have to be a problem in a city if you find a smaller community within the city. Having found that community, though, you must still do your bit in contributing to its success. As in every other context, your contribution will make other people happier, improve your sense of self-worth, and tend to help you to be happier too.

Meet the neighbours

It is more difficult in a city than in a smaller place, but getting to know your immediate neighbours can still pay dividends. Greet them consistently. At first you may get no response, but everyone responds to a smile eventually. Remember that they are unlikely to value you unless you are valuable to them. You can be valuable just by being pleasant.

If you see a neighbour obviously having difficulty with something, offer to help. Your offer may be turned down or it may be accepted. Either way, you will make the area a better place to be.

You can also be valuable simply by caring about what you have in common with your neighbours. Do your bit to make the immediate area as pleasant to live in as you can. What you can do may be limited, but keep your eyes open for ways in which you can contribute, and do it. This will be good for everyone, good for your self-respect, and good for your happiness.

Mistakes to Avoid Everywhere

If you are going to be happy with people, you must make sure that they are happy with you. I do not mean that you must take total responsibility for their overall happiness, but you must not do anything which makes other people feel that they would be happier if you weren't around. There are exceptions to this, but as a general rule, people should not find you unpleasant or hurtful.

You can avoid much unpleasantness and hurt by making allowance for a few simple facts about human nature, and about the world.

Forgetting people's names

People are very attached to their names. At some deep level, you feel that your name is who you are. If someone forgets your name, you are likely to feel slighted, to feel that they don't care about the fact that you are a person, and certainly that they don't really care who you are.

Don't do this to other people. When someone tells you their name, remember it. It doesn't matter what techniques you use to help your memory to do its job, but you will find it easier if you can somehow attach the name and face to some aspect of the character which you care about.

If you remember someone's name when they were not expecting you to, they will feel good about you, and you can feel good about yourself too. This is more true in cities than in villages; equally, in a village you are more likely to cause deeper offence by forgetting a name.

Assuming you'll never meet again

When someone whom you do not know does something which annoys you, it can be very tempting to "give them a piece of your mind", or to be unpleasant in some other way. You assume that you're never going to meet this particular idiot again, so you can indulge yourself by telling them just what you think of them. There is greater temptation to this in a city than in a village, because you are more likely to think that you will get away with it, but wherever you are, it is a small world.

Obviously, you could be wrong. It might be years later that you come across this individual in a different context. They will remember, and they will remember you as an unpleasant person with a quick temper and a vicious turn of phrase. They won't remember that they were in the wrong and that you were quite right to tell them what for. How are you going to be happy in this relationship now?

If you had, in the first place, assumed that here was a person you might wish to be able to talk to at some future time, you would have handled them much more politely, no matter how bad their behaviour towards you. Then, when you do meet again, you are in a much better position: they may even remember what they did wrong and how well you handled it, and then they may want to apologise. Even if they don't, it doesn't matter.

Of course, this is another case of short-termism versus long-termism. Letting rip at someone whom you never expect to meet again gives you a short-term good feeling, at the expense of a risk of a long-term bad feeling. Keeping your cool may cost you the short-term satisfaction of letting off steam, for the longer-term benefits of knowing that you did keep your temper and knowing that if you meet the fool again, there is a chance of a civilised relationship.

Breach of confidence

Don't leak! There will be times, especially as you become obviously happier with yourself and the rest of the world, when people want to discuss their personal problems with you, or to trust you with other confidential information. This is a great responsibility, but it has a terrible temptation with it.

What you may hear in a confidential conversation might just be so fascinating that you want to share it with someone else, someone who can be trusted to keep their mouth shut, of course. They might treat this information as confidential and tell no-one, or they might find it so fascinating that they just have to share it with someone else, someone who can be trusted to keep their mouth shut, of course. And so it goes on ... Eventually, it becomes clear that you were never to be trusted in the first place, and how will you feel then?

How you will feel then should be just the same as when you leaked in the first place. Dreadfully, and properly guilty. It should make no difference that the rest of the world now knows that you are not to be trusted. It is quite sufficient that you yourself know that you cannot be trusted.

The alternative is to be trustworthy. That way you retain other people's respect, but much more importantly, you retain your own self-respect, which you need in order to be happy. Remember that, while village life is notorious for gossip, breach of confidence is just as bad in a larger community as it is in a small one.

There is more to keeping a confidence than just not telling what you know. You should also act, as far as possible, as if you didn't know what you have been told in confidence. There are two exceptions to this. Obviously, if the information was given to you so that you could act on it, then you can do so. Secondly, if you come across confidential information which tells you that some deception or planned violence is afoot, you have not only the right, but also the duty, to warn the potential victims. This is true even if the information stems from your employer, and even if your employer is the state.

Honest people have the right to assume that their secrets are safe. Criminals do not.

Dishonesty

Dishonesty is commoner in larger communities than in smaller ones, but why should you ever be dishonest? People are dishonest in order to obtain what they want, when they think they cannot obtain it honestly. It doesn't work very well.

You can't enjoy something which you have obtained dishonestly anything like as much as you can if you have obtained it honestly.

More relevantly to this part of the book, all your relationships with other people suffer if you are ever dishonest with anyone. If you are prepared to let dishonesty become part of your life, you will always worry about when to cheat and when to be honest instead. You will be much happier, and have a simpler life, if you never allow any dishonesty at all.

A consequence of this thoroughgoing honesty is that most people, certainly honest ones, will recognise that you are honest yourself, and they will trust you. This will help you in all your dealings with all people.

Violence

Violence is commoner in cities than in villages, but the nature of violence is the same everywhere. Violence never helps a relationship. The first use of force is always wrong. The morality of meeting force with force is arguable. If you want to be happy with other people, never use violence, or threats of violence, against them, and never be guilty of incitement to violence. To do so would destroy your own happiness anyway, since you can never be happy in the long term about anything which you have obtained by force or threat of force.

Perhaps I should also mention a common misconception about death by violence. Some people think that violent criminals are a serious threat to society. In fact, violent criminals are rare, and have been responsible for relatively few deaths throughout the course of human history. The vast majority of deaths by violence occur in wars. The most dangerous people on the planet are those who are prepared to believe that starting a war can be morally right, and are prepared to encourage large numbers of other people to slaughter as many of "the enemy" as possible. A single politician can be responsible for more deaths by violence than the entire criminal fraternity of the country.

It is therefore important to understand the nature of politicians, and for this, it is as well to consider ...

Chapter 17

Society as a Whole

Utopia does not exist. Every society is in some ways unsatisfactory. It is just that some countries are worse than others. To be happy in your country, and in the world as a whole, it is as well to understand it as well as you can.

A deeper understanding of the way your country functions might make you sad, but the old saying about ignorance, "Where ignorance is bliss, 'tis folly to be wise" is nonsense. A deeper understanding will help you better to cope with things as they are, and equip you better to help change them. You cannot make intelligent changes to something you don't understand.

Without understanding, you might just feel that there is something indefinably not quite right, or maybe seriously wrong, without being able to identify what it is. This kind of feeling has led, in the past, to bloody and unstructured revolutions, the political equivalent of vandalism, which is the consequence of a desire for change without intelligent thought as to what to change and exactly how.

When you do understand society as a whole, you will not only be better equipped to run your own life happily, but you will also be better able to use your political influence intelligently, and to cope with future changes in society.

The most fundamental things to understand are the types of laws there are, the nature and amount of taxation, and the nature of politicians, the people who decide on what the laws and taxes are to be. When we have looked at these things, we will look into the future, and see if we can find a way for you to run your life so that the political future will not be a problem for you.

Good Laws

In any society, there are two basic types of law, objective law and subjective law. The easiest way to tell them apart is to try to identify who would be the victim when the law is broken. If it is clear who the victim is, as in the case of all crimes of violence and theft, then the law is objective, and necessary for civilisation. If there is no identifiable victim, or the only apparent victim is the person alleged to have committed a crime, then the law is subjective, and probably designed to limit individual freedom.

Roughly speaking, objective laws are good, and subjective laws are not. Let's look at some of the things which are ruled out by objective law in civilised societies.

Violence and Threats

Murder, rape, kidnap, robbery with violence, and assault are all illegal, and properly so, in all civilised societies. So, too, are threatening behaviour, demanding money with menaces, extortion and intimidation. All such things are an infringement of the basic human right to life and are properly illegal everywhere.

It is slightly less obvious, but still true, that crimes against property are objectively illegal. Property rights are human rights. You own what you own, and you have a right to keep it. For this reason, burglary, theft, arson, and criminal damage such as vandalism are all illegal, as objective crimes against people. Shoplifting, pilfering, poaching, and similar crimes against companies and other such institutions are just as illegal, even though the actual victim is often not an individual person, but a group of people, no one of whom may be noticeably hurt by the crime.

Cheating and fraud

Cheating is the obtaining of anything valuable by means of deception or breach of promise. It includes not only the traditional ideas of fraud, such as embezzlement, but all issues of breach of contract, obtaining money by deception, and misleading trade descriptions, all of which are objectively illegal.

In many countries, there is a requirement that anything sold by way of trade must be of sufficient quality to meet its stated purpose, which is a perfectly reasonable objective law in circumstances where the buyer cannot conduct a thorough examination and test of the product before committing to buying it.

Negligence and dangerous behaviour

In most civilised societies, the legal system contains the idea of the duty of care. The idea is that by being careless, we can hurt other innocent people. Probably the commonest breach of this type of law is the causing of death by dangerous driving.

Laws which are intended to handle cases of accidents where there is an identifiable innocent victim, and an identifiable individual who caused the accident through carelessness or negligence, are objective laws, and therefore good laws. This does not mean that it is right to look for someone else to blame or to sue if you have an accident after deliberately doing something risky.

Protection of weaker members

Some people are too young, too old, or too ill to be responsible for their own decisions. The care of such people is properly the responsibility of their families and of charities. In some countries, some of this care is taken over by the state, which pays for it out of taxes.

How much of this care should be taken over by the state is the subject of a great deal of political debate. There are three types of answer: all of it, some of it, or none of it. If you believe that the state should take over all such care, you are denying people's right to care for their own children and for anyone else they care about. If you believe that the state should take over some such care, then how much? The answer to this is subjective: there is no objective way of deducing a correct answer to this question. There is only one other answer, and that answer depends on the assumption that you have no duty to pay for the care of anyone whom you do not choose to support.

To what extent, then, should there be laws to protect children, the old and the sick. To answer this, we must look again at the nature of crime. For there to be a crime, there has to be a criminal, and there has to be a victim; the criminal gains something at the expense of the victim. Exploitation is the issue here. It is impossible to exploit a mature and competent person who can make rational decisions as to what to agree to, but children, the very old and the sick can be exploited.

It is easy enough to outlaw child labour on the objective grounds that a child cannot rationally make a fully informed decision, but how old is old, and how sick is sick? Who needs to be protected from whom, and by whom? There are no easy answers to these questions, but the way to judge any such situation when you encounter it is to remember the simple and objective rule that if there is a victim who suffers some loss due to force, threat of force, criminal negligence or deception, then there is a crime and a criminal somewhere. If the apparent victim suffers only as a result of their own weakness, then there may be a sad situation, but there is no crime, and no criminal.

Rules made to be Broken

On top of all the good, necessary and objective laws there are in all societies, we are loaded with all sorts of laws, rules and regulations, the details of which are not arrived at by logical deduction from unarguable premises, but, as often as not, from heated debate based on some people's feelings about how other people should be controlled. If you doubt this, observe your legislators in action, assuming that they permit this in your country.

Such subjective laws generally have a purpose which many will agree is desirable, but they also have a cost, and the cumulative cost of all of them is very substantial. The people who monitor and enforce all these regulations do not contribute anything to the wealth of the society in which they work, but they are paid for by those of us who do.

You probably do not pay much attention to all the rules and regulations which exist. As a basically good person, you probably just assume that other people are basically good, and that all laws, rules and regulations are there for good reasons. This makes it possible for you to be controlled by people who are prepared to take advantage of your good nature. Evil always depends on good in this way.

So, how are you going to approach the plethora of rules and regulations which surround you? And what does that question have to do with your happiness? If you are faced with one of the army of enforcers of subjective rules, remember that the enforcer is dependent upon you the producer for survival, and not the other way around, despite the powers they may have to destroy your livelihood: knowledge of this fact will allow you to retain your self-respect no matter what they do to you. If you are the enforcer, do not expect to be happy: the thrill you get when you wield the power granted to you by subjective law does not last, and does not contribute anything to your basic happiness.

Are all subjective laws there as rules made to be broken? No, but if you find your freedom restricted by a law which seems to make no sense, then breaking that law may get you into certain difficulties with the enforcers, but the fact of breaking it will not, in itself, make you unhappy. If, on the other hand, you break an objective law, stealing, cheating, using violence or threats, you will make yourself unhappy, because such crimes are fundamentally contrary to human nature. Cheating includes getting a living by means of subjective law: this will make you unhappy.

It is for these reasons that your happiness depends upon an understanding of the difference between objective and subjective law, so let's go into just a little more detail.

Victimless crimes

If ever you find yourself tempted to break the law, or, even worse, if you find yourself accused of committing a crime, ask yourself who is the victim of the alleged crime. If you cannot identify one, do not allow anyone to make you feel guilty about the alleged crime. If they do try to make you feel guilty, ask them who the victim is, and, if they cannot identify one, point out to them that they are trying to make you into a victim, and that they are therefore guilty.

I will give you an example. A near neighbour of mine was arrested for growing cannabis. He was growing cannabis because his wife was suffering a rare disease for which cannabis is the best treatment; the doctor approved of this, but was not permitted to prescribe it, because of subjective legislation, and was obliged instead to prescribe other drugs with much more dangerous side-effects. Who was the alleged victim? It was alleged that the victims of my neighbour's crime were the people to whom he might have sold cannabis, if he had chosen to sell it, which he hadn't. The actual victim? The man whose house was broken into and whose property was damaged by the police, and his wife, whose illness worsened when she was no longer able to get the best treatment.

There were, of course, yet more victims of this crime. Who paid for the police and the time of the legal professionals involved? Who paid for the legislation in the first place?

Over-protection

Let us continue with this example, because it illustrates something more about subjective law and the consequences of it for all of us. The alleged victims of the crime, you will remember, were the people who might have bought this illegal drug.

How can someone, who chooses to enter into a bargain, be a victim of the other party to that bargain? The answer is when there is fraud or cheating. This can happen in any straightforward purchase when the seller misleads the buyer as to the nature of what he is selling. You can argue that anyone selling drugs is unlikely to draw the purchaser's attention to the possibility of addiction and any dangerous side-effects there might be, and that they are therefore cheating, and guilty of an objective crime. If this is the case, why have we not made tobacco and alcohol just as illegal as cannabis and heroin? And what about coffee and chocolate?

What if someone is stupid enough to wish to buy a dangerous and addictive drug, knowing the risks? If they are among the large minority whose poison is tobacco, they simply go to a shop, and buy their favourite dangerous and addictive drug at a price low enough that they aren't likely to resort to criminal activity to raise the funds necessary to support their habit. If they are among the smaller minority who prefer heroin, they have to pay a much higher price for a drug which is also cheap to produce. The extra money goes to people who are prepared to use violence to protect their trade, a trade which would not be as lucrative if competition were permitted, as it would be if it were legal.

All drug-related crime, therefore, stems from subjective legislation intended to protect people from their own stupidity. In the final analysis, however, you cannot protect people from their own stupidity.

Your happiness depends upon your choosing not to be stupid. Laws intended to prevent you from suffering from the consequences of your failure to make intelligent decisions will not make you happier, in fact, quite the contrary.

Encouragement of irresponsibility

Why the contrary? How can legislation intended to protect you help to make you unhappy?

To understand this, consider the alternative. Let us suppose that you were completely free to make all your own decisions about everything and to take the consequences of those decisions, subject to your not committing any objective crime. You would not only have greater freedom, but also more money, since you would not be paying so much tax.

As it is, if something goes wrong in your life, do you look for someone else to blame, getting angry with some untraceable bureaucrat who failed to make a regulation to prevent your suffering? Are you expecting that you should be fed, clothed and housed at the taxpayer's expense? Can you be happy with this? When you understand that anything paid for by the government comes from money which is obtained by threat of force from people who have earned it, you will not be happy to benefit from it.

If the legislators are encouraging you to expect someone else to be responsible for your decisions, and for your life, are they being fair to you? Are they helping you to be happy?

"Jobs for the boys"

This brings us to the matter of unemployment benefit, and the welfare state in general. Why is there a poverty trap? Why is it that, once you are dependent upon state benefits, it is extremely difficult to get out of the trap? If you earn some money, you may lose more in so-called benefits than you gain in earnings. How can this be?

If the opposite were true, if you could always improve things by earning more, you might have quite an incentive to work your way out of the benefits system altogether. Who would gain? You would gain, and so would the taxpayer. Who would lose? Whose livelihood is dependent upon there being plenty of recipients of so-called benefits to be "helped"? Who would have no excuse for the pay they demand if there were no-one to "help"?

Are you on the other side of the counter in the benefits office? Are you happy in your work? What if you succeeded? What if you got the great army of unemployed back into real productive work? Unthinkable isn't it? They will always be there won't they? You had better make sure they are, because otherwise you will be out of a job yourself. Are you happy in your work? Money is taken from productive people and transferred to the unemployed. This is a good thing, isn't it? You get a cut of this money. That's good too, isn't it? Wouldn't it be dreadful if there were many fewer unemployed? You'd have to find some other way of getting a living.

Of course, you and your colleagues could keep yourselves going by making the rules more complicated. With more complicated rules, you need more people to administer and interpret them, so you can require more money to keep the system going. Have you done this already? Are you happy in your work? If you work really hard, you might get to wangle a way of having more people in your department, which gives you an excuse for a bigger salary. Have you done this already? Are you happy in your work?

Maybe you have nothing to do with the welfare state, but you still work for central or local government. Are you familiar with all the techniques for justifying your pay and maintaining your department in the face of all those wicked people who want taxpayers to pay less to support you? Are you sure you have done everything possible to secure your position? Are you happy in your work?

Regulation

One of the most dangerous recent political developments common to a number of Western countries is the introduction of regulators, in the form of individual people who are given the power to make regulations binding upon whole industries, solely on the basis of what seems right to them, rationally or otherwise. This is the logical end-point of the idea of "enabling legislation", the passing of laws by legislators, which delegate to individuals the power to make rules and regulations without further reference to the legislators themselves.

This is subjective legislation at its worst, where a law arises neither from logic, nor even from debate, but from an individual's opinion.

If you wish to be happy, do not accept a job as a maker of rules, because you cannot do so without making a number of assumptions about life which are incompatible with your long-term happiness, no matter how conscientiously you think you are doing your job. If you are affected by the decisions of such a person, recognise them for what they are, and think very hard about how you will regard the rules they make, rather than simply accepting such rules as if they were as inevitable as the law of gravity.

Taxation

Taxation is the only known successful way of raising the money necessary to pay for those things from which all members of society benefit, regardless of whether they individually choose to pay for them or not. For example, if your country has a properly constituted army, whose function is to protect you from foreign invaders, you will be protected by it, regardless of whether you contribute to its cost or not. Because some people are so short-sighted that they think it might be good to take advantage of those others who choose to contribute to that cost, it has become necessary to raise such money by taxation rather than by voluntary contribution.

The difficulty we all have as members of society is deciding what should be paid for out of taxation.

Legitimate objectives

We have seen that the use of force is generally objectively criminal, but surely you have a right to use force in self-defence against violent criminals. In a civilised society, people are not normally permitted to take the law into their own hands and exercise this right. Instead, we have the police, whose function is to defend the individual citizen from the violence of criminals, and the armed forces, whose only proper function is to protect the citizens of a country from the violence of foreign invaders.

We also need the courts in order to determine objectively whether a person accused of a crime is indeed guilty of it. All these things are paid for by taxes, no-one having yet found a convincingly better way of paying for them, but the portion of our tax money used for this purpose is, in a sense, paid voluntarily, in that very very few taxpayers would argue that these things should not be paid for out of taxes.

It would also be useful to have, in a civilised society, a reliable means of convincing criminals not to re-offend. In the absence of this, we have prison and probationary services, which are also paid for out of taxes, pending the invention of a better system.

Since everyone benefits, or should benefit, from the presence of the police, the armed services, the courts and so on, it is only fair that everyone should help to pay for them. It is also reasonable to argue that anything which is needed by everyone, which cannot be provided by private enterprise, and which everyone benefits from if it is present, should also be paid for out of taxes. Can you think of any other examples?

It used to be argued that the state had a proper role in running major industries, but it can be seen from the consequences of privatisation of state monopolies that virtually anything which can in principle be done by the private sector is better done by the private sector.

Other objectives

In practice, most tax money goes to benefit a subset of the population, not everyone. When you are aware of this, you might notice that, whenever anyone says that the government should do something about a particular issue, they rarely draw attention to the fact that what they propose costs money, all taxpayers pay, a few people gain something, and, more often than not, one of the intended beneficiaries is the person clamouring that the government should do something. Some such people get quite a handsome income from their cut, whilst presenting an impressive show of all the good they are doing, and never mentioning the costs or who exactly pays.

Taxpayers

Who does pay? There is a clever little myth, which is widely believed, that virtually all of the adult working population pays tax, no matter who they work for, even if they work for the government. This is simply not true. The only people who really pay tax are the people who personally make payments to the government or whose businesses do so. The people who actually sign the cheques or pay cash over the counter to the tax collectors are relatively few, and it is on them that the whole system depends.

Obtained by force or threat

Do you pay tax? If you think the answer to this question is "yes", ask yourself what would happen if you were to decide not to pay it. If you can't answer this one because the tax is taken off your pay before you get it, then you do not really pay the tax yourself. You probably have a predictable net take-home pay from which you budget your expenditure, without thinking much about your nominal "gross" pay "before tax". Either the tax is paid by your employer, or you are paid by the government, which operates an elaborate hoax in order to maintain the fiction that you are just as much a taxpayer as anyone in private industry.

If you think you are a taxpayer, ask yourself when you last received a piece of paper issued by a collector of taxes pointing out to you that unless you pay the amount they demand by a certain date, "steps will have to be taken to recover it either by ... the seizure and possible sale of your possessions, or by proceedings in court", or some such wording. True taxpayers are people who, if they do not pay up, receive such warnings, and eventually run the risk of having what they own taken away by force.

Maximisation of revenues

There are people in government trying to solve the problem of setting the overall rate of tax so as to maximise income from taxes. This is quite an interesting problem. If tax rates are very low, increasing them increases the revenue to the government, but when they are very high, increasing them causes so many business failures that revenues actually go down. So what rate of tax can they fix upon so as to get as much out of the true taxpayers as possible without actually destroying too many of them?

The fact that this question has even been asked reveals a great deal about the psychology of some people who work in the public sector. Should the maximisation of tax revenues ever be an objective of government, or of anyone who works for any government?

Summary

In short, it is reasonable to raise small amounts of tax to pay for the protection of the individual citizen from violence. This little could almost certainly be raised without threat of force, since most true taxpayers would be happy to pay for such services. You may be able to think of other government services which benefit everyone and which you do not mind paying for, if you pay tax, that is.

Most other tax is raised by means of threats to a small minority of people, and is used to pay for the livelihoods of other, less productive minorities. You may be happy about this, but not if you personally are on the receiving end. At the back of your mind, there will always be the question, " ... at whose expense?"

Politicians

Most prominent amongst the minorities who live off tax revenues are the politicians, the successful ones that is. Do you know any obviously happy politicians?

Have you noticed a curious phenomenon involving politicians? They seem to be involved remarkably often in scandals of one sort or another. When a prominent politician is exposed as having been dishonest in their sexual relationships or their business dealings, the news media seem to expect the rest of us to be surprised. Yet, such dishonesty is exactly what you should expect to observe. Why?

Dishonest by nature

There are exceptions to every rule, and so what I have to say here cannot apply to every individual politician, but most of them obviously believe that it is OK for them to live off the rest of us, whilst they argue about the rules by which we should be controlled and about the amounts of tax which can be taken out of the productive sector of the economy. Do honest people live like this?

Self-perpetuating

Imagine a person who thinks that some aspect of society should be changed. To bring about this change, they go into politics, and get the law changed. Do they stop there? Not usually. Having found that they can get a living by arguing about things, they find new things to argue about. For ever. Regardless of the cost to the people paying.

The more effective ones achieve what is called "high office". In senior positions in the government, they can personally make decisions affecting the lives of millions of people. This kind of power can be very addictive, and they are always upset when they are finally voted out or otherwise dismissed.

Issue-dodging

Have you ever listened carefully to a political interview on the radio or television? Have you noticed how the politician often ignores the actual question, but takes advantage of the opportunity to speak and uses it to say whatever he wanted to say regardless of the question asked? When you understand the fundamentally criminal nature of politicians, you should not find this surprising.

What is slightly surprising is that the interviewers and their colleagues in the media behave as if they expect the rest of us to take politicians seriously, and to believe at least some of what they say. The only plausible explanation I have come across for this is that there is a symbiotic relationship between politicians and political commentators in the media: each depends on the other for survival. If this is the case, then the political commentators, other than, perhaps, the satirists, are as dishonest as the politicians.

How their magic works

What has all this got to do with your happiness? To remain happy, you must not allow yourself to be tricked by dishonest politicians or other people who seek to have power over you. To avoid being tricked, you must understand just a little about how professional magicians work, and how their most basic method is also used by politicians.

The trick is to cause the audience to concentrate on a distraction from the real action. You may see this most easily if you study a budget speech; these often lay great emphasis on any reduction or abolition of a tax, and glosses over new or increased taxes as if they were minor details. You can also see the general principle whenever it is announced that the government is going to do something widely seen as worthwhile: the benefits are always strongly sold, and the costs scarcely mentioned at all.

Oppression

If you live in a relatively free society, politicians will not often do you much harm, but you should be aware of the power they have to affect your livelihood. If you are employed by the government, your job may not be as secure as they might have led you to believe, and if you are in private industry, watch out for regulations and taxation, and for the penalties surrounding both sets of rules.

If you live in a less free society, do not let the politicians con you into helping them to oppress your compatriots. Where do they get their oppressive power? From you! They certainly don't get it from anyone else. By co-operating with them in oppressing the people of your country, you will destroy your own happiness, and you won't even help the oppressors themselves to be happy.

Wars

The worst thing politicians ever do is to involve their people in wars. Wars are obviously a major cause of death amongst the people actually fighting in them, but they also create all manner of other havoc, including death, by indirect means. Most famines this century have been a consequence of war. One shell can destroy a factory which took years to build, and wreck many people's livelihoods, thereby creating poverty. Both the First World War and the Second World War were followed by periods of great economic difficulty. The Vietnam War cost the United States so much that the U.S. dollar is now a token currency, no longer backed by gold.

Whenever the politicians talk about going to war, they talk about your national interest, even if the fighting is half a world away. They never mention that your national interest is best served by not paying for such an expensive waste of resources, and not sending some of the potentially most productive young people away to be killed. They never mention that it might be in your national interest not to be seen as a warlike nation. But a war is a great thing for distracting you from domestic problems created by those same politicians.

Do not let anyone distract you from what is actually going on. Your happiness depends upon being in touch with reality.

Revolutions

When those who govern a country no longer have the consent of the people they govern, a revolution is inevitable.

Past revolutions

In the past, most revolutions have been bloody affairs, and in only a few cases has there been much improvement for the ordinary people. What has occurred most often is that one tyrant is replaced by another, or one bunch of thugs replaced by another.

Recent revolutions

Recently, however, there have been some revolutions which have been much less bloody than most earlier ones, and which have left the ordinary people rather freer, even though many of those who relied upon the state to provide them with a livelihood have found things harder, as happens after all revolutions. I refer, of course, to the collapse of communism in Eastern Europe.

Only a few years before, these revolutions would have been unthinkable. This is a general characteristic of revolutions. Not many people see them coming.

The next one

I have come across four completely independent predictions of the next major political revolution in the world, each argued from a different standpoint. The next such revolution is likely to be a tax strike in the Western world, when the relatively small number of people who are true taxpayers decide to stop paying. It is not clear how soon this will occur, but it seems inevitable.

The first, and weakest, argument is that, with the exposure of the true nature of the parasitical élite classes, the productive classes will no longer be tricked and will cease to support them.

The second argument is that the relatively few people who are true taxpayers are mostly business people who normally demand good value for money in everything they pay for. They are not getting good value for the money they pay in taxes, and eventually they will simply refuse to pay.

The third argument is that an increasing proportion of tax money goes into the welfare state and that the welfare state is failing. Instead of just creating a safety net for the very old, the very ill and the very poor, it has created a welfare-dependent underclass and a huge population of elderly but fit people whose contributions to the system during their productive lives are no longer sufficient to pay for their state pensions. As it currently exists, the welfare state is unstable, and no politician would dare to put forward a scheme for dismantling it gradually. Collapse is therefore inevitable.

The fourth argument comes from a study of history. Taxation has a very long history, but the current level of taxation has no historical precedent. In the Western world at present, overall taxation (total fiscal pressure) is in excess of 40%, having risen to that level in just a few decades. In the course of history, overall taxation levels in excess of 10% have always led to revolutions. History never repeats itself exactly, but there are reliable patterns, and this appears to be one of them.

Be prepared

How can you be sure that you will survive such a revolution? The answer is simple to express, but possibly challenging to achieve. Arrange your life so that you are not dependent upon public money.

If you are a public sector employee, it may not actually be necessary for you to leave your job, provided that the organisation you work for and your job within it would both survive if it were privatised by force of necessity. For example, do not worry if you are a nurse: your hospital could become a private enterprise or a charity without your job being put at risk.

If you are living on investment income, you might wish to consider getting rid of your government securities. Given how the income from them is raised, your could start thinking of them as guilt-edged rather than gilt-edged.

You do not have to accept that the tax strike is likely to occur soon. I could be wrong. Nevertheless, knowing what you now do about taxation, you will only be happy if you do whatever you can to avoid being dependent on it yourself. It is better to work productively if you can.

Chapter 18

The World of Work

If you have a job, trade or profession, then the relationships you have at work are the most important outside your home, and maybe the most important of all, since your livelihood, and therefore your life, depends upon them. If you do unpaid work, as a full-time housewife and mother for example, most of this chapter still applies to you even though you are effectively paid in kind rather than with money. If you are unemployed, retired, still too young to be earning a living, or not working for some other reason, it is still vital to understand the world of work, because, unless you are leading a self-sufficient existence on a desert island, your life still depends upon work, work done by other people.

Civilisation, society, and ultimately human life itself is only possible because people work, and work for each other. You are, quite properly, concerned with your own self-interest, but you achieve this through working with and for other people, and (generally) being paid for what you do.

You Are What You Do

What you do tends to define who you are. Have you ever noticed that when you meet new people, the conversation often turns quickly to the matter of what you do for a living? It may not be discussed for long, but it is usually one of the first things people want to know about each other.

I once read about a man who had made enough money early in life that he retired when still in his thirties. When he was asked by new acquaintances what he did, he would answer their questions literally, and talk about his hobbies. People would assume when he mentioned playing golf that he was a professional golfer. If he mentioned writing, they would assume he was a professional author.

We like to pigeon-hole people according to their jobs, to identify them according to how they get their livings.

Your sense of identity

Because of this, your own sense of who you are also depends upon your livelihood. There is nothing wrong with this. What you do in order to get what you need to survive is indeed fundamental to who you are.

Some people go to work only in order to make a living. Others love their work and would do it even if they had to do something else as well in order to live. Many are somewhere in between, enjoying what they do, but wishing they didn't have to do it. It doesn't matter which of these categories you are in: what you do, and why, is still fundamental to who you are.

Your sense of worth

Not only does your work define a large part of your identity, but it also has a profound influence on your sense of self-worth, and self-worth is essential for happiness.

If you are to be happy, you must have self-respect. If you are to have self-respect, you must see yourself as valuable. If you are to see yourself as valuable, you must either be valuable or deceive yourself. If you deceive yourself, you will never be truly happy. Therefore you must be valuable.

So, you have a choice when you go to work. Will you be valuable? Will you do something which other people really value, and earn your living that way, or will you just work the system solely for your own benefit, and get your living that way? Which will make you happy? Will you be a producer or a parasite?

If you are a parasite, and unhappy because you know deep inside that other people cannot value your work, how can you become a producer, do something valuable, and give yourself the sense of worth which will be essential for your future happiness? Let us look in more detail at ...

Producers and Parasites

A producer makes or does something which people want to buy or are willing to pay for. A parasite not only produces nothing tangible, but would also find it impossible to sell what he does if the organisation in which he does it were to vanish.

If your income ultimately depends upon taxation, there is a significant chance that you are a parasite. There are some exceptions. The police and the armed forces have to be paid for out of public funds, as we have seen. Truly valuable work is also done by some other public sector employees, such as medics, grave-diggers, road-sweepers and some teachers, and a few of the people organising such work have valuable careers too.

What people willingly pay for

Bus drivers, plumbers, garage mechanics, farmers, and shop-keepers are all producers. If, like them, you make things, do things or supply things which people willingly pay for, and your customers come to you for what they know you can do or supply for them, you are not a parasite.

Even if you have a fairly anonymous job working in a factory, never meeting any customers, you can get a good feeling about what you do when you see the goods produced by your factory. There is something special about seeing something in a shop window and being able to say to yourself, "I made that". You can get this feeling even if you personally only had a small part in the manufacturing or even the design process. It is called pride in your work. You can have this only if you are a producer.

What's good for the company

A great deal of productive work is done in companies, where no one individual does everything, but each individual contributes to the success of the whole.

The greatest producer of all is likely to be the boss of the whole outfit, especially if he (or she) started out with nothing and built the business up from scratch. Such people are often despised as exploiters of their workers, whereas, in fact, they are nothing of the kind. Without such people, and the work they do, the workers would be much worse off, and the customers would be without the products which they want.

If you work in a company, you can judge your own value quite easily. Is what you do good for the company? Are you making a genuine contribution to the effectiveness and profitability of the organisation? Can you take pride in your work?

Parasitism in the workplace

Even if you are in a manufacturing company, you might still be a parasite. Many companies, especially large ones, carry "dead wood", people fulfilling outdated roles or operating in such a way as to make themselves indispensable, without actually contributing much to the company.

If, at the end of the day's work, you can feel good about what you have contributed to the company, you are not a parasite. If you think in terms of what you can get out of the company, then you probably are.

If you are leading a parasitical existence within a company but the company itself is a producer, in that its products are voluntarily bought by members of the public or by other private sector companies, you are in a good place, and you will not need to change your job in order to become a producer. You will only need to change your attitude and how you do your job.

Parasitical organisations

As long as the police, the courts and the prison services fulfil the role of protecting the citizen from acts of violence, they are not parasitical. When the police, courts and prison services are subverted into the enforcement of arbitrary rules, which have more to do with oppressing people than defending them, they become parasitical. When the armed services are used, not to defend the country against invaders but to interfere in conflicts in other countries, or, worse, to control the activities of people in their own country, they too become parasitical.

All other organisations paid for from taxes are in essence parasitical. Their leaders point to the good that they do, or attempt to do, and make themselves appear as worthy members of society; they also manage to get themselves paid substantial salaries. The people running them never admit to themselves, nor to anyone else, that their income is obtained from producers by force or threat of force. Those which have a productive function generally operate better in the private sector, where their income does not depend upon force.

What about other organisations, such as government departments, which cannot effectively be privatised? As an example, consider the United Kingdom Department of Trade and Industry. While researching this book, I asked a number of business people about this department, and many of them had good things to say about it. Nevertheless, *all* of them agreed that it would be better if the department were abolished and the cost of running it were taken off corporation tax, and *none* of them believed that this would ever happen. This is typical of a parasitical organisation.

The cost to your self-respect

If you work in a parasitical organisation, you are working as an accomplice to the criminally minded people at the top. The work you do may actually benefit people, but it cannot benefit them as much as if they had not been taxed as heavily in the first place, because you have had your cut of the money, and so have your bosses and their bosses, and the tax inspectors, the tax collectors and a number of other bureaucrats. The same work done in a private company would carry much less of an overhead. Parasitical organisations do not and cannot deliver overall net benefits to the societies in which they operate.

You may look at the benefits you deliver to people, and take pride in your work, but only if you hide from the costs. When you recognise the costs to other people, and the suffering created, you will recognise that you too are a parasite.

If you work for a company which depends upon contracts with the public sector for its income, then you might as well be in the public sector for all the good it will do your sense of self-worth, depending, as you do, upon money obtained from producers by threat of force.

Wait a moment! This is a book about how to be happy, not about making yourself miserable by destroying the self-respect you once derived from pride in your work. But happiness is dependent upon honesty, and self-respect founded upon hiding from some of the truth is ultimately bound to collapse. In the long term, therefore, you will need to admit the truth to yourself, and the sooner you do it, the sooner you can achieve true and lasting happiness.

The way to do this is to recognise that your life has been parasitical, resolve to become a producer rather than a parasite, and then change your way of life. This might have substantial short-term material costs, that is to say, in the short term you are likely to be financially worse off. If you take being a producer seriously, the longer term benefits will far outweigh the short-term costs. In the longer term, you will find greater financial security, independence from many of the whims of politicians, and self-respect and happiness for yourself.

Contribution

Your contribution to making the world a better place for everyone to live in is, as I have implied before, crucial to your happiness. It is at work that you should be making your greatest contribution to the world. It is at work, too, that you are paid back directly for your contribution, and get the wherewithal to live. The contribution you make at work is therefore vital, in that your life depends upon it, as well as your happiness.

You may think that it can't be that vital, because you would still survive if you didn't work, but how would you survive? If you have savings or rich relatives, that wealth came from work, or should have done. You might be able to claim benefits from the state, but they are paid for by other people's work, and, given the fragility of the welfare state, they are not as reliable as you might wish to think. However you get your money, what you buy with it depends upon work done by other people.

Good for everyone

Society, therefore, depends upon people working. Civilisation itself depends to some extent upon the work you do to support it. All our lives depend upon the work done by those who make a genuine contribution by producing what we need and want. Your contribution is an important part of this.

Who is your job good for?

You may doubt that your work is important for everyone. Think about it for a moment. If your work is unpaid, someone is supporting you, presumably because they value your work. If you are paid, who pays you? Why do they pay you? What for? Where does the money come from? In any normal business, there are customers who choose to buy what your company produces. Your job is part of what makes that possible, and your company is creating new wealth in the very act of producing what the customers want.

Your work is good for your firm's customers. It is good for the other people who work with you in the same company. It is also good for the people who live off the taxes paid out of your wages or salary, and the taxes paid by the company on its profits; some of them may contribute a little to the well-being of society, but it is your work and your money which is making possible whatever good they do too.

Doing your job

If you are in private industry, therefore, you can take pride in your work, but only if you actually do it! The good feelings you can get from work only come when you are confident that you are making a genuine contribution. Of course you should be able to expect to be paid fairly for what you do, but the good feelings which come from receiving the pay itself are transient.

The money looks and feels good, but if you don't feel that you have earned it fairly, it will never help to make you happy. You may feel a little resentful if you think that you are underpaid, but if you concentrate on being truly valuable to your company, by working hard and contributing whatever you can to its success, you will soon be in a much stronger position when you ask for more pay. Even if your employer pays you less than you know you are worth, you will be happier doing your best and accepting less than you deserve for it, than you would be doing less than your best.

Many companies, especially large ones, carry some staff who are there not for what they can do, but for what they can get. These people are parasites, and they are never truly happy. If you are one, you can change your ways, become helpful, especially to people junior to you in the hierarchy, and start to earn some happiness along with your pay. If you are a real producer, do not become too resentful of the parasites in your company: they are unlikely to be as bad as the ones paid for out of your tax money; it is just that you can see them at close quarters, and so you are more aware of them than you are of the hidden ones that you are paying for through taxation.

Attitude

Your happiness depends upon your attitude to life. Your attitude is nowhere more important than it is at work. You can choose your attitude. You can choose to approach your work with the notion that this is where you do all you can to make the world a better place, and that this is where you earn pride in what you do, self-respect, and consequently much of your happiness. There are other possible attitudes, but they are not worth considering.

Doing more than your job

When you approach your work in this frame of mind, you will naturally do more than what is required of you as the minimum. When you have done what you absolutely have to do, you will be finding other things to do which will help, or you will be learning more about your work and how it fits into the functioning of the whole enterprise, or you will be working out how to do things better, faster, cheaper or more reliably.

Helping others

When you have a good attitude, you will find yourself helping your colleagues, both junior and senior, in their work. You will do whatever you can to help keep the operation running smoothly, and to bring new plans to fruition. You may find yourself making coffee, cleaning, fetching, carrying, helping to move the furniture, anything. What you will not find yourself doing is saying, "That's not my job", or "I'm not paid to do that." The specific job for which you are paid must, of course, take priority over anything else you might do, but, if you have a helpful attitude, and are always willing to do more than is required of you, you will go home happy about what you have done at work.

The good example

Your happiness with your attitude will show. People imitate one another. If you are well-liked and well-respected, people will copy you. Your happiness and helpfulness will tend to make you better-liked and better-respected, so there will be a tendency for your good attitude to be copied, thus making the whole place better for everyone to work in.

This is only true if your helpfulness is genuine. If you are perceived to be always on the look-out for opportunities to appear to be helpful, no matter what the current requirements of the job for which you are principally paid, you will be seen as someone trying to curry favour, and you will not be respected for this. Your helpful attitude comes into its own when you notice that one of your colleagues is having difficulty with something, and you help out as a matter of common decency to a fellow human being, or, when you are asked to do something in addition to your normal duties, and you just co-operate without grumbling.

This kind of example is inspiring, and you may find that you can single-handedly turn around the atmosphere of a whole department, or even a whole company, just by your own attitude. That really will help you to be happier.

How to climb any ladder

When you do your job as well as you possibly can, and do your best to learn how to do it better, and also put in whatever effort you can to do more than your job requires in order to make the whole enterprise more successful, you will be a natural candidate for promotion.

Be a bit patient, because in most places opportunities for promotion do not come up every month, but when you are sure that you could do the next job confidently, or that you could do it at least as well as anyone else, go and ask. Your boss might just be waiting for you to show enough initiative to ask for promotion.

If you do not get the job, do not give up hope of getting it, or something better later, and on no account give up your attitude. If you eventually reach the conclusion that you are never going to get what you deserve, find a job elsewhere; if your attitude is right, this will not be difficult. When you tell your erstwhile boss about your new job, you might get offered the promotion you were after, in which case, you can either accept it, or go to your new job anyway.

If you are promoted, or start a new and better job, knowing that you are in your new role because you have genuinely earned it, you will not be unhappy about this. If you wangle your way into a job you do not deserve, by currying favour with the "in" people, or by any other unfair means, you will not be happy in your work, at least until you change your attitude and behaviour, and start truly earning what you get.

Constant improvement

Doing your best does not mean doing the same all the time. To maintain your happiness, you will need to commit yourself to a policy of continuous and never-ending improvement. If you take your work seriously as the source of most of your self-respect, you will not find this difficult. The better you do your job, the happier you will find yourself, and the more you will want to improve.

Security

We all want security. It is natural to want to feel safe, and it is difficult to be happy whilst feeling insecure. Job security is obviously very desirable, and it is tempting to choose your job solely because it seems to offer secure employment.

Illusion

If you do choose your employer on the basis of promised security, and you do not believe that your employer will get rid of you if you do not make an adequate contribution, you may well be falling for an illusion. How can your employer promise job security?

If you go to work for a normal business, there is always a risk that a more efficient competitor might drive your employer out of business, especially if your employer does not require you and your fellow employees to more than earn their livings by contributing to the success of the enterprise.

If you go to work for a monopoly, what guarantee is there that the monopoly will hold in the long term? Even monopolies have competitors: you may work for the only supplier of electricity in your area, but people may choose gas or oil instead, or they might even move out of the area if your electricity is too expensive.

If you work for the government, a promise of a secure job may be a major temptation, but just as much of an illusion. The laws which guarantee your position can be changed, and governments can fall.

If someone promises you job security in order to persuade you to work for them, you are very likely to be being tricked into doing something of which you will not be truly proud. Any promise of job security is founded upon some assumptions about how the world works, and particularly on the assumption that the world will continue to work that way. As all past revolutions, including the recent collapse of totalitarian communism in Eastern Europe, have shown, you cannot assume that the world will continue to work in the way it does at present.

For the sake of your own happiness, do not fall for the illusion presented to you by anyone who offers you job security in order to get your services.

Make your own

You want job security, and you can have it, but you can't have it given to you. The only way to get job security is to make your own.

Even in times of very high unemployment, such as in the great depression of the 1930's, large numbers of people did have and keep jobs. They were the ones who concentrated on what they could do which was of value.

When a company gets into hard times and has to slim down, the best workers are never fired. The most valuable people are always kept. If a company goes bust, the very best people find other jobs easily enough. Those who understand that they must produce more than they consume are always employable, and usually employed, and they are happy too.

The most reliable way to make your own security is to make your own business. Make sure that your customers are ordinary people or other businesses, and supply to them anything you can which they will willingly choose to pay for. Then strive for ever greater efficiency, reliability and quality of service. If you are the best at what you do, or amongst the best, your income will be secure as long as you keep an eye on what your customers actually want, and make sure that they are aware of what you do.

There is, of course, much more to running a business than this, but if you consistently exceed your customers' expectations, you are very likely to have a successful business.

Internal security

Finally, you must have faith in yourself. Without faith, you will not achieve, but anyone with normal abilities can rely upon themselves to earn or make what they need, provided they are prepared to believe in themselves and put in the necessary efforts. Believe this, and believe in yourself, and you will be secure in your future.

Chapter 19

Manipulation

I have already said several times in this book that manipulation is a bad thing which undermines the happiness both of the person doing the manipulating and the person being manipulated.

This is so common and so serious a cause of unhappiness that I think it warrants a whole chapter to itself. To defeat it, you must understand it. To be happy, you must defeat it. By defeating it, I mean never falling victim to it, and never succumbing to the temptation to use it yourself.

Who Does It?

Let us look first at the people who do succumb to the temptation to use manipulation. Nobody ever does anything without a reason. Therefore people only use manipulative techniques to achieve something that they want, and they do this without due thought to the effects on their own happiness. Let's look at a few examples of this.

Parents

Parents have to control their children while those children are too young to look after themselves. Some parents are tempted to try to retain control after their children are grown up. Some lay the foundations for this while their children are still small.

Spouses

The strong emotions between husband and wife can be used unfairly by either party as a weapon against the other. Some people are tempted to use such emotional weapons just for the sense of power it gives them.

Politicians

Who loves power? If you really love power, you might be tempted to go into politics. Mao Tse Tung's wife said that power was more interesting than sex. What is the purpose of political power? If you want it for your own gratification, will it ever make you happy?

Bosses

In a healthy organisation, the boss's instructions to subordinates are designed to help the whole organisation achieve its objectives. This is in the best interests not only of the boss but also of the subordinates. But some bosses just enjoy ordering people about.

Churchmen

How do clergy survive? Do they provide something which people willingly pay for, or do they obtain their income dishonestly? The answer has to be that there are some of each. How voluntary are the offerings which the congregation put into the collection? The answer to this varies not only from place to place but also from individual to individual.

It is not unheard of for clergymen to tell their people that there is a moral requirement for them to put money into the church. This can happen in any faith and in any denomination.

Advertisers

Advertising varies hugely in its honesty. At one extreme, an advertiser might make a straightforward presentation of the product, the advantages of owning it, its price and where and how to buy it. At the other extreme, an advertiser can mislead purchasers into a subconscious belief that the product will enhance their lives in some way not related to the way in which it physically functions; the subtlety of this is that it can be done without making any false statements whatsoever.

Criminals

What is a criminal? Is it just someone who breaks the law, no matter how unjust the law? Or is a criminal someone who obtains or tries to obtain something of value by means of force, threat of force or dishonesty, even if the law permits what they do? The answer to this question depends on the idea of objective law. People who get what they want by means of force, threat of force or dishonesty are objectively criminal in their way of life. This includes all the manipulators mentioned in this section.

How do they Do it?

Apart from the crudest and most obvious criminals, successful manipulators rely heavily upon false authority. Thinking can be hard work. Isn't it much easier to be told what to believe and what to do by people who do the thinking for you? If you rely on other people's authority to save you from thinking for yourself, you are a ready victim for the manipulator, who will tell you what to believe and tell you what to do.

A genuine authority will always be prepared to explain the reasoning underlying what they say, and be prepared to listen to any evidence which might show them to have been wrong. False authorities might make a show of something like this, but eventually retreat to the argument that they know best because they are who they are, and suggest that it is not for you to challenge their authority. Often, they use rituals or uniforms to enhance their apparent authority, the more elaborate and awe-inspiring, the more effective.

Having established an apparent right to tell you what to do or think, how do they get you to behave irrationally in such a way as to help them towards their own ends?

The guilt trap

Having established themselves as a moral authority, anyone can muddle your conscience by telling you that you should feel guilty about something which would otherwise not trouble you.

If they point to something you have done, you might be in a position to argue that your actions have no victim and that there is no cause for you to feel guilty. This way, you could weaken their authority, unless they can produce a convincing counter-argument that there was indeed a victim of which you were unaware. All this can be perfectly rational, which is not the manipulator's real territory.

Where the manipulator can get to you is by telling you sternly that you should not feel what you feel, or should not think what you think, because it is wrong to have such feelings or thoughts. Any arguments you might produce about the non-existence of victimless crimes will fall on deaf ears. After all, the manipulator has no interest in rational argument. What the manipulator wants is control over you, which depends on you behaving irrationally, which in turn depends on rational thought being condemned as wrong.

Your conscience is so vital to your happiness that you must prevent any false authority from planting irrational beliefs in it. If this has already happened to you, you will have to work quite hard to root out any irrational beliefs which have got into your conscience. This work is worth the effort: it will free you from manipulation and let happiness into your life.

The duty trap

Do you remember Nelson's famous signal to his ships just before the Battle of Trafalgar "England expects every man to do his duty" or Kitchener's famous poster "Your country needs you"?

The duty trap is very similar to the guilt trap. The method is to use an authority figure to muddle the victim's conscience. In this case, the idea planted is that you should feel guilty if you do not do what the manipulator asks. This type of manipulator never mentions the advantages to themselves of you following their instructions. (Lord Nelson did not inherit his title and nor did Lord Kitchener inherit his!) Instead, they point to a higher and usually ill-defined cause.

Anyone who has the courage to refuse to be manipulated in this way is dubbed a coward or a traitor. This is an interesting misuse of language since it takes great courage to stand up to such manipulation, and the few who do so usually have a more profound love of their country than those who want to send their fellow countrymen to be killed in a foreign war.

The fear trap

Political oppressors keep their subjects under control by making them afraid of physical violence. Manipulative parents can use this method, but they also use the threat of withdrawal of affection, which plays on the deepest fears of a child, even when the child is an adult. Religious demagogues use the fear of the wrath of God. Others, such as leaders of certain religious sects, have wielded considerable power by means of the threat of withdrawal of peer group approval. Bad employers sometimes use the threat of dismissal.

The more deep-seated the fear, the more effective it can be as a weapon of control. The less aware the victim is of the method being used, the more effective it is too.

The false expectation trick

Unless you are trying to avoid something you fear, everything you do is in the expectation of good feelings. Some manipulators achieve their ends by creating false expectations of good feelings. Others offer short-term rewards which have longer-term costs for their victims. Have you ever heard a parent offering an ice-cream as a bribe?

The false expectation trick is most often used by the poorer sort of advertiser. You can spot this most readily in television commercials which have a sexual undertone but where the product has very little to do with sex. Once you are aware of the trick, you can get a fair amount of entertainment from watching television commercials, trying to observe what benefit is being implied by the design of the advertisement and asking yourself how the product is supposed to deliver that benefit. You will find some honest advertising, which is a good thing, but you will also find some very dubious benefits being implied, especially by the advertisers of cars, chocolates, coffee and alcohol.

False expectations are also much used by politicians. Unfortunately, our choice of politicians is rather limited. Of course, you vote for the one who offers the least implausible expectations. Wouldn't it be nice to be able to vote for someone in whose honesty and competence you were completely confident? They would all like you to believe that they are totally honest and thoroughly competent, but, if they were, would they have careers as politicians? Wouldn't they be happier doing something else?

The rhythm method

The most effective politicians are great orators. Orators know a few things about the human psyche that most of us don't know. One of the things they know is also known by the people who choose the music played in shops, and by the writers of some advertising slogans.

The use of certain rhythms bypasses the rational part of the mind and affects parts of the mind which are less rational but which are involved in behaviour. When you find someone's words echoing around your head, suspect that you might be being manipulated and make a special effort to think about what is really going on. If you find yourself in a shop with music, ask yourself what the true reason for your purchase is, before you part with your money.

Fashion

Music, especially music with a steady beat, is often to be found in clothes shops, especially those more concerned with fashion than with the practical purpose of clothes. Fashion itself is a clever invention of the clothes manufacturers, the purpose of which is to get us to buy more clothes than we actually need.

Why might you buy more clothes than you need? You might do this to avoid feeling that other people might think less of you for being less well-dressed than you could be. What you are fearing is the loss of approval of your peer group. When you act on this fear without recognising what it is, you are falling victim to a manipulator.

I do not mean to suggest that clothes should not be beautiful or that all clothes designers are wicked people. Far from it! One of the proper functions of clothing is to help you to look good, and clothes designers can earn their money honestly. It is just that, in the world of fashion, there are people who want you to be irrational when buying their products.

How Does it Work?

The manipulator wants you to do something which is not in your best interests. To do this they have to convince you that by doing what they want, you will either achieve something you desire or avoid something you fear. Of course, anyone who wants you to do anything has to convince you in the same way. People who want to trade with you honestly must also convince you that by dealing with them, you will gain something you want or avoid something you fear, but the honest trader does not want you to do anything which is not in your own best interests.

The honest trader can afford for you to be rational, but the manipulator must get you to behave irrationally.

Getting you to behave irrationally

All the techniques I mentioned in the previous section are aimed at getting you to behave irrationally. There may be other methods which I have not yet detected, but the aim of all of them is to get you to behave in a way that the manipulator wants, regardless of your own goals, and ...

Preferably without you noticing

The manipulator cannot afford to be recognised! Even the armed criminal who does not disguise the nature of the threat takes steps to conceal their identity. Successful parasites are open about who they are, but not at all about their methods: many of them even conceal their methods from themselves.

Once you notice what a manipulator is doing, you are on the road to freedom. How do you get to notice? You will recognise what is being done to you by the manipulators in your life when you identify that some of your actions are not rational, and are not what you have deliberately chosen. How will you notice this? Remember that earlier in this book, I recommended that at the end of each day, you spend some time reflecting on what you have done, and understanding why you did it. This is when you can recognise who has been manipulating you and how. It is no coincidence that the worst religious sects use sleep deprivation as part of their initiation methods.

Recognising the manipulators and their methods is only the first step towards freeing yourself from them, and we will come back to the question of what else you have to do shortly, but first we must consider another of the tricks used by manipulators.

Pattern building

Once you are in the habit of doing something, your subconscious mind will try to defend the habit, good or bad. If you try to change a habit, your mind will come up with all manner of justifications for keeping it as it is. Many of these may be just as irrational as the habit itself.

A manipulator's position is much strengthened if you are in the habit of doing what they want. One of their aims is what is called the "click-whirr response". The best demonstrations of this can be seen on a military parade ground, where a whole battalion of men make the same movements together in response to an order barked by one man ... and they do this without thinking!

If anyone can get you to produce a predictable response to their chosen stimulus, they control you. Your response will only be truly predictable when the pattern has been built. Look out for people trying to get you into any habit which might be to their advantage but not to your own.

Don't Do It!

Why might you wish to use any of these manipulative techniques on anyone? You might wish to get something from them, but if you get it, it will only give you the same benefit as if you had stolen it: you will never be happy about having it. You might just enjoy the feeling of power, a very short-term benefit, like a drug; and, like a drug, it will make you no happier in the longer term. Finally, you might believe that you are doing some good for your victim, controlling them to prevent them from making their own mistakes, but people have a right to make their own mistakes, and you will not make yourself happier by spoiling other people's freedom in this way.

Manipulators destroy their own happiness

Whatever you might try to achieve by means of manipulation will never do you any good. Anything you do achieve will feel the same as unearned wealth, nothing like the real thing.

More importantly, if you use manipulative techniques, you will know deep inside that you are cheating. All these techniques rely on some sort of deception. They are all dishonest. Knowing that you are dishonest will always make you unhappy: it is one of the universal barriers to happiness mentioned at the start of this book. Hiding from your own dishonesty will involve self-deception, the antithesis of self-knowledge, and will also destroy your happiness.

Addiction to power

It may be difficult to give up dishonesty if your livelihood has depended on it for some time, but it will be even harder for you to give up if you are in the habit of manipulating people just for the thrill that the power gives you.

Power is as addictive as any hard drug, and at least as difficult to give up, if you are hooked. If you were an alcoholic, you would, on joining Alcoholics Anonymous, have to admit, as a first step, that you have no power over your addiction. For someone hooked on power to admit that they have no power is unthinkable.

If you get such a thrill from wielding power that you resort to manipulating people, or even if you do it to achieve some other aim, the first thing you must do is to observe the effect on yourself. It does feel good when people do what you want them to, but does the feeling last? It does not. To get the thrill again, you have to do it again, but the thrills do not make you happy, any more than taking drugs makes you happy. Once you recognise this, the time has come to turn all your manipulating skills on yourself, and set the rest of the world free from your tyranny. If you have power to control other people, you certainly have power to control yourself!

How to Counter Manipulation

Falling victim to a manipulator is almost as bad for your prospects of happiness as acting as a manipulator. I say almost as bad because the victim of any form of crime is generally hurt in the short term but not as unhappy in the long term as the criminal. In the case of manipulation, it is slightly different because, to fall victim to a manipulator, you must relinquish some of your self-control, and, as we have seen, self-control is vital for happiness.

Given how easy it is to be tricked by a skilled manipulator, and how bad the effects of this are for all concerned, it is worth learning how to defend yourself. Once you know that techniques of manipulation exist and that there are people out there who know no better than to use them, you have the basic tools of self-defence than you need.

Recognise it

The first step in your self-defence is to recognise any attempt at manipulation. If someone seems to expect you to do something, ask yourself why. Your obedience may be expected in the workplace, and you may not know enough about the business to have a full understanding of why you are being told to do something, but everywhere else, you should never be expected to do anything without knowing why.

The two big clues to manipulation are these. Clue 1: someone offers you a benefit of some sort without being clear as to exactly how you are to benefit and what the costs to you are. Clue 2: someone tells you that someone else will benefit, without mentioning the fact that they will themselves be taking a cut of what you pay out. Either of these clues can tip you off to an attempt to manipulate you.

Analyse it

The one thing the manipulator cannot afford is for you to do your own thinking. Many of them try to rush you or bully you into a quick decision (in their favour). Some of the worst of them resort to sleep-deprivation techniques.

Whenever you find yourself being persuaded into a commitment of any sort without having a clear understanding of all the costs and benefits to you, stop and think. Analyse everything as carefully as you can. What exactly is being asked of you? Who benefits? Answer these questions as fully as you possibly can. In particular, ask whether the cost to you is limited. Even a dishonest trader will only cost you the one-off purchase price of the shoddy goods on offer. A tyrant could cost you your freedom.

Once you have identified the costs and benefits, you may conclude that someone is trying to con you. If so, analyse the techniques they are using as carefully as you can. Remember that rational thought and understanding are your best weapons of defence against such people. You may find some of the techniques I mentioned earlier, or maybe others. In any case, once you understand how a piece of trickery works, you cannot be fooled by it.

If possible, draw attention to it

As I said before, what the manipulator most fears is your understanding. Manipulators can be dangerous people. Once you understand how one is working, you may have a difficult decision to make. Obviously, you will not allow yourself to fall victim to their power, but how much do you say about them and to whom?

Provided that it is safe for you to do so, I would recommend talking freely about what you have discovered about their methods. In some totalitarian countries this might be too dangerous for you, so be very careful about who you talk to, but remember that the more people understand what is going on, the sooner you will all be free. If you don't feel safe exposing the manipulator's methods, you might still judge that it is in your interest to let the manipulator know that you understand what they are doing and how: to do so will weaken their power over you, unless they are of the type who readily resort to violence if they feel threatened. Alternatively, you might just decide to be quietly uncooperative: a manipulator with plenty of potential victims won't waste much effort on you.

Be very careful about the rationality of your behaviour

Whatever you decide to say about any manipulators in your life, the key to your happiness still lies with self-control. Remember the question I posed early on in this book. If you do not control yourself, who does?

Watch yourself. Understand why you do what you do. If you catch yourself behaving irrationally, stop and ask yourself why. If you catch yourself being manipulated, understand what the manipulator is doing, how and if possible why. Having identified what is going on, decide rationally what you are going to do. Then do it.

If you catch yourself trying to manipulate other people, stop. It is not rational for you to continue, as it will not make you happy. Earn what you want honestly instead.

Avoidance is best

If you can manage it, the best way to deal with manipulative people is simply to avoid them. This can be difficult, but it is worth a try.

Are there any manipulators in your life? Probably there are, since they are so common. You may be able to defuse them by making them understand that you know what they are up to. Draw attention to what they are doing and point out to them exactly how their methods work, just in case they don't understand themselves. This may not work with public figures, but it might work quite well with people closer to you.

What do you do if you find that a manipulator in your life is incorrigible? The best answer is to dump them. This can be very hard if you are dealing with a tyrannical member of your own family, but if they won't mend their ways after they have been identified, what else can you do, other than to continue to be a victim?

As for the more public figures, is ostracism a cure? Most politicians and other parasites seem to rely for their self-respect on the respect apparently given to them by other people. What would happen if this were withdrawn? What if we all just stopped respecting, or pretending to respect, those apparently élite people who rely for their parasitical existences on their ability to manipulate enough of the rest of us? Would they lose what little self-respect they seem to have, and give up? Would you play golf with a tax collector? What about his boss? Or his boss's boss? What respect do you show to the people who decide how much tax we "should" pay?

Chapter 20

Damaged Relationships

You have many relationships with many people, and not all of them will be perfect all of the time. Of course it would be better not to have this problem, to be able to maintain all your relationships in good working order, and I hope that what you have already read in this part of the book will help you to do better in this respect, but you cannot expect perfection.

It is not always appropriate, but if a relationship goes wrong for any reason, you are likely to want to rescue or repair it. Sometimes, there is little or no hope of being able to do this, but if you approach the problem thoughtfully, carefully and with due humility, you can do a great deal to enhance your chances of making things better.

Confrontation and Reconciliation

Ignoring a fundamental problem in a relationship will not make it go away. If the relationship is going to be repaired, if reconciliation is ever going to come about, then, the problem has to be faced by both parties. However, just confronting the other person with the problem, without having given a good deal of thought to it yourself, is unlikely to bring about any sort of improvement. First, you must ask yourself ...

What went wrong?

The answer to this question is often glaringly obvious, but, if it is not, then look for the source of anger. Who is, or should be, angry with whom and why? Remember that anger is a response to pain, and that sometimes it is not expressed in its natural form, but gets diverted into depression, despair, apathy, or even humour.

Having found the anger, the chances are that you will discover that it was caused either by deliberate wrong-doing, or by misunderstanding. A failure to act might be a case of wrong-doing but is more likely to be a misunderstanding over the importance of something which was to be done but has been left undone.

Now that you have identified either a misunderstanding or something which appears to be both wrong and deliberate, the time has come to ...

Discuss it

This can be very difficult, especially if emotions have been running high. The key is to keep control of your emotions, but this might involve treading a difficult path between emotional outbursts on one hand and coldness on the other.

A simple and obvious misunderstanding can be fairly easy to resolve, although you must be prepared for someone to be angry with you for failing to understand something which was clear to them. Where there is apparently deliberate wrong-doing or culpable negligence, always be on the look-out for this being the result of a less obvious misunderstanding; remember that incompetence is much commoner than malice.

Misunderstandings are always caused by a mismatch of people's mental models or "maps" of the world. Your understanding of the universe and of the way everything in it functions (including people) is incomplete and also inaccurate in certain details. So is everyone else's! It can be difficult to grasp the fact that not everyone has the same map as you do: they have different gaps and different inaccuracies. Where you have a misunderstanding, or even just a difference of opinion, compare your maps.

Where there are differences, they will show up as differing beliefs. Where the beliefs are about facts, they can be checked against the real world. If you have different beliefs about matters which will always remain matters of faith, the most important thing is to recognise that neither party can be shown to be right, and that it is therefore reasonable to agree to differ.

Asking questions and echoing/reflecting

When you are trying to sort out a misunderstanding, the last thing you want is to be accused of not listening or not trying to understand. Therefore listen, try your best to understand, and make it clear that you are doing both of these things. Listen not only for what is said but for what is not said. Sometimes people make their feelings clear not by what they say but by their tone of voice, the way they move or their choice of phrasing.

In order to understand what someone believes, especially if it differs from what you believe, you will almost certainly have to ask questions. The best questions to get someone talking are the so-called open questions, of the "how" and "why" variety, which do not admit of single-word answers. When you get an answer, make it clear how much of it you have understood by summarising in your own words what you have understood, and if necessary asking for clarification of anything which you have not understood.

It is often a good idea, especially when trying to mend a damaged relationship, to get people to talk about how they feel. Sometimes you can trigger this by saying something about how you think they feel, and asking whether you have understood that too. The emotion you are most likely to uncover is anger, but you may also come across pain, despair, or even fear. Hopefully you will also come across a desire to make the relationship better.

Remember that, at this stage, you are seeking understanding. You will understand any of the negative emotions more easily if you see them as reactions to a problem, in the sense that we defined a problem earlier, a mismatch between the situation as desired and the situation as perceived. Try to understand how the other person perceives the situation, and what their desires are. When you understand both of these things, you are well on the way to mending any damaged relationship.

Talk and be honest about your feelings

Any dialogue of this sort should be two-way. If you are the one who first wants the relationship to improve, you will usually get on better if you listen first and talk later, but the time will probably come, usually after the other person feels understood, that they will be ready to hear about your point of view.

When you come to talk about your own feelings, and your own point of view, you will probably get on best if you follow a few simple guidelines. Firstly, be prepared to stop if it becomes clear that the other person doesn't really want to hear at the moment: if you press on because you believe that this is your only chance, you are likely to cause it to be your only chance. Secondly, never say anything you know to be false, and never assert as definite fact something which is just your opinion: your honesty must be absolute. Thirdly, talk as calmly as you can about how you feel, and do this without placing or implying any blame for your negative feelings. Fourthly, always be ready to answer any questions you get, as clearly and as straightforwardly as you can. Finally, if you are interrupted, keep your cool, listen and try to understand the reason for the interruption, and make it clear what you have understood.

Forgiveness

Whenever a damaged relationship is healed, there is forgiveness. When you forgive someone, you admit that they have done wrong but you agree to treat them as if they had not. How can this be consistent with the absolute commitment to honesty advocated in this book?

In forgiving someone, you do not deny that they did wrong, but you express faith that they will not do the same thing wrong again. Your faith may be misplaced in any particular case, but the principle is founded upon the belief that people can change. It would be dishonest to forgive someone if you believed that change was impossible, but you can actually make change more likely by forgiveness, so there is no inconsistency.

Forgive freely

It is to your advantage to forgive people readily. Forgiveness tends to lead to happiness both in the forgiver and the forgiven.

Make it as clear as you can that you know what they did, and that you are prepared to trust them not to do it again. Never let them think that you did not know what they did wrong, and never let them think that you are gullible. Alas, you will have to withhold your forgiveness if they make it clear that they have no intention of behaving differently in the future, but at the slightest sign of repentance, be ready again to forgive.

Do not be afraid to ask to be forgiven

When you have done wrong yourself, and you have admitted it to yourself and decided to behave differently in the future, you can approach people you have hurt directly or indirectly and ask their forgiveness. You may have to face some unpleasantness, their anger or their pain, but you will admit that that is no more than you deserve. Where you find people ready to forgive you, you will find happiness, both for them and for you.

Your repentance as a prerequisite

This only works if you have honestly decided not to repeat your offence. You must be committed to a better way of life, and get people to believe this and to trust you in the future. Without this repentance, and people's acknowledgement of it, any apparent forgiveness or conciliatory words are a sham, and won't help anyone to be happy.

Do it again and again

What do you do when someone you have forgiven lets you down by repeating their wrongdoing? If you believe that they have no intention whatsoever of mending their ways, then forgiveness is impossible, but otherwise you have a choice.

If you choose to believe that, despite their good intentions, they will never reform, you are choosing, in effect, to bear a grudge, which will never make anyone happy. If you choose to believe that, no matter how often you have been let down in the past, there is always hope for the future, you are allowing things to improve, which will improve the chances of happiness all round, although it won't guarantee it.

By forgiving again and again, you are doing your bit for happiness, and you can be happy about this. Everything else is up to the other party, but you are allowing scope for them to be happy too, so they can choose the way of happiness for themselves, by proving that your trust in them is well-founded.

But do not deny justice

Believing that someone will not repeat an offence is not the same as pretending that they never committed it in the first place. The truth of the past must never be denied, and it follows from this that people must face the consequences of what they have done, regardless of their intentions for the future.

It is a simple fact of nature that actions have consequences, and the concept of justice is an extension of this observation. When someone behaves badly so as to hurt someone else, they have a natural duty to make amends as best they can. Denying this leads to unhappiness, whereas accepting it leads to happiness. This is true both for the offender and the victim.

As an extreme illustration of this idea, consider the case of a violent criminal who, having attacked someone, realises that this sort of thing does not lead to happiness, and resolves to lead a non-violent life in future. How can he make amends to his victim? The victim will not want to see him on the streets until the mental trauma of the attack has healed. The most effective way of making amends might be to go to prison for a few years. Prison does not seem to help criminals to repent but, regardless of the state of mind of the offender, it does give the victim a chance to recover from the crime.

When to Get Out

Most of this chapter has been about mending damaged relationships. This is because, in most cases, that is the way to greater happiness for all concerned. There are, however, exceptions. There are times when the best way to handle a damaged relationship is to abandon it. The purpose of this section is to help you to identify cases of this sort, and to show you how best to handle them.

Destructive relationships

People can always change, but if you observe that someone does not even wish to change and that their behaviour towards you is consistently evil, you may have a case for abandoning the relationship. If you find that the things they say and the way they behave leave you feeling disempowered or dehumanised, you are facing the kind of evil I have in mind.

The signs to look for are these: allegations that you are incompetent, uncaring or arrogant; fits of anger with no real justification; negative reactions to any idea of change, especially if it is your idea; and consistent pessimism.

You can't be blamed for how you feel

Faced with any or all of these, you are likely to feel miserable. You are very likely to feel a powerful dislike towards anyone who behaves like this. Do they claim that you should love them, rather than hate them? If so, they do not understand that feelings of love are deserved by those who earn them, not by those who claim them as a duty. Your explaining this is unlikely to get you anywhere in circumstances like these.

Are you being manipulated despite everything?

Having read this far, you should by now be able to recognise when someone is trying to manipulate you. You can try your best to get anyone who tries to manipulate you to change their ways, selling the change to them on the basis that they will be happier for it. Alternatively, you can break the pattern of manipulation simply by recognising it and refusing to fall for the techniques.

Some people, however, are such powerful and skilled manipulators of others that you might find yourself unequal to the task of facing them down. With these people, as with those whose attitude is so negative as to be irredeemably dispiriting, the only solution is to ...

Cut your losses

When you do decide that a relationship is wholly beyond repair, and that staying in it is not compatible with being happy (and only you can make this decision) get out. You have already talked about it, discussed it as best you can, maybe taken your problems to other people for their counsel, tried every avenue of change you can, but nothing has worked.

Face it: nothing is going to work. Don't worry about the short-term cost. If you understand and can put into effect what you have learned from this book about contribution, the cost of leaving will be short-term. If you have been financially dependent upon the person or group of people you are going to leave, it is a wise idea to have some sort of a job to go to, so as to avoid the risk of homelessness, which can be a terrible trap in itself, but whatever you do, get out.

There is urgency here. The longer you stay, the unhappier you will be, the more emotionally debilitated you will become, and the harder it will become to make any change at all. Do not be too quick, however: you must first try everything you reasonably can to bring happiness into any relationship you are in – only when you have been baulked at every turn by a consistently negative reaction must you give up, but when you do, go quickly.

"Money is the material shape of the principle that men who wish to deal with one another must deal by trade and give value for value. ... Your wallet is your statement of hope that somewhere in the world around you are men who will not default on the moral principle which is the root of money."

Ayn Rand

PART FOUR

Being Happy
With Things

We live in a material world. Whether or not you are materialistic, as some people put it, you still have to handle material objects in order to do almost everything you do do. Things, that is real pieces of physical matter, are very important to us as human beings. Other creatures also depend upon physical things for their survival (they eat some things and use other things to build their nests and so on) but only human beings spend so much effort on making changes to physical objects.

You may find some people who claim that material possessions are unimportant, and that all that matters is a good conscience, and good relationships with other people and with God. They have a point, in that material possessions are not sufficient, and you do need a clear conscience and healthy relationships in order to be happy, but if you watch these people in their daily lives, you will observe that they too rely heavily on things. They rely particularly upon things made in factories by people whom they would decry as materialists, they wear shoes they didn't make themselves, they eat with cutlery they didn't make and they write with ballpoint pens they wouldn't know how to make.

Material things are vital to us. We depend upon them. Some people fight over them, others seem to dedicate their lives to obtaining them, and others to trying to prove they don't need them. Your happiness depends, in part, upon having a healthy relationship with the inanimate world of things, hence this part of the book, but if you are to be happy with things, you must first know their limitations.

"You can't live on just groovy emotions alone. You have to work with the underlying form of the universe too, the laws of nature which, when understood, can make work easier, sickness rarer and famine almost absent."

Robert Pirsig

Chapter 21

Know Their Limitations

Although you are dependent upon things, they can't do everything for you. In a sense, they can't do anything for you, since you have to control them if they are to be any good to you at all. If you are unrealistic about what things can do for you, you are laying yourself open to the possibility of being made unhappy when your unrealistic expectations are disappointed. Yet again, we find that happiness is dependent upon realism. So, let's look at what this realism entails.

Things Can't Make you Happy

It is not within the power of any physical object to make you happy. When put as simply as this, it seems unarguable, but it is tempting, sometimes, to think that the cause of your unhappiness is the lack of some physical possession. If you are unhappy because there is some object you want but which you haven't got, it isn't the lack of it which makes you unhappy, but the interpretation you put on that lack. The proof of this is that there exist happy people who also lack what you lack.

Despite all this, there may be something you want which you haven't got, and there need be nothing wrong with the desire, as it is natural to desire good things. The problem arises when you find yourself saying ...

"If only I had a ... "

It doesn't matter at all how you complete that sentence. Whether you want a new dress or a great big ranch in Texas, the idea that you could be happy if only you had one is poisonous. Poisonous as the idea is, we must look at it a little more closely.

Good feelings on acquisition ...

When you acquire something which you have wanted, you get a good feeling, especially if you buy it with money which you have earned honestly. The bigger and more expensive the thing is, the stronger the feeling. The feeling is also stronger if you have been wanting this thing for a long time. But these good feelings you get ...

... don't last

It isn't long before you find yourself wanting something else. There needn't be anything wrong with such a desire. The problem arises when you find yourself believing that having this next acquisition will make you happy. It might give you some sort of good feeling, maybe joy, but not happiness. If you keep seeking this good feeling, you might find yourself suffering from ...

197

Shopping addiction

An addiction to shopping is a compulsive behaviour. Gamblers, alcoholics, drug addicts and compulsive shoppers have a great deal in common. If you are a compulsive shopper, you are carrying round a nasty little meme, which keeps saying, "Buy it – you'll feel good."

This particular meme survives well because it tells the truth, or part of it. The antidote is a slightly bigger meme, which tells more of the truth. It says, "If you buy it, you will feel good for a short time." Unfortunately, what the antidote says may not always be wholly true, as there are some things which you will always be glad of having bought. What it does for you is to start an internal argument, which will help you to make rational decisions about what to buy. This is yet another case where thinking and rationality will protect you from unhappiness.

Even if you buy something for good reasons, the good feelings will not last for ever, and nor will the physical things that you buy.

They Perish

Jesus said that, wherever your treasure is, your heart will be too. This is as good a definition of the word "treasure" as any. If you treasure something, you have an emotional attachment to it. Such an emotional attachment to material objects is bound to lead to disappointment. There are a number of reasons for this, but one of the most important is that material things tend to deteriorate, on account of the ...

Second law of thermodynamics

You may have no interest in physics, but one of the laws of nature discovered by physicists is important here. Simply put, the second law of thermodynamics tells us that, left to themselves, things tend towards disorder. What this means in practice is that all the effort we put into making things, collecting things, and creating order and beauty around us only has a temporary effect.

Rust, moth, worms

I do not mean to say that it is wrong to try to create order and beauty around you. All I am pointing out is that, if you let yourself develop too great an emotional attachment to anything material, you are risking unhappiness. How great is too great? Think of it this way: if you feel sad when you find evidence of rust on your car, moth-holes in your cardigan, or woodworm in that nice antique table, you are too emotionally attached to it.

By all means create or buy things of beauty if you will enjoy them and if you can accept that it is in their nature to perish. If your enjoyment is going to be spoiled by something as inevitable as the fading of a watercolour painting exposed to the light, don't get one. For exactly the same reason, avoid things which deteriorate so slowly as not to be noticeable, but which can get broken, such as beautiful glassware, unless you are prepared to live with the risk of it getting broken, and you can be sure of not feeling too much emotional pain when it happens.

What you feel when a material thing wears out, disintegrates or gets broken is, of course, up to you. You decide the rules which define how you will feel in any circumstances, including these. If you want to be happy, don't give yourself rules which tell you to feel unhappy if something gets broken. If you give yourself a rule which tells you to be unhappy if the second law of thermodynamics affects your possessions, you will be unhappy because you cannot successfully defy the laws of physics; but you don't have to give yourself such a rule.

If you don't like the idea of things deteriorating or getting broken, you might choose to surround yourself with physically stable valuables, such as gold and diamonds. These are not much better because they attract thieves.

Thieves

The other thing which happens to material possessions is that they tend to get stolen. There are people around who have not learned that unearned wealth cannot help them to be happy, so they steal things. Some theft is carried out by petty criminals and some is institutionalised, but the effect on you is similar.

The effect is that, if you own something, you cannot guarantee to continue to own it. This is very hard to accept emotionally, because the need for a sense of security is a fundamental human need, and we get part of our sense of security from the feeling that we can keep what we have made or earned.

Nevertheless, if you are to be happy, you must accept that there is a risk to your possessions not only from the second law of thermodynamics but also from lawlessness in society. The key is not to let yourself become so emotionally attached to an object that, if it is stolen, you will make yourself sad.

There is something to be learned here from Croesus, the legendary king of Lydia, whose commercial success was such that we still have the phrase "as rich as Croesus" in our language today. When his country was invaded and defeated by the Persians in 546 BC, the peace terms he negotiated with Cyrus, the Persian king, were very clever. It was agreed that the invading army could take all the money in the treasury and all the finished goods that had been produced in the capital city Sardis, but were to leave the farms in the countryside and all the means of producing wealth (mostly looms) untouched in the towns. Within a very few years, Lydia was once again a wealthy country.

What do you learn from Croesus? It isn't what you own that defines your wealth. It is what you are capable of producing. If you are a truly productive person, all the thieves and parasites there are around will not destroy your wealth, unless you let them destroy your capacity to produce wealth. Don't be made unhappy by the fact that they take things from you. You can always make some more, in the same way as you can replace anything that wears out or gets broken.

The key is to understand that wealth can be created. Croesus understood this, but Cyrus probably did not. It would seem that Cyrus believed that the only way to acquire wealth was to take it from those who had it. This is the thinking of the thief and the parasite, and it does not make for happiness.

Even if you understand that wealth can be created, it does not follow that you are personally able to create it. If you are elderly, disabled or housebound, it might be extremely difficult for you to create new wealth. This will make it harder for you to cope with the loss of your possessions however that loss is caused. There is no easy solution to this, but it is still wise to avoid making rules for yourself which would cause the pain of such loss to make you unhappy.

Fashion and technological advance

Even if your possessions remain intact and they remain *your* possessions, some of them may become outmoded simply because of changing fashions, or they may become obsolete because of improvements in technology.

Your reaction to this is up to you. If you are unhappy because your once prized possession is obsolete, it is just because you have attached too much emotional significance to that thing, or to other people's opinions of it; outdated equipment can remain useful. Be realistic instead. Expect whatever you have to have its day and then to be past it. Don't set yourself up to be unhappy when the inevitable happens.

Function vs. Form

Things are not always what they appear to be. Not only is this true of political or social situations, but it can also be true of material objects.

A thing is what it is. It may (like a fake or a toy or a cheap imitation of a useful product) have been made to look like something else,. It may even have been a useful product, which has ceased to be useful without changing its appearance, like a clock with a broken spring, or a broken down car.

You must therefore not judge things solely by their appearance. To do so is to set yourself up for a disappointment. To do so routinely could put you on the path to unhappiness, which can follow from a failure to handle the material world successfully. How then, can you assess what a material object actually is?

It's what they do that counts

From your point of view, a thing is characterised by what it does to you or for you. (Even if you are a scientist seeking the true nature of the thing, your experimental work on it tells you what it does under certain kinds of investigation, and what information it can give you about how the universe works.)

When you are thinking of buying something, your first concern is whether it will do what you want it to. This is even true when you are buying things solely for their appearance, as we shall see later.

Whenever you use something, you are concerned with what it does. You may not care how it does it, but your ability to use it depends upon your understanding of what it can do. If you drive a car, you must have learned what to do with the various controls in order to affect the behaviour of the vehicle, but you may not know how they operate. If you use a computer, you are very unlikely to have a comprehensive understanding of how all its internal components function, but you know what your computer does for you.

You might have an opinion about the external appearance of your car, or maybe even of your computer, but it is the internal workings that define what such an object is, not what it looks like outside.

What they do often defines how they look

Some things look the way they do because they have to be the shape they are in order to do the job they do. It is said that form follows function. For example, an aeroplane has to be the shape it is in order to fly. Some machines even have a kind of natural beauty arising from the way they are designed to perform a particular function as well as possible, and the same thing is true of some buildings, particularly bridges.

For some things, how they look is what they do

Not everything has a physical function to perform. If you hang a picture on your wall, the only effect you are looking for is an aesthetic one. The function of the thing is to look good. The same is true of wallpaper, ornaments and so on. Paint has a functional purpose, in that it preserves the surface beneath it, but the colour of the paint is usually a matter of taste.

This brings us naturally to the subject of ...

Art

You have a right to any opinion you may have about anything to do with art. Never let anyone try to give you feelings of inferiority on the grounds that you do not share their opinions about a work of art, or about art in general.

There are people around who use their "superior" knowledge or taste in order to manipulate people who are less sophisticated. The less harmless ones just try to score points at parties so as to make other people seem ridiculous, but actually end up making themselves look ridiculous. The more dangerous ones argue that it is in the national interest that large amounts of public money be spent on preserving items for the country, only a tiny proportion of whose inhabitants care about the works of art involved, but all of whose inhabitants are impoverished by the expense. Such people take a small cut of the budget to support their own luxurious life-styles. Are they happy? I doubt it.

If you are an artist, by all means do what you enjoy. Produce any work of art which satisfies you. If someone wants to buy what you want to sell, by all means enjoy the profits, and live off them if you can do so and wish to do so. You might even get rich that way. You can be happy about all this, provided that you do not argue that you have any right to be given a living at the expense of people who do not wish to buy your work: any such move will destroy your happiness.

How does it make you feel?

Whether or not you are an artist, and whether or not you know anything about art, there is a simple way of telling whether a work of art is any good from your point of view. Remember that your point of view is the only one that matters.

Look at a painting. Concentrate on it. Gaze at it. Stare at it. If you can, be absorbed by it. Now, how do you feel? Good? Great? Calm? Disturbed? Amused? Tearful? Does it, in fact, do anything for your emotions whatever, or do you just feel blank? In the answers to these questions, you will find your opinion of the painting, the only opinion that matters. You will also know whether you wish to own it. You may recognise it as a powerfully emotive work, but you might still prefer not to have it on your own wall. Again, only your opinion matters.

Everything I said in that paragraph about a painting, you can adapt easily enough to any sort of work of art, such as theatre, ballet, literature, and even music.

How much can you expect from it?

Good works of art can have quite a beneficial effect on your feelings, but art itself will not make you happy. If you do expect art to make you happy, you are making a rule for yourself which will ensure that you are unhappy. Happiness comes from within you and follows from choices you make; it does not come from feelings induced in you by a work of art, no matter how profound.

Are you living in the real world?

One of the problems with art is that, in order to enjoy it properly, you have to detach yourself from the real world to some extent. It is possible to become so absorbed by art that you lose touch with reality, whether you are producing your own work of art or enjoying someone else's. This may not be a bad thing for a short time, but it can become addictive, especially if you are not dealing successfully with reality on a day-to-day basis.

Your happiness depends upon living in the real world. If you are escaping from the real world on a regular basis, whether through, drink, drugs or art, you have a problem which you must solve in order to become truly happy. (I should mention here that television, films and fiction are all art-forms, which are more commonly used for routine escape than other art-forms, but any sort of art, be it painting, sculpture, music, gardening, or whatever, can have this effect.)

Having said that there is a risk that, through concentration on art, you might lose touch with reality, I should also say that some of the greatest art can help you to see reality in a new way, and thus deal with it more successfully.

As with anything else, in order to be happy, you have to make your own judgement as to whether any interest you have in art is helping you to relate properly to the real world. If it is getting in the way, or distracting you too much, then you must change your habits. Never forget that there is great beauty in the natural world, and great beauty in people: you can enjoy these things at least as much as any work of art, and they are real.

Art as an investment

Have you ever thought of investing money in art? Can you spot a winner? Can you identify the work of art which you can buy cheaply today and sell for a fortune in a few years' time? Why should you wish to?

There are people who have made money in this way, but most of them say that they bought what they really liked because they liked it, and subsequently sold it because they had to. As often as not, they are sad to part with their treasures. Why should you wish to copy them?

If you want to make money, productive work is the most reliable method. Buying something in the hope that it might become more valuable is gambling, and it does not lead to happiness. Buying shares in a productive company may be seen as an exception to this, provided that you have a real interest in what the company does, rather than just in its value on the stock market. Buying works of art in the hope that they might become more valuable is not only risky, but also unproductive: it won't help you to be happy, but if it is just a hobby, and you can afford to lose your money, it won't destroy your happiness either. If you buy a work of art (or go to a show) because you value the artist's work, this may well enhance your happiness, provided that your expenditure is within your means.

Chapter 22

Know Their Uses

Although material objects cannot make you happy, many of them have been carefully designed by other people just so that you can use them. There are all sorts of things which you use in the ordinary course of daily life, and if you use them to help you to achieve well-chosen goals, they help you to be happy. Understand them, learn what they can do for you, and use them to achieve what you want. Remember that, when you were a young child, you had to learn how to use many things which you now take for granted, and do not be afraid to learn how to use new things.

Extension of Self

If you are going to be happy, you must be able to handle the real, physical, material world with confidence. Confidence, as we have seen, is faith in yourself. However, when you are handling material things, the scope of that faith broadens somewhat. The reason for this is that, when we handle tools successfully, our "self" expands. Let us look at a few examples.

Knife, fork and chopsticks

Were you brought up in a Western household, eating with knife and fork, or an an Eastern household, with chopsticks? Have you learned, as an adult, to use the eating implements common in the other hemisphere? Have you ever watched a European adult in their first struggles to master chopsticks, or a Chinese person in their first encounter with knife and fork? You can learn a lot from a study of this!

Let us suppose you are a European with no childhood experience with chopsticks, and you are learning as an adult to use them. You quickly discover that holding one stick in each hand is not helpful. Next you concentrate on getting the grip right as you hold two sticks in one hand. At first, you get aches in parts of your hand you had never thought of before, as tense little muscles struggle to keep hold of the things. Next you get the idea of one stick being more or less stationary, while the other one can be moved, but still you are concentrating on just which bits of your hand are doing what with which bits of which chopstick, and your food is getting cold.

After a while, you master the skill of handling your chopsticks, you can pick up anything in your bowl from a whole king prawn to a single grain of rice, as you choose. By now, you are not thinking of what your fingers are doing, you are just eating, maybe not even concentrating on the food, and certainly not on the process of getting it from your bowl to your mouth. If you do stop to think about this, you look at the tips of the chopsticks, not at the hand that is holding them!

When you have reached this level of skill, which will have taken dozens of Chinese meals, your chopsticks have become part of your self. When you hold your chopsticks, your consciousness extends right to the tips of the sticks, rather than stopping at the skin of your hands. Although you have no nerves in the sticks themselves, you can feel what they are in contact with by means of the nerves in your hands. You can even concentrate your mind into the tip of a chopstick as you probe a piece of fish to see how tender it is!

When you were a child, you went through a similar process of learning with your knife and fork, which you now use so unconsciously that, while you are eating, they are part of you.

Car

If you drive a car, you will have gone through a similar learning process. If you are an experienced and skilled driver, you no longer think about the movements of your hands and feet as you operate the controls; you merely think where you want to be on the road, and you go there. The car has become an extension of you.

This self-extension can be so complete that you will flinch if your car is bumped by another, even if the impact is so slight that you are uninjured, and even if the car itself is undamaged. It just feels as if the car is part of you, and in a sense it is.

Every expert driver feels at one with the vehicle. The same is true of a cyclist or a pilot. True control of the material world comes from a sense of oneness with it. You will not be truly happy as a driver until you reach this level of skill.

The disadvantage of this sense of oneness is that you run the risk of feeling hurt if your car gets damaged, and you are likely to feel sad when you find that it is wearing out or rusting away. It can be hard to grasp that the thing rusting away is just a thing, and is not physically part of you, and it is not you that is rusting away!

To be happy with your car, you must be in control of the extent to which it becomes an extension of you. While you are using it to get around, let it be part of you, but do not let it become such a part of your life that you will be unhappy if it gets damaged or destroyed. You must own it, but not let it own you.

Telephone

Where are you when you talk to someone on the telephone? Last night a friend telephoned me from two hundred miles away. There is nothing exceptional about this in the modern world, but it gives us an example of this idea of the extension of the self.

As we spoke, we did not discuss the telephone system, nor even think about it, we merely used it. We spoke as if we were in the same room together, not hundreds of miles apart, but where was he? I think, although I am not sure, that he was telephoning me from his house, which I know quite well, but I don't know which room he was in, and I am fairly sure he didn't know which room I was in either, so where was I from his point of view? We were present to each other, but just in each other's ears!

In this sort of way, you can be with more or less anyone you like anywhere in the world. Your sense of self can reach thousands of miles around the world and you can influence people anywhere this way. In a sense, you are there with them.

Computer as typewriter

As I type this, I spend only a very small part of my time thinking about which fingers are where on the keyboard in front of me. In my mind, I am imagining talking to you, although I cannot see you, and, as I talk, my words appear on my computer screen. What has happened is that the computer, acting as a typewriter, has become an extension of me: I am using it in the same way as I use my voice when I am speaking to someone, not thinking about how to enunciate the words, but just talking.

Computer *per se*

Really skilled computer users use their machines as extensions to their minds. The computer does not think, as such, but acts as an aid to thinking, particularly with its ability to store large amounts of information and recall it accurately and present it in a variety of ways.

Control of Material World

What is the use of all this? How does an ability to extend your sense of self into inanimate material objects help you to be happy? The answer is that this is how we, as human beings, actually control things skilfully, and the skilful handling of things is so much a part of being human that it has a bearing on our happiness.

The infant's problem

When you were born, you came into the world with virtually no physical skills. You could suck, swallow, breathe and cry, and that was about all. You couldn't do anything constructive with your hands. At that stage, however, you were unaware of all the things you would have to learn in order to become a successful adult.

As you grew up, you discovered various things you would like to be able to do and you learned how to do them. With each new skill, you learned more about what you could do, and what was beyond you, and the boundary between the possible and the impossible kept changing.

Very early in this process, you learned where your own physical boundaries were. Which bits of the world are part of you, and which bits are not? Physically, you end at your own skin, but you didn't know that at first. You had to learn that your mother was a separate being whom you could not control in quite the same way as you could control your own fingers. You had to learn that clothes are not part of you, but that skin is.

Possibly the infant's biggest problem is to learn where its boundaries are. Have you, as an adult, successfully solved that problem yet?

Where are your boundaries?

Obviously, you are aware of the physical boundary at your skin which defines the difference between you and not-you in a physiological sense. That is not the problem.

When a craftsman is using a tool of his trade skilfully, the tool, as we have seen, becomes part of him, in the sense that, when he is thinking of what is happening at the tip of the tool and not at the end of it that he is holding, his boundary is at the tip of the tool.

Knowing where your boundaries are in this sense helps you to be happy. Confusion over what you can do and what you can't can be very upsetting, so let's look at the process of learning a new skill again.

The phases of learning a new skill

There are four phases of learning any new skill. They are known as unconscious incompetence, conscious incompetence, conscious competence and unconscious competence, in that order. Let's return to our chopsticks example and look at these four phases.

Before you learned that there are people who eat with chopsticks, you never knew that such a skill existed. You were incompetent with chopsticks, and you never knew! This was unconscious incompetence. This is where all babies start with all skills. Next, you discovered that the skill exists, but you knew that you could not handle those sticks correctly: you were consciously incompetent.

As your skill with handling the chopsticks grows, you pass through the stage of conscious competence, where you can get them to do what you want but you have to concentrate on it, until you reach the point of unconscious competence, where you use them skilfully without even being aware that you are doing so.

The most important stage to understand for the sake of your happiness is the second one, conscious incompetence. When you know that you have not learned now to do something that some other people know how to do, it is very tempting to use the words "I can't". Avoid these words like the plague, because they can limit you. When you are tempted to think "I can't", remind yourself that you must be at the second stage of a four-stage learning process, the third stage of which is conscious competence, when you can say "I can". If, at this second stage, you do have to say something, never say "I can't", say "I haven't yet learned how."

Means to an End

Whatever skills you learn, and whatever material things you use, in other words, whatever you do, let it always be for a purpose. Have an end in view. Remember the two great evils: purpose without action and action without purpose. Know your goals, and always make sure that your use of material things and the skills you need to handle them are directed towards the achievement of those goals.

Power for power's sake always corrupts

It is sometimes said that power corrupts. This is an oversimplification. Admittedly, there is a tendency for people who exercise power over other people to become corrupt, even if they were not corrupt beforehand, but power over the material world does not necessarily corrupt a person.

It can be corrupting, however, if it is power simply for the sake of power. This is what the vandal exercises: he uses the power to destroy things simply for the sake of the feeling of power. If you do this, there is a great danger of making yourself unhappy. Even if you do not use your power over things destructively, but use it instead simply for the pleasure it gives, there is a danger that you might make yourself unhappy.

If, for example, you dedicate your youth to developing a sporting skill, you might well enjoy it at the time, but in your later years you are likely to regret it, especially if you suffer long-term health problems as a result.

There is a risk of becoming too emotionally attached to any skill you may have, whether it is physical or mental. Any skill can be lost through accident or the deterioration which comes with old age. It is up to you to choose your rules in such a way that you will not be made unhappy by the loss of any skill you may have. This is possible, no matter how much effort you put into developing the skill.

Power for a purpose

If your goals in life are well thought out and themselves consistent with happiness, then anything you do towards achieving them will help you to be happy, unless you cause someone else to suffer. Learning a new skill, therefore, will help you to be happy, if that new skill helps you to achieve a more important goal.

Use things

Likewise, you can use any material thing in whatever way you like, provided that you don't hurt anyone, which, of course, you can do by using things which do not belong to you without the owner's permission. Remember that property rights are human rights, and you cannot violate them without making yourself unhappy.

Do whatever you like with the material world. You can manipulate your physical possessions in any way you please. Do not, however, use people. You can reach agreements with people if they benefit in some way from co-operating with you, but do not use them in the same way as you would use things. Things do not have feelings, but people do.

Use them up if need be

Some things are in limited supply, and other things wear out. If you are unclear about your goals, you will feel a need to keep some of anything of which you only have a limited supply, just in case you need it another time. You will also try to avoid wearing anything out, for the same reason. What might you need it for? You might need it to achieve some goal which is not yet clear to you.

Happiness comes (in part) from achieving well-defined goals, so do not let this feeling prevent you from achieving a goal which is clear to you. To miss a good goal in order to give yourself a better chance at one you haven't even thought of yet would not be a good idea, and would not help you to be happy.

Furthermore, things are often not as limited as they seem. If your life is properly productive, you will be creating wealth, and you can apply part of this wealth to replacing things, maybe not with identical copies of the ones you have worn out or used up, but with something which can be made to serve the same purpose.

Chapter 23

Control

If you are to be happy, you must be in control of your life. We have seen how important self-control is for this, and how important it is not to be controlled by other people, but what about your ability to control the material world? You must be in control of at least those parts of the material world which have a direct bearing on how you live your life. It can be hard to achieve this, and there are limits to what is physically possible, but the alternative to being in control of things is to drift through life feeling like a victim all the way. So what can you control, and how?

Your Body

The one material object which you and you alone have an absolute human right to control is your body. You do not have a right to use it to hurt anyone else, but you are entitled not to have it controlled by anyone else. You can forfeit that right by engaging in criminal activity such that you have to be restrained by the proper authorities so as to protect other people from your violence, but as long as you live honestly and peacefully with the rest of the human race, you may do what you like with your body.

Having a right to control your body does not give you the ability to do anything with it, and nor does it give you any sense of what you ought to do.

What I want you to do now is to think of your body as a physical, material object. Admittedly, it is part of you, so it can be difficult to think of it just a thing, and the idea of separating mind and body is not often very helpful, but if you can do it now, it will make what I am trying to say a little clearer. See your body as a very complex machine, of which you are the sole owner and the only operator, and keep this idea in mind for the remainder of this section.

Your most precious possession
This wonderful machine, your body, is the most precious thing you own. Without it, everything else you own would be worthless.

Look after it
If you damage it badly, repair and recovery take priority over everything else. If you damage part of it irreparably, your life will never be the same again. You only have one body. In the course of time, it will deteriorate, but by looking after it carefully, you can limit the effects of old age to some extent.

Keep fit, but don't overdo it

If you let yourself become so unfit that your body doesn't work properly, your happiness will be adversely affected. If you want your body to perform as it should, you must take a reasonable amount of exercise, and keep in practice with the things that you need your body to do for you. Because exercise and keeping fit bring pleasant feelings, there is a risk of becoming addicted to them. Remember that the purpose of keeping fit is to be able to use your body for other things.

See it as the means to every end

This complex machine which you own, control and maintain as best you can, is the one thing which you use to do everything that you do do. First comes thought, but after thought comes action, and all action involves the use of your body. Whenever you say something or write something, you are using a part of your body just as much as if you are doing something more obviously physical, such as painting or swinging an axe.

Everything you will ever do in your life depends on getting your body to do what you want it to.

Tools

Your body alone cannot do everything you might wish. This is especially true if you are physically disabled, but it is true of everyone. You can't take the cork out of a bottle without a corkscrew or put a nail in the wall without a hammer. Maybe you can't get around without a wheelchair. With the right tools, you can do pretty much whatever you want. If you are disabled, you need more and better tools, but the principle is the same for everyone.

Tools are an extension of the body

As we saw earlier, when you use a tool or a machine with unconscious competence, it becomes part of you. In effect, it becomes an extension of your body. Any skills you learn for handling things of this sort are in fact skills of bodily control. Although you are thinking in terms of what the tool or machine is doing, you are using your body to control it. Through the use of any such tool, you use your body to control other parts of the material universe more effectively.

Uniquely human

The use of tools and machines is uniquely human. No other species designs, makes and builds machines. This is part of why the successful use of tools and machines has such a bearing upon happiness. To be happy, you must be fully human. To be fully human means to be competent at these uniquely human skills, and to control those things which you own by using whatever skills, tools and machines you need, and to use all your skills, tools, and machines to help you to achieve your rationally chosen goals. Anything less than this is less than human, and will make you less than completely happy.

211

Generalisation of tools concept

It is very easy to think of tools just as things like hammers, screwdrivers and spanners, but I would like to broaden the idea to cover anything which you use for a purpose other than the joy of using it. With this idea in mind, you can take more or less any manufactured object and ask what its purpose is. If it is anything other than a work of art or a toy, the chances are that it is, in this sense, a tool.

This idea can be taken even further ...

Zeug

The German word Zeug (pronounced "tsoish") is not easily translated into other languages, but the concept is so useful that I'd like to try to explain it. To do this, let's first look at a few compound words.

The verb "spielen" means "to play", and the word for toy is "Spielzeug", meaning (more or less) anything you might play with. The verb "schreiben" means "to write", so what does the word "Schreibzeug" mean? A pen? A pencil, perhaps? What about a piece of chalk for writing on a blackboard? Or one of those tiny paintbrushes used for Chinese calligraphy? Of course, it means any or all of those things. A Schreibzeug is a writing implement of any sort. Likewise "Flugzeug" means an aircraft of any sort, be it an airliner, a helicopter or even a glider.

What about "Zeug" as a word on its own, not as part of a compound word? It means the "whatever-it-takes", the "whatever-you-need-to-do-it" or the "where-withal". This does not have to be a physical object or tool of any kind; it can cover knowledge, skill, training, confidence or whatever combination of abstract and physical things is necessary to achieve the end in mind.

Therein lies the point. If you want to achieve something, anything, whatever purpose you have in mind, you need the Zeug for that purpose. If you haven't got it yet, get it, or make it.

Be a Tool-maker

Human beings are unique in the animal kingdom in that they use tools for virtually everything. It follows that human beings are not only users of tools but also makers of tools. As I have pointed out before, happiness means being fully human. This means being able to create new means of doing things when necessary, not necessarily unprecedented ways of doing things as inventors do, just things which are new in your life.

Necessity as the mother of invention

You will not create anything new unless you have some need which you cannot easily satisfy. When you have some aim, purpose or goal, no matter how big or small, and you can't immediately see how to achieve it, you are lacking something. What you lack is some aspect of the Zeug necessary for the purpose.

How do you overcome this problem? Of course the answer depends upon the particular problem. Sometimes it can be as simple as going to a shop and buying the tool you need for the job. Other times, you might have to create something which didn't exist before. I am writing this book for a purpose I could not achieve any other way. I remember my father building a flight of steps in our garden when I was a child, to make a steep slope safer. These things are essentially the same, the creation of something new (although books and steps have a long history) in order to achieve a particular purpose. This is tool-making.

Imagination necessary

If you are to do anything new, you need to use your imagination. If you never do anything new, you will stagnate and you will not be happy. It follows that using your imagination constructively can help you to be happy. How does this idea apply here?

When you want to achieve something, and you are aware that you have not got the Zeug for it, the thing to do is to imagine life as it would be after having achieved it, and then imagine remembering how you did it. This simple little trick can be very effective at opening your mind to ways of doing things, and it will help you to be inventive. Once your imagination has shown you in this way how to do something, you then have to get on and do it, and that may involve new tools.

Metatools

There is just one more concept worth mentioning while we are on the subject of tools and tool-making, and that is that when you make a new tool, you use tools to make it. Those tools were themselves made by means of other tools, and so on. If you trace back the ancestry of any tool in that way, you will eventually come to a human being using his hands on a piece of the natural world, such as a stick or a stone.

There is nothing to stop you from using raw materials in this primitive way. Equally you can use the most sophisticated of modern machines. Whatever you use from the great family of tools whose development has gone on in parallel with that of the human race, you are doing something completely natural and fully human, using physical objects to help you to achieve your aims. And if you use one tool to help you to create another, you are furthering the development of the human race in a fundamentally proper way.

Of course, to make or use tools, you need ...

Skills

The greater part of any skill is in the mind. Even in the case of an apparently purely physical skill, you build up new neural pathways in the brain as you practise, as well as toning up the muscles involved. A purely mental skill involves nothing but neural pathways. It is these neural pathways which allow you to control the physical world in the way you want, firstly through your own mental skills, and secondly through your physical skills, which allow you to control your body as you wish, which is the means by which you control other material things.

213

Joy of learning

Learning something which you want to learn is enjoyable. It is no fun having to learn something for no other apparent reason than that your teachers in school would be unpleasant to you if you didn't. When you want to know something, or want to know how to do something, in order to use your new knowledge or skill to achieve something you want to achieve, you will learn what you want, and enjoy the process of doing so. It is a great shame that this natural source of joy can be tainted by unpleasant experience at school, but even if you hated school, you can still enjoy learning new things if you choose to do so.

Never too old

There is no age limit on the ability to learn. Admittedly, you may get a bit slower as you get older, but the more you keep your brain in the habit of taking on new things, the faster you will remain. And by taking a new interest in life, you can speed up the working of your mind and be rejuvenated. The joy of this can help to bring new happiness to your later years.

It is even possible to learn new physical skills when you are older. Taking up pole-vaulting in your nineties is unlikely to be a good idea, but if there is something which a contemporary of yours can do, the chances are that you can learn to do it too, if you really want to. The most likely barrier to this is the "I can't" belief. Keep telling yourself that if anyone can then you can, and set about learning the basics. Enjoy the learning process, and you will soon also be enjoying using your new skill to achieve what you want.

The "I can't do maths" trap

The natural world is well-behaved. It never breaks the rules. Nothing ever defies the law of gravity, for example. Two apples plus two apples makes four apples, always. If you are going to be happy with physical things, you must accept that they behave logically even if their behaviour sometimes appears bizarre. In dealing with them, you must be rational, because physical things do not care about your irrational beliefs, desires or wants; they follow their own logic, regardless of what you want.

Over the centuries, mankind has developed a system of logic by means of which we can describe and predict what the physical world does. This is called science, and at the heart of all science is mathematics, which is just formalised logic.

In order for you to be happy in dealing with the physical world, you must be logical, and it can help to have some skill with mathematics, so that you can calculate things. The alternatives to calculation are guessing or relying on an expert, who may not be as clever as he makes out, or may even be trying to trick you by means of his claim to be an expert.

Do you think you can't do mathematics? Where did you get this "I can't" belief? At school, probably, where you were expected work hard to solve artificial problems which had no relevance to life as you then saw it. No wonder you were put off! Millions are! A few people enjoy the problem-solving for its own sake, and some of these go on to university to study mathematics or one of the sciences, but many such people are less than successful in other parts of their lives.

A very few people have discovered that it is possible later in life to learn to think logically and even to express this logic mathematically. These few have always had a specific motive for learning such mathematics as they need. One example who springs to mind is a young man who hated school but loved motorcycles: hopeless at school, he went on to work as a motorcycle engineer, learning as he did so more applied mathematics and physics than his school could ever have taught him.

You too can learn as much formal logic and mathematics as you want, if you want to. Only two things stop you. The first is not being able to see the advantages of understanding the regularity of the world. The second is the "I can't" belief, which you can just dump, knowing that other people have managed to dump it too.

Physical skills

When you learn a new physical skill, you start by doing whatever it is carefully and slowly, paying close attention to every detail. With practice, things come more easily, until eventually you reach the stage of unconscious competence when you can do whatever it is without thinking.

Everybody knows that practice makes perfect, but do you know why? As you learn by practice, new connections are established in your brain, and new neural pathways are built up. This is true with any repeated behaviour, whether it is something you are trying to learn or a just an established habit. Repeat it, and the pathways become stronger. Stop and they weaken. When they are weak, you are out of practice and your skill is lessened.

Would you believe that daydreaming can help you to improve your physical skills? That would be an oversimplification, but some of the world's most successful people, especially in sport, have learned that by constantly visualising the fine details of a successful performance, they can improve their skills more than by practice alone. If you repeat over in your mind the details of a skilful performance, many of the relevant neural pathways will be built up usefully. Add this to your physical practice and you will be a winner.

Using your physical skills successfully brings a joy of its own. All joy of this sort has a double-edged implication for happiness. If you use the skill just for the joy of using it, you run the risk of developing a compulsive behaviour and making yourself unhappy. If you use it to help you to achieve something you believe to be worthwhile, it will help you to be happy.

Mental skills

More or less everything I have said about physical skills applies equally to mental skills. Maybe you find mental arithmetic and spelling easy, but have difficulty remembering names and faces. Or vice versa. If there is something you have difficulty with, you are probably only aware that it is a difficulty because you know of people who seem not to have that difficulty.

If anyone can do it, then you can do it. Find someone who has the skill you would like to have and ask them how they do it. They may not find it very easy to explain, but if you persist, you will find someone who finds easy that which you find difficult, and who can explain how they do it.

Copy them! It is as simple as that, but you will only manage it if you want the skill for a purpose of your own, and you are prepared to put in the effort of copying other successful people, and practising. It can be done, but you must want to, and you must believe that you can. Keep telling yourself that if anyone else can do it, then you can do it: this will give you the "I can" belief you need.

Most mental skills are useful, and fun to use, but as with all things which are fun, there is a danger of addiction. Crosswords, for example, may be seen as useful mental exercise, but the fun of solving them can get you hooked. If you let puzzle-solving become a compulsive behaviour, it can undermine your happiness.

Artistic skills

Artistic skills are for the artist to enjoy. If anyone else enjoys what the artist does, then so much the better, but that is not the point. If you want to be artistically creative, and you have the time, do whatever you want, and enjoy it. If there is a particular type of artistic skill you would like to master, find someone skilled at it, and copy their techniques, and their thinking. You may even be able to do this at your local college.

Art can add a great deal to your quality of life, but it can also be addictive. If you want to be happy, by all means enjoy your artistic skills, but do not let art take over your life, and on no account use it as an escape from reality. Your happiness depends upon being in touch with reality, not on escaping from it.

Chapter 24

Do Not Be Controlled

Does the idea of being controlled by material things seem strange? I do mean being controlled by them, not by means of them! Of course, strictly speaking, nobody is completely controlled by material things, but it is possible for you to have irrational beliefs which can make it seem as if you are not in control of your own life but instead spend your time meeting the apparent demands of the material world.

You will have guessed already that I am going to say that if your life is like this, then you will not be happy, and you may feel tempted to skip this chapter because you are sure that you control things and things do not control you. Stay with me, however, and you may discover a few things which will help you in two ways. Firstly you might just learn how much less control you have than you could have, and why, and this could help you to be happier with the things you own. Secondly, you may learn about some problems that other people have with material things, and this could help you with your understanding of them, which, as we saw in Part Three, can certainly help you to be happier.

Goldratt's Third Law

In an extraordinary book called "The Goal" (published by Gower, 1989), Eli Goldratt gives nine rules about running a manufacturing business. His third rule is relevant to everyday life, and it is this:

Statement of law

"Utilisation and activation of a resource are not synonymous." Now that is somewhat technical language and its relevance to everyday life is not very obvious, so let me re-phrase it: "Operating something is not the same as using it." This is still a bit subtle, so let's look at a few ...

Examples in everyday life

Goldratt's basic point was that there is no point in running a factory producing products that no-one is buying, nor in running part of a factory at top efficiency churning out components of a product faster than they are used in making the complete product. What is the equivalent in everyday life?

You switch the television on because it is there, believing that there is no point having the thing if you are not going to watch it. You get a new car, and you take it out for a drive, not in order to get to a particular place, but because you think that if you have the thing, you might as well drive it rather than just leave it parked in your driveway. Someone gives you a sandwich toaster for

Christmas, and, although you have never liked toasted sandwiches, you use it because it seems wrong not to.

These are all examples of failure to understand Goldratt's third law. The television, the car and the sandwich toaster are all tools in the sense I used the word earlier: they are all things which can help you to do things which you cannot do alone with your bare hands. That is fine as long as you use them to achieve your own goals, but when you start using them, or "activating" them as Goldratt would say, just because they are there, you are no longer behaving rationally. Instead you are being controlled by these material objects, and the result is bound to be that you will become less happy.

Whenever you use any material thing, know why you are doing so. You will be much happier if you make sensible decisions as to what you use for what purpose than if you do anything without having a clear purpose in mind.

Toys as opposed to tools

Perhaps you think I am going too far here, and not taking into account the fact that some material things are toys, and can be used just for the sheer pleasure of using them. This can, indeed, apply to all the examples I have just given, but the basic argument is unchanged.

Toys as tools

Your car might be a toy, and you may get great pleasure from just driving it. That is fair enough, as long as you are aware that that is why you are driving it, and you are doing it deliberately.

In a sense, a toy is a tool. It is a device which helps you to enjoy life more than you would be able to if you did not play with it. It works only if you use it with the purpose of enjoying using it.

What's pulling your strings?

You can be quite happy using any material object for any purpose you want, including for the pure pleasure of using it. If you use something because you think you ought, but with no other clear purpose, it will leave you feeling dissatisfied, and this sort of behaviour can ultimately leave you feeling unhappy. You do not owe it to anyone to make use of anything for any purpose which is not wholly your own. To give you another example, if someone gives you a hideous scarf as a present, you do not have to wear it!

To be happy, you must remain in control of yourself. If you ignore Goldratt's third law and use things just because you think they ought to be used, you are being controlled by those material things, and because they have no desire or ability to make you happy, they will not make you happy. Your happiness is up to you.

Losing your Soul

When Jesus asked the immortal question, "What does it profit a man if he gains the whole world but suffers the loss of his soul?", he may well have meant to make more than one point. We have already seen the risk to you of resorting to dishonest methods to obtain your wealth, but can you still lose your soul or destroy your happiness by means of wealth acquired honestly? Maybe ...

Some people think that materialism is in effect a religion, and that there are other people, always wealthier than those making the accusation, who worship their material possessions in much the same sense that conventionally religious people worship God. I am not aware of any objective justification for this idea, even though it can sometimes seem that your material possessions are taking over your life. This is not the same as having materialism as a god or your material possessions as little gods.

Ancient concept of a god

There is an academic called Julian Jaynes who has written a fascinating book with a very tedious title, "The Origin of Consciousness in the Breakdown of the Bicameral Mind." In it, he puts forward the idea that, before the human race developed consciousness as we now understand it, normal mental activity was very like what we now describe as schizophrenia and regard as mental illness. He argues that we invented language before consciousness, and that for some thousands of years people acted on the basis of what they were told to do by voices which they hallucinated.

These hallucinated voices, according to Jaynes, were identified as the voices of the gods. It is interesting to note that, in the societies which he describes, it was not uncommon for people to carve effigies of what are believed to be representations of those gods, and that this same behaviour is often shown by people in the modern world who suffer from hallucinated voices, although Jaynes does not mention this detail himself.

Are you really in control?

It is very unlikely that your life is controlled by hallucinated voices, whether or not they appear to emanate from statues, as this phenomenon is now unusual enough to be regarded as abnormal. Nevertheless, there is still a risk that you might not be fully in control of your life, and that your relationship with material objects may be part of the cause of your lack of self-control.

We have already seen the risk of failure to allow for Goldratt's third law, and the risk of resorting to dishonesty to acquire material possessions, but there are yet other ways in which you can find your life influenced by material things to the extent that your own control of your life might be diminished.

Addictive materialism

You have probably experienced that special kind of feeling that comes from having spent your money well and bought something well worth having at a reasonable price, or even better, at a bargain price. This is a good and healthy feeling. It feels good for several reasons. Firstly, doing something rational which leads you towards a rational goal should always feel good. Secondly, trading of this sort is purely human, and it feels good to do something so characteristic of humanity. Thirdly, if it is the sort of deal with which both the seller and the buyer are genuinely pleased, everybody wins, and you can be happy about it. Fourthly, you can enjoy using your purchase for its intended purpose.

When something feels good for so many reasons, you can find yourself wanting to repeat the experience, but the joy of buying things can get out of control. The problem is that the joy you feel when you make a good purchase is a side-effect of buying something, not the primary effect. If you buy things just in order to get that feeling, you will feel something, but it won't be as good. If you do not understand how the feelings associated with shopping arise, there is a danger of getting into a compulsive behaviour, in which you spend all you have, or more, on trying to get that elusive feeling. By then, you are a "shopaholic", and you have a psychological problem.

This is could be seen as another instance of being controlled by material things. If your relationship with the physical material world is such that you keep buying more than you honestly need or want, you will not be happy with the things you buy. Could you describe the situation in terms of having lost your soul? If so, the first step of the solution is what used to be called repentance, which we discussed in Part Two.

To be happy with things, you must always know why you buy what you buy. That way, you stay in control.

The problem of too many possessions

If you buy more than you really need, keep things after they have ceased to be useful, or have things given to you which you do not really require, you can end up with too many possessions. When this happens, you can find yourself spending too much time, sorting, shifting, storing, cleaning all these things. You are looking after their needs and not your own. In a way, your life is being dominated by all these things which you think you own, but which affect you as if they owned you.

Regaining Control

If you feel that your life is to some extent controlled by material things, or that your relationship with the material world is such that you are not fully in control, it is time for you to take or regain control of things. The first thing to do is to develop a ...

Rational purchasing policy

This will stop you from being manipulated by dishonest advertisers, packaging designers and shopkeepers. (Many such people are honest, but some are not, and you should be able to tell the difference.) It will enable you to break any habits verging on shopping addiction. And it will prevent you from adding more clutter to any excess of possessions you already have. All this will help you to be happier, as you will be more in control of your life, but how do you do it?

The answer is quite simple. Never buy anything without knowing exactly why, and being able to explain, at least to yourself, just how this item will help you to achieve something worth achieving. Plan every purchase, and resist the temptation to buy things on impulse, especially items which last. This sounds like hard work. It can be, but it is worth it. Try it!

Now that you have stopped adding unnecessarily to your collection of possessions, the next item on the agenda is to ...

Take control of what you already own

The first step towards control is observation. Watch yourself. Do you spend any significant proportion of your time just looking after material things? Look around the place where you live, carefully assessing what you own, and asking yourself whether there is a good reason for having each item. When did you last move house? Were you surprised at how much stuff you had? Does the answer to that question make you dread the idea of moving again?

The answers to those questions will give you a good idea of how well you are already in control of what you own. Now, if you find that you do have a number of things which have the effect of reducing your sense of control of things, in that they are taking up your time or inconveniencing you and not helping you to be happy, the time has probably come to start ...

Throwing things away

The process of doing this can be time-consuming but it is worth it to get back your sense of control. You must be ruthlessly rational here. Do not throw away something truly valuable just in order to get the feeling of being able to do so!

The method is to go through everything you own, and ask yourself two questions about it. Do you know it to be useful? Do you believe it to be beautiful? If the answer to both of these questions is no, then here is a candidate for throwing away. Not so fast! There is a third question. Could it be useful to someone else, or is someone else likely to believe it to be beautiful? If the answer to this is also no, then get rid of it. Immediately! Do not put it on one side for reconsideration later, or for later disposal. Into the bin! Now!

You are now left with the things you truly need or want, and some candidates for giving away.

Giving things away

If you are to be happy about giving things away, there are two rules to follow. Firstly, only give things to people who want what you give them. Secondly, never burden people to whom you give things.

There are several ways of burdening people with gifts, all of them worth avoiding. You can make people feel that they owe you something. You can make them feel that they cannot throw away your gift if they happen to disagree with your assessment that it might be useful or beautiful, albeit not to you. You can burden them by offering them something on long-term loan, intimating that you will eventually want it back even though you have no use for it at present. You can even make life difficult by demanding something back at an inconvenient time after having given the impression that you would not do so. You can imply, as you hand over your gift, that they should have been wise enough to get one of these for themselves and that they should feel a burden of guilt for relying on you to supply it. Avoid all these; they never help to make anyone happier. Let there be no strings attached to anything you give away.

Finally, what about parting with things which you do know to be useful or believe to be beautiful, things which really are precious to you? Provided that you avoid any burdening of the people to whom you give things, such a gift can be an excellent expression of love. If you give something you value to someone else, and you do it in genuine love, you will feel good, and rightly so, but if you do it just in order to get that good feeling, it won't work.

Poverty

The opposite of the problem of having too many possessions is poverty. In poverty, too, you are unlikely to be able to develop a shopping addiction. However, if you are poor, you still run the risk of being controlled by material things. Even though it is less of a risk in some ways, you may run a greater risk of becoming too attached to the few things you do own. A rich person, especially a productive one, has a good chance of being able to replace anything which gets stolen, broken, used up or worn out, but this is much harder for a poor person.

Of course, that is just one of the difficulties which arise from poverty, probably the greatest of which is lack of choice, lack of freedom. Nevertheless, there are people who deliberately choose poverty over wealth. In fact, Jesus of Nazareth even recommended this idea to some individuals. Poverty clearly presents problems, so why should anyone ever choose it? What could the advantages possibly be? Let's look at the idea of a ...

Vow of poverty

We have seen how a vow of obedience might be to the advantage of the monk who commits himself to it, but what about his vow of poverty?

In the cloister, the monk has nothing which he can call his own. Everything there is owned by the community, rather than by any individual monk. Consequently, the individual monk has nothing to lose. He cannot be a victim of theft or burglary, and nothing he has can ever wear out or get broken. If something valuable owned by the community is lost, all the members of the community share equally in that loss, and can support one another.

By means of his vow of poverty, the monk protects himself from many of the risks run by those of us who live in a more material world. This does not mean that his standard of living is necessarily low. The monastery may be quite wealthy, and he may live quite comfortably, but that is not the point. The point is that he cannot be hurt by the loss of anything which he owns, because he does not own anything. If he does become attached to anything which is owned by the community, then he has a problem, but only to the extent that his commitment to his vow of poverty has broken down.

Poor in spirit

What Jesus said about this issue was, "Blessed are the poor in spirit." Unfortunately, he was not totally specific in what he meant by this, but it seems, from other things he said, that he meant that happiness depends to some extent on being able to let go of your possessions.

A very poor person, like someone who has taken a vow of poverty, owns almost nothing, and so is less likely to lose what they own, although the little they do have may be very precious. The challenge is to those of us who do own plenty of things not to be hurt by losing them, and not to fear the risk of losing them.

I mentioned earlier that when you use a tool or a machine skilfully, it becomes part of you in a sense. If your material possessions become part of you to the extent that you can be hurt if any of them get lost, stolen or damaged, then, I think, you are not "poor in spirit" in the sense that Jesus meant. Certainly, your happiness is vulnerable. It is more or less inevitable that some of the things that you own will get lost, stolen or damaged at some time, and if you don't want this to make you unhappy, you must learn to be "poor in spirit".

Freedom as consequence

When you have learned to be poor in spirit, you will find a new freedom, and with it new happiness. Recognise that the things you own are not part of you, and always be prepared to let them go. You can survive without almost all of what you own, so do not grieve that the material things in your life are not necessarily always going to be there.

If you are not too attached to things, you will not fear the material cost of following your conscience, so you will find yourself freer to do what you believe to be right in all circumstances. This, in turn, will make you happier.

You may think that some of the things you own are irreplaceable, and so they may be, but if you look at them purely as functional objects, and ask what they do for you, you may find that virtually all of them could in principle be replaced by other items which perform much the same function. If you are hanging on to something which is irreplaceable only because it is irreplaceable, you have probably not yet learned to be poor in spirit, and you may be being controlled by something other than your own self-control.

The more productive you are, the easier you will find it to replace things. If you are burdened by the belief that wealth cannot be created, but only transferred from one person to another, or destroyed, then more things will appear irreplaceable to you than if you understand how wealth is created, and how your efforts fit into that wealth creation process.

Thus we have the interesting apparent paradox, that the people who are happiest with poverty, and are least distressed by the fear of being separated from their possessions are those who are best at creating wealth. These are also the people who control things, and are not controlled by them. Be one of these people!

Be in control of the things you own, but do not be afraid of losing some of the things you own, as it is virtually inevitable that you will. If you can, be creative and productive. That way, you will be less able to be hurt by thieves, robbers, parasites, fire, flood, storm, wear and tear or rust.

You can be happy with material things if they do not control you, and if you do not let them become too much part of you.

Chapter 25

What Do You Want?

If you ask yourself what you want, it is very tempting to answer the question in terms of material possessions that you might like to have without thinking carefully about why you want them. You may also find yourself answering in terms of what you don't want, or what you want to get away from. Neither of these types of answer is very helpful.

In this chapter, we look again at how to choose your goals rationally. In particular, we will be concentrating on material goals, but no material goal should ever be an end in itself. It only makes sense to have a material goal if the material thing you want has a specific purpose. It must be a means to an end, something you need to have in order to achieve a goal which is important to you.

Attaining your goals is different from deciding on them, and is covered in the next two chapters.

We have to start with the question of what you want to achieve. In Chapter 2, I recommended that you write down and analyse everything you want to achieve. The analysis should have led you to an agenda, a list of things to do. Nevertheless, I want you now to take a step back from that and look again at ...

The "WHAT" problem

For the time being, don't worry about how you are going to achieve the things you want to achieve. Think only about *what* you want.

If you find it difficult to define what you want to achieve, you might find it helpful to write two obituaries for yourself, one as it would be written if you were to die today, the other as you would like it to be written after your death at a ripe old age. By comparing the two obituaries, you will discover what you want to achieve in life.

From this process, or from what you did when you read Chapter 2, you should have a list of things you want to achieve. This list will naturally include your principal goal, your most precious ambition, your main aim or objective in life. There will also be a number of sub-goals which will help you to achieve the principal one.

We will be concentrating on that principal goal, although what comes next applies to any sort of goal.

How will you know when you've done it?

When you set a goal for yourself, or, indeed, for anyone, you must have some way of recognising when that goal has been attained. If there is no way of recognising the attainment, then it is not a goal.

The usual example authors give to illustrate this idea is the goal of getting rich. How rich? If you cannot answer that in terms of exactly how many millions will suffice, then you do not have a goal, but rather a direction. The danger is that, however rich you get, you will be able to conceive of being richer still, and end up losing your soul in a never-ending struggle for greater and greater riches.

This is not too bad an illustration of a possible problem, but I think there is a more useful way of looking at it. You will not fall into this trap as long as you remember that money is a means to an end rather than an objective in its own right. Only limited objectives can be attained, and any limited objective only requires a limited amount of money.

What might you want to achieve next?

Setting a goal, and then, possibly, achieving it, is not necessarily the end of the goal-setting process. You can change your mind about what you want to achieve, and you will probably do so as you progress through life and get to know yourself better, and get to understand reality better. There is nothing wrong with this, no stigma attached to changing your mind about what you want to achieve.

Moreover, after having attained a goal, you will not only feel happy about having attained it but also wish to do something else next. This is natural and good and part of living life to the full.

For both of these reasons, it is a good idea always to look a bit beyond what you might think of as achievable now, and ask yourself what you might like to do next. The answer to this question might uncover a more important goal, but it is more likely just to tell you about something which you should not preclude.

It is up to you to think about all these things. No-one can do it for you. I cannot tell you the answers, because those answers are yours, not mine. If you are going to be happy, you have to live your own life. It is up to you, and no-one else, how you choose to live your life. Nothing has a greater impact on your happiness than the choices you make or fail to make.

What to Do ...

Now, what are you going to do? Having decided on your main goal in life, what do you do next? The answer to this must depend upon your goals, because any alternative would amount to activity without purpose, which would not help you to be happy.

The "HOW" problem

It follows that the next problem to solve is the matter of *how* to achieve your goals. This is exactly the same question as asking what to do next. This may seem like quite a difficult problem to solve, in which case, the time has come to apply ...

A problem reduction technique

You start with writing down whatever it is that you want to achieve (your goal). Next, you write down the major steps in your life that are necessary to achieve it, not worrying for the time being that some of these may be a bit daunting in themselves. You may find that there are about half a dozen such major steps, maybe only two or three, maybe ten or more, but not a huge number. If you find the sheer number of steps overwhelming at this stage, you are looking at too fine detail too soon: take a step back and look for the major features of the big picture. You can think of these major steps as sub-goals in their own right.

Next, for each sub-goal, repeat the process outlined in the last paragraph. By now, you will have a few dozen sub-sub-goals, as it were, but each of them should be more obviously within reach than the main goal you started with.

Some of these sub-sub-goals may need to be broken down into yet larger number of smaller steps, and so on. Repeat the process until you have a large number of very small things to do.

At this stage, it is easy to be put off by the sheer number of little steps to take. In Chapter 9, I mentioned a Chinese proverb which says, "A journey of a thousand miles begins with a single step." You can stop yourself being discouraged by the large number of things to do by reminding yourself of a few relevant facts. Each such step brings you nearer to your goal, so taking each step makes you happier in itself. No single step is beyond what you can achieve, and therefore the ultimate goal is not beyond what you can achieve. Anything worth doing always has some degree of complexity. At each and every moment of your life you do something by choice: it must be a good thing to know which choices will bring you closer to your goal.

Alternative ways

There are very few journeys for which only one route is possible. Whatever you want to achieve, there is almost certainly more than one way of doing it. So, your long list of things to do may not be the final answer to the question of how you are going to achieve what you want.

As you go through life, you may find that some of the things you thought you were going to manage quite easily turn out to be more difficult. Again, do not become discouraged. You will manage to do some difficult things, and in some cases you will find easier alternatives which still get you closer to your goal.

The key is to keep reviewing your successes and your failures in the light of the goals you are pursuing. When you find that something isn't working, try something else, and keep reviewing the situation. All successful people do this.

What you Need to Have

In your long list of things to do, you will find at least a few mentions of things you need to have which you currently do not have. These things, both material and abstract, are things which you see as required resources, things without which you will not be able to achieve what you want to achieve. It is very important to ask yourself ...

What do you really need?

There are two basic ways of getting a wrong answer to this question. Either you can fail to think of things you do need, or you can think that you couldn't do without some things which might just be nice or a bit useful. There are therefore two stages in making a list of things you need.

Firstly, from your list of things to do, form another list of material objects, money, skills, relationships, and time which you will need. Getting each of these things is something to do in its own right, which needs to go on the list of things to do, and be broken down into small manageable steps, and then be analysed to see if it implies that there is something else you need.

Next, go through your list yet again, and remove from it anything which you do not really need, but which is there just because you think you might like it. If you do acquire something which you don't need, you will end up giving it houseroom, perhaps cleaning it or playing with it, or otherwise tending to its needs without it helping you to do what you want to do with your life. Although you think you might like it, it is unlikely to help you to be happy. Having said that, I must add that we do all need some recreation, and so it is fair enough to have some things which you use in your leisure activities, but do try to avoid things which tend to take time or other vital resources away from the process of attaining your goals.

Material resources

In order to reach your goals, you will need some material things. That is what this part of the book is basically about. Whatever you do in life, whether working towards your goals or not, involves material things, and, as we have seen, a proper relationship with and understanding of your possessions is essential. But, what about the things you need in order to reach your goals, but which you haven't yet got?

Getting what you need is a sub-goal, or perhaps a set of sub-goals. We will go into this in greater detail in the next chapter, but there are a couple of points to make here. You would never even have thought of the possibility of getting the things you need if it were completely impossible; we only think of possibilities. Remember to tell yourself that if anyone can do it, then you can do it. It is also worth pondering the idea that, as you go through life, you will spend money on things: choosing how to spend what you spend on the basis of how well your purchases help you towards more important goals, will help you to achieve those goals, which will in turn make you happier.

Financial resources

As we have seen, any money you get must be acquired totally honestly if you are to be happy about it. This does not mean that you must never borrow it, and it may be that that is the only way to get what you need in order to achieve your goals, but if you are going to borrow it, honesty requires that you must be confident of being able to pay it back and that you do so when the time comes.

We will return to this whole subject at much greater length in the next part of the book, but I want to point out here that everything I have just said about material resources also applies to financial resources. You will not have thought of anything impossible: difficult maybe, but not completely impossible. If you can identify the financial resources you need to achieve anything you really want to achieve, you will find a way of getting that money, honestly.

Personal resources

To achieve any goal, you need certain resources within yourself. These are of two kinds: skills and confidence. Skills can be learned, and, as we saw in Chapter 9, confidence can be built. The important thing is to identify the personal resources you need, so that you can go about doing what is necessary to acquire them.

Other people

It may be that you have need of a skill which is beyond your capacity to acquire. Do not let this put you off. There are other people on the planet, and someone somewhere will be able to help you. It may be that you can hire someone with the right skills: if so, the problem reduces to one of acquiring the necessary financial resources.

If the skills you need cannot be learned or hired, you will need to persuade someone to help you for some reason other than the simple one that you are willing and able to pay them. I am sure that, having studied Part Three, you will be able to think of something!

Time

Time is our most precious resource. It is the most perishable commodity which exists. If you don't eat an apple while it is fresh, it will deteriorate, and eventually become completely inedible. This process is gradual, but the deterioration of a moment of time is instantaneous. Once gone, it is gone for ever into the past, never to be retrieved.

Think how much time you will need for each little step, and organise your life so as to fit those little steps in. Where are you going to find the time? We discussed this earlier, when we were on the subject of reflection, but the issue is slightly different here.

It is not that you are necessarily looking for regular chunks of half an hour or so per day. It is a matter of how you apply the time you have. You have enough time to achieve what you want to achieve, but only if you use it. As each minute arrives, you can use it to help you to achieve your objectives, or you can let it go to waste. That is your choice, and it is on this choice that your success depends.

Chapter 26

You Can Have Anything

Is there some material object which you want very much? Provided that you want it for sound reasons, that there is no physical reason why it is impossible, and that you are prepared to proceed honestly, then you can have it. We are not given to wanting that which cannot be had under any circumstances. The question is not, "Why can't I have one?", but "How can I get one?" If the only answer you can find to the question "how?" involves objective crime, i.e. theft, fraud, cheating, violence, threats, or dishonesty of any kind, then obtaining the thing you want will not bring you happiness, so forget it.

If you concentrate on just one goal, material or otherwise, you will almost certainly attain it. If you have a large number of goals, there is less of a chance of achieving all of them, unless they are all part of one consistent whole, as they should be if they are sub-goals derived from a principal goal. You have to make choices in life, and this includes deciding which potential goals are most important to you.

While you can have anything you want, you cannot have everything which you might conceivably want. You must choose, and then be consistent, because if you tell yourself that you have chosen one goal and then pursue another, the chances are that you will reach neither.

Material Goals

If you have a material goal, you want to own some material object, be it a house, a car, a particular work of art, or anything. The first thing to realise is that, if you have any such material goal, then you have chosen it. It is possible to choose such goals without careful thought; in fact, some advertisers would like you to do just that. If you achieve a goal that you have not thought about in advance, the chances are that it will not make you happy. If you want to be happy, choose your goals carefully: remember that they ...

Shouldn't be arbitrary

Someone once said, "Beware of your dreams, because they will come true!" Your mind has a tendency to dwell on things, because the brain tends to repeat established patterns. The brain then tends to behave in such a way as to bring about a situation in which the world matches the pattern. This can be to your advantage, if you choose carefully what to dwell upon, what to have repeating itself in your brain. On the other hand, if you let any old meme establish itself in your mind, without giving thought to whether it would be useful or not, it is unlikely to make you happy.

When you have chosen a material goal, you will be allowing a repeated pattern to build up in your mind, and in your brain, a pattern which represents the thing you want, and which will help you to get it. If this pattern is not to be arbitrary, it follows that it must be ...

For a purpose

Any material goal should ideally have been derived from your overall aim in life. Consequently, you should be able to relate any material goal you have to your overall aim in life. If you find yourself saying, "I want a ... ", ask yourself, "What for?" If you can't find an answer to that question, the goal is arbitrary, and unlikely to help to make you happy, especially as the chances are that it will conflict with your main aim in life.

It follows that, if a material object is to help to make you happy, it must have a specific purpose, which will help you towards the attainment of some other more important goal. In other words, it is a tool of some kind, in the general sense we had earlier. It has a job to do! Knowing what that job is will help you, when defining the sub-goal of getting that object, to be ...

Specific

The more specific and definite a goal is, the better is the chance of your reaching it. In the case of a material goal, the getting of a material thing, you will help yourself a great deal if you can be totally specific, and absolutely exact about the particular thing that you need.

This is not to make a case for misplaced perfectionism. The thing that you want has a specific job to do for you, a particular purpose to fulfil, and it is this that you need to be absolutely precise about. From this precision, you should be able to be specific about the thing that you need.

Your brain works better in its task of getting you what you want if it can have a clear image if the object in question. It can therefore be helpful to specify for yourself some attributes of the thing which are not actually necessary to its function. If, for example, you have decided that a particular model of car would best suit your needs, imagine it in a specific colour: the colour is not essential to the working of the car, but it does help with the working of the subconscious mind, because the clarity of the image will help your brain to set up the relevant neural pathways.

If a material goal is definite and specific in the way I have described here, then there is something else about it, which is very important. That is, it will be ...

Finite

How could it be otherwise? Material goals and financial goals are so closely related that it is worth mentioning again a problem which people often give themselves with their financial ambitions, which you could also easily give yourself with material ambitions.

Do you want to be rich? If so, how rich? Where do you stop? With money, there is no limit to how rich you could get: you can go on getting richer and richer and richer until eventually you die, but what would be the point? If you define a particular amount of money that you need for a particular purpose, you can get that amount, use it for its purpose and feel good about it: this is the benefit of having a finite financial goal.

Similarly, with material possessions, what is the point of accumulating more and more stuff, simply for the sake of accumulating it? There is no limit in principle to the sheer number and bulk of possessions that you could accumulate, but what would be the point? If you decide you want a thing, or a set of things, for a particular purpose, you can get it, use it for that purpose and feel good about it. That way, you'll be much happier. Naturally, what you decide that you want must be ...

Available

If you are honest with yourself, as you must be if you are going to be happy, you will admit that, for the time being at least, some things are out of your reach. The proverb I mentioned earlier says that a journey of a thousand miles begins with a single step, not that it is completed by means of a single step.

You will not make yourself happy by constantly pondering desirable material possessions which are out of reach. Admittedly, such pondering can help you to work out ways of bringing whatever you desire within reach, but it is better most of the time to concentrate on getting what you are confident that you can get, provided that that brings you closer to what you ultimately want. Military strategists have been aware for a long time that having a limited objective is one of the keys to success in any campaign; once having achieved one such objective, you can gather your forces ready for the next one.

Thus you will proceed from one reachable goal on to the next higher goal, provided always that your goals are ...

Non-contradictory

If you have one overriding aim in life and all your goals and sub-goals help you to achieve that aim, you most likely won't have the problem of contradictory goals. If you find that you are trying to achieve something you want but at the same time that effort is making it more difficult for you to achieve something else which you also want, then you have contradictory goals.

The only solution to the problem of contradictory goals is thought. It is up to you to think hard about what you really want and how you are going to get it. Although you might find it helpful to talk to someone else about all this, only your very own answers to these questions will do you any good when it comes to matters of your own happiness.

Planning

Everything you do deliberately is planned. The only things you do without planning are to have accidents and to have instant reactions to events. Even a spontaneous purchase is planned, albeit only moments before it occurs. When you do something unconsciously out of habit, the planning took place so long ago that you are no longer aware of it, but you could not have developed the habit without planning.

Sometimes you will lay plans for something months or years ahead. This is what is usually thought of as planning, and we all know that it is necessary to bring about anything complex or difficult. If you just decide spontaneously to go out for a walk one day, you still make some basic plans, even for the simple action of picking up your keys on the way out of the door: even if your walk is just a ramble, with no previously decided route, you still plan the next few steps ahead just before you take them.

You are therefore making plans for a very large part of your waking life. All that varies is the depth, range, complexity and thoroughness of your planning. If you want to do anything successfully, including acquiring material wealth, you have to plan it first, because it is impossible to achieve success at any level without commensurate planning.

If you can't plan it, you can't do it

If everything you do deliberately is planned first, it follows that if something you would like to do is possible, then it must be possible to plan it. From this it follows that if you cannot form a plan for doing something, then the doing of it is itself impossible.

What if you are sure that your goals can be achieved but you think you can't form a workable plan of how to achieve them? Either you are deluding yourself as to what is possible, or a plan can be made, but the difficulty and complexity of the planning process is overwhelming you for the time being.

Delusions of any sort do not lead to happiness. Happiness is dependent upon having an honest relationship with the real world. If you come to the conclusion, after trying your best to work out a plan for achieving a goal, that no such plan is possible, then you must abandon the goal before you waste your life dreaming of the impossible. Look for something worthwhile to do, plan it, do it, feel good about it, and then think again.

If you are finding the idea or the process of planning overwhelming, remember the section in Chapter 25 where you read about a ...

Problem reduction technique

... which I will remind you about now. Anything you want to do can be broken down into a number of smaller steps, each of which might be quite large, but is not as daunting as the whole project. Each such step can, in turn, be broken down into a number of smaller steps. If you do this repeatedly until you are left with a very long list of very simple things to do, you have solved your planning problem.

Do not fear the complex

When you break down a short list of large steps into a long list of small steps, the very length of the resulting list might put you off. Don't let it! As you go through life, you will do a very large number of things. Having your very long list of things to do will help you to do those things which help you towards your goals rather than spending time on things which have not been planned with such thoroughness.

Any fear you have of complex plans arises from an irrational desire for easy solutions. This is the attraction of being told what to do by someone else, as opposed trusting in your own ability to work out what you want to do for yourself. Self-control leads to happiness, whereas looking for someone else to control your life for you does not.

Writing things down

If you are making a long and complex plan for achieving something which you believe in, you may have difficulty holding it all in your mind at one moment. This might be part of the cause of a fear of complexity. It is only since the human race has invented writing that we have been able to manage very complex tasks.

Writing things down makes them easier! It helps you to clarify your plans, even to turn dreams into plans. It helps you to manage the complexity of having a large number of small things to do. It helps you to keep track of which large steps you have not yet broken down into smaller steps.

Planning feedback loop

When you have written your plans down, you are also in a much better position to see how well you are getting on. You can cross things off your list as you complete them, and you can also review your list from time to time to see whether it needs updating.

This last bit is most important. Planning a task, especially a complex one, is not a once-off process. Whether or not your plans are written down, they should not be completely static.

As you complete some steps, new information will probably come to light which has a bearing on other steps in your plan. Keep reviewing your goals and your path to them. Do not be afraid to change your plans, or even your goals, in the light of new information. Every time you do something, it will either lead you closer to your goal, or it will not: either way, you have new information which potentially has a bearing upon what you should do next. Take it into account, along with any relevant news you may hear, and any change in your own feelings about your goals.

Once a plan is written down, it is not necessarily final. As far as possible, you should, as the saying goes, plan the work and then work the plan, but what you learn whilst working the plan can help you to improve the plan.

Programming the Mind

When you have a goal and a plan for achieving it, the next thing is to do whatever is necessary to carry out the plan. All the actions involved start in your mind, and therefore you need to be in the right state of mind. If you think of your brain as a kind of computer, what you have to do is to program that computer correctly with the details it has to have of the goal and of the plan.

Basis of self-hypnosis

The easiest way to do this is by means of a simple form of self-hypnosis. You can put yourself into a shallow hypnotic trance quite easily, and there is no danger of getting stuck in it.

The first thing to understand is that a shallow trance is so much a normal part of life that you experience such trances routinely without ever having recognised them as such. Whenever you watch television or read a book and become "absorbed", you are in a shallow trance. The characteristic signs of this are a partial loss of the sense of the passage of time and a slightly reduced awareness of your surroundings.

To get into a shallow trance deliberately, you must be comfortable and relaxed, preferably in a quiet place and reasonably sure of not being disturbed. The only other thing which is really necessary is concentration. Once in your trance, all you have to do is tell yourself what you are going to achieve and imagine it happening: that is what you have to concentrate on. While in your trance you can enjoy a kind of foretaste of what the success will feel like at some future time.

The process is very simple. Regular visualisation of successful completion of your plans is what programs the mind in such a way as to help you to complete them successfully. It can also help you to see in finer detail just how you will go about completing them.

The so-called "secret" of riches

Several books have been published which purport to reveal a great secret which has been known to wealthy and successful people throughout the ages and which will be revealed to you if only you pay for the (often overpriced) book. The "secret" is just this process of self-hypnosis with creative visualisation, as it is called.

Some authors even seem to promote the idea that *all* you have to do is to visualise the future you want, and it will come about; this kind of wishful thinking simply does not work. I do agree that it is extremely useful to have a clear image of what you want, but it is not sufficient; you need discipline, thought and control too. The belief that change can be brought about without effort can be a great limitation on the process of change.

Positive thinking

Because the brain tends to work in such a way as to initiate actions which bring into reality that which has been visualised, it is very important only to visualise success. If you think about what you don't want to happen, and imagine what life would be like if things went wrong, your brain will work out how to bring these disasters about and tend to make them more likely to happen.

This is the essence of the idea of positive thinking. By constantly filling your mind with good ideas, beautiful images and success-creating thoughts, you will improve your life. This is not very difficult. It can be difficult to eliminate the negative, and this is at least as important. When ideas of how things could go wrong cross your mind, take only just enough notice of them to know what to avoid, and then dismiss them.

Time

The process of programming your mind in this way is not instantaneous. It takes time to relax and visualise how you want the future to work out. I said enough in Chapter 5 about how to find time for important mental processes, so I will not labour the point here. You can do it. It is up to you to work out just how.

Regularity

In this process of programming your mind, you are actually building up new neural pathways in your brain. This can only be done by repetition. In this respect, it is very similar to the process of learning. It is not sufficient to dream just once of an ideal future and how you might bring it about. You have to go on and on working at the image, pondering your plans with such concentration that you lose track of irrelevancies. You have to do this not just once but again and again with unbroken regularity and as frequently as you practically can.

That way the practice of positive thinking and creative visualisation will become a habit, and one of the most useful habits you could possibly have. This habit corresponds to a set of neural pathways in the brain which will help you to achieve anything you really believe is worthwhile. You could misuse it and work out dishonest ways of acquiring what you think you want, but this always backfires and generates unhappiness. When you use this habit to help you to do what you know is right, it will help to make you happy.

Constructive dreams

Although the term most usually used for this type of mental programming is "creative visualisation", I think a better term might be "constructive daydreaming". There is more to daydreaming than just visualisation. When you daydream, you are there, as a whole person, in your daydream: you experience everything almost as if it were real.

The art is to keep deliberate control of your daydreams. Dream deliberately of doing the right things in your life and enjoying the consequences. The principal consequence of doing the right things is happiness. Enjoy it in advance, and without cheating! The dream may not be reality in itself, but it can form an honest part of bringing about that reality, and there is no reason why you shouldn't enjoy it, provided that you are honestly using the technique to help you to do what is right.

Whole brain thinking

The brain has two halves. In most people, the right hemisphere processes images, feelings and intuitive impressions, while the left hemisphere processes language, reasoning, symbolism and logic. Success comes from getting these two halves to work together towards the same objectives rather than interfering with one another as they each work towards different objectives.

If you think about the process of conceiving a goal, planning how to attain it, and programming the mind, with this understanding of the operation of the two hemispheres, you will see that it goes like this. The right hemisphere has an image of the ultimate goal; the left hemisphere works out what has to be done to achieve it; the two then work together on visualising the details of the process. Finally the two work together to bring about the desired result.

This process only works if you give the two halves of your brain time to communicate with one another to work out together what you want and how to get it. This is where the self-hypnosis and creative visualisation come into their own.

Chapter 27

Getting It

You have decided that there is some material thing which you want to have for some definite worthwhile purpose, and you have worked out a plan for getting it, but a plan is not enough. What is required now is action. If you want to have something, you have to do something about getting it, but can you do it?

You Can do it

This is the point at which things can start to go wrong. Regardless of how good your plan is, nothing will happen if you don't do something about it, and the most likely thing to stop you is "I can't" belief. You have to replace this with "I can" belief. If you believe that you cannot do something, you are certainly right, just because of that belief, no matter what justifications you may have for it: the belief alone is enough to stop you. If you believe that you can do something, you are almost certainly right, regardless of the obstacles.

How, then, can you replace "I can't" belief with "I can" belief? The answer lies in the very fact that you have a plan.

Can it be done at all?

The fact that the plan exists demonstrates that what you have planned can be done. Every step of the plan is possible, or it wouldn't be in the plan, and the number of steps is finite, or you could never have written it down. Therefore it can be done, but ...

By whom?

That's you! You probably wrote your plan with the assumption that you were going to carry it out. You, not anyone else. You are therefore the person to do it.

Even so, the important thing is to get the right things done. It matters less who actually carries out each task. Provided that you are fair and honest at all times, you can have other people perform some of the tasks on your list. How you persuade other people to help you in matters like this is a separate problem, but you will understand from Part Three of this book that there has to be some advantage to them in helping you.

If you do get other people to help you to attain your goals, never forget that they are *your* goals, it is *your* plan which is being carried out, and it was *your* decision to get other people involved. If those other people do not perform as you wish, that is not sufficient reason to abandon hope of completing your plan and achieving your objective of getting what you want. It is *your* responsibility to make it happen, and it's no good blaming other people for letting you down.

Taking responsibility for your own decisions, even when they don't work out exactly as you intended, helps you towards happiness. Blaming other people for anything, even when they are in the wrong, never helps you to be happy yourself. If, therefore, your decision to delegate some of the things which you need to get done is not working out, find another way of getting them done.

Doing It

If you want to achieve anything, the most important thing is action. You have to do something. What you do will change the situation and, if you are following a good plan, it will change things for the better. If what you do does not improve matters, this gives you useful information about how to change your plan; in other words, if the outcome of your action is not what you desired or expected, don't give up, but try doing something different.

When you take action, you have an effect on the material world. Deliberate actions having an effect on the material world are necessary to the achievement of any human goal. Even if you just speak to someone, you are setting the air in motion, and changing the electrical activity in your listener's brain. Observe the consequences of what you do, and use those observations to help you to decide what to do next.

Failure to take notice of the effects of what you do can lead you to failure and unhappiness. More commonly, people fail through inaction. Why is this? Let's look at some of the reasons why you might just not do anything useful, and some of the attributes you need to make sure that you do act.

Belief

In order to do anything, you must believe that it can be done. More importantly, you must believe not just that someone can do it, but that you can do it. As we have seen, establishing this belief need not be too difficult.

Believing, however, is not enough. There is a danger here. Some people seem to think that if you have enough faith then what you want to happen will happen, regardless of what actions you take or how you fail to act. This is a silly idea which can be found in some religious circles, and amongst some purely secular folk who have got the wrong idea about positive thinking. It is also possible to pick up the same silly idea from books on creative visualisation. Faith and positive thinking are necessary for success, and creative visualisation can be helpful, but they are not sufficient: action is necessary too.

Discipline

If you do not have discipline, your actions will tend more towards chaos than towards order. You need order to bring about a desired result. Therefore you need discipline. Self-discipline comes first, but if you have people working for you or with you, you need them to have discipline too. Discipline is actually a type of ...

Control

If you are in control of a machine, that machine does what you require it to do, no more and no less. Although control is never absolutely perfect, one can get fairly close to complete control of a physical object like a machine. It may take training and practice, but it is quite possible.

Controlling other people is a completely different matter. Complete control of another human being is wrong, and will never help you to be happy. Threats, dishonesty and manipulation won't help either, so how can you control other people, and to what extent? The only way is to influence what those people focus on. If you study influencers and what they do, whether they be political orators, military leaders, business managers or preachers, the one thing they all have in common is the practice of changing what people focus on. If you want people to help you to achieve your goals, you have to work out how to apply this principle.

Whether you are controlling material things or influencing other people, still the most important aspect of control is ...

Self-control

There is so much elsewhere in this book about self-control that I will not reiterate it all here; I will just point out that, if you are to control anything, you must first control yourself. If you doubt this, ask yourself how you control anything. You control physical things by moving parts of your body in a deliberate way. This requires you to be able to control those parts of your body with the required degree of accuracy, which means controlling part of yourself. In so far as you control other people, you do it by what you say or write, which requires at least as much control of yourself.

Patience

As I write this, it is very early in the morning, and the shops are not open yet. Soon, I will go out to buy some milk and some bread, but in the mean time, I have to be patient. When I bought a car earlier this year, a few weeks passed between deciding to do so and completing the purchase. Buying a house usually takes longer still.

Generally speaking, the more valuable something is, the longer it takes to acquire. This unpalatable fact flies in the face of the idea of instant gratification. I observe, however, that when something is sold on the basis of instant gratification, the gratification passes away almost as instantly as it came.

Better to be patient. Decide what you want, accept that you aren't likely to be able to get it instantly, do what is necessary to get it, and take the time it takes.

Rome wasn't built in a day

The old saying that Rome wasn't built in a day carries both wisdom and folly in a single short sentence.

The folly is the unstated assumption that Rome was deliberate. It isn't as if a town planner came across the site, noted the course of the River Tiber, surveyed the seven hills and decided that here would be a good place for a new town, then planned it, laid it out and had it built.

The wisdom is that, even if it had happened that way, the process of building would have taken more than a day. When you look at how Rome actually happened, more wisdom is to be found. Each building represents a dream brought into reality by organisation and hard work: a goal realised. Each building is followed by another building, just as in life, you develop new goals having attained older ones. This all takes time.

Don't give up too soon

Things often take not just a long time, but longer than you think you can bear. When you have been trying to achieve something for longer than you originally thought it would take, it can be very tempting to give up, just because of all the effort you feel that you have wasted.

There is a danger here. While there may be rational reasons for abandoning a goal, the fact that you have already spent a long time trying to reach one is not, by itself, a rational reason for abandoning it. In the time that you have already spent, you will have made some progress towards the goal, even if, like Edison and his light bulbs, you have just learned a thousand ways of not achieving it.

The rational way to think about this problem is this. Given what you now know about the goal and what is involved in attaining it, consider the following questions. Do I still want it? Starting from where I am now, what will I have to do to get it? How long will it take? Forgetting what it has already cost, will it be worth the time and effort which it will cost from now on?

You may suffer a bit in the mean time

In Latin, the same word is used for "to be patient" as for "to suffer". This is why the medical profession uses the word patient to mean "sufferer". Suffering is so much of a problem that there is a whole chapter devoted to it later, but a brief look at the subject is relevant here.

A problem, as we have seen, is when the situation as observed differs from the situation as desired. When a problem persists, what you have is suffering. While you are implementing the solution to a problem, this particular form of suffering continues until you observe the new situation, which, as a result of your efforts, is now as desired.

With the suffering in patience comes wisdom

When you are reasonably sure that there will be an end to the suffering, and that you are doing what is necessary to bring about that end, it need not be too hard to bear. In fact it can harden your resolve to do those things which you have to do, and thus strengthen you.

The strength which you gain by living through difficulties on your way to achieving something you believe to be worthwhile is a form of wisdom. You may have met this type of wisdom in older people who have been through hard times for good reasons and kept their hope and integrity. You may have noticed their happiness.

Work

Although you will sometimes get what you want just by asking for it and being patient, more often you have to work for it. Work means making an effort to achieve something. The alternative is leisure. To be happy, you need some of each. It follows that ...

Work is not a bad thing

Why should you think that work is bad? Many people hate it, but why? The answer is actually quite simple. If you are working for someone else solely in order to earn money for yourself without either caring about helping your employer to achieve their objectives or working in a carefully chosen way for an objective of your own, the work will not help to make you happy. In itself, however, work is not bad.

You have to do it to get what you want

The work you do helps you to achieve your objectives in life, or, if it doesn't, you should change it, or at least add to it something which does help. If you don't know your objectives, this is impossible, so work will not help you to achieve them. If you do know what you want to achieve, there are two completely different ways in which work can help you to achieve them. Either, you can do something which directly helps you to get what you want, or you can accept employment and use the money you earn to get what you want.

If, for example, you decide that you would like a pond in your garden, you can do the digging yourself, which is work which you will almost certainly enjoy, as it is directed towards an objective of your own, or you could use money to pay someone else to do the digging. If you choose the latter method, the money probably has to be earned, and it is possible to enjoy this too, provided that you are honest in your dealings with your employers and that you do not despise what they are trying to achieve.

Work can help make you happy

Work, then, can be enjoyable, but does that mean that it can help you to be happy? Leisure can be enjoyable, but does not of itself make you happy, so what about work? The answer is that work will always tend to help to make you happier, provided that it meets a few simple conditions.

Always have your work aimed at some finite objective which you care about. Never do anything dishonest or despicable. Take enough leisure time to make sure that you are not losing sight of your objectives, and to regain the strength you need for your work. These things are all that is necessary to ensure that your work will help you to be happier.

If you are in a position to choose your career, choose something which you enjoy, rather than that which pays most. If you really enjoy it, you can become good enough at it that it is virtually certain that someone will want to pay you to do it: just find that someone! If you can live by doing something you love, your work will certainly help you to be happy, even if you never get rich.

Contribution

We have already seen that a sense of contributing to the world can help to make you feel happier, but what relevance does this have to the problem of getting what you want? If you are going out to work for an employer in order to earn money to use to get what you want, ...

Don't expect something for nothing

You may be tempted to think of your employer as a source of wealth for you. In a way, that is fair enough, but if that is all you see them as, then your work will not help you to be happy. Remember that employment is a kind of trade. Your employer offers you money in exchange for your best efforts at helping them to achieve their objectives. Having entered into the agreement, your employer is obliged to keep their side of the bargain, but what about you? You could give less than your best, and still get the money, couldn't you?

You won't get it

Why should you? Why should you be paid when you don't keep to your side of the bargain? In the short term, you might think that you are getting away with it. After all, your employer seems to have more money than you, and your need is great, so isn't it right that your employer should contribute to your upkeep? Why should you have to work for it too?

There are many answers to this question. The simplest is that, if you are not doing enough for your employer for them to be better off employing you than not employing you, they will eventually work out a way of dispensing with your services, and why not?

There is also another answer, which has more of a bearing on your own personal happiness, and that is ...

The problem of unearned wealth

If you do manage to get an employer to pay you more than you truly earn, you won't be happy! You will also have the same problem if you try to survive on state benefits, and it can come with living on inherited wealth or being kept by a wealthy patron.

The problem is that unearned wealth is an illusion. Nothing is valuable if you do not value it. The sign that you value something is that you are prepared to work to get it and to keep it. If you get something which you do value and you get it by means of work, you will feel good about having it. If you get something by any other means, it is much harder to feel good about it, and if the means you use are dishonest or unfair, it is impossible to feel good about it. In other words, if you get what you thought you wanted by any means other than honest effort, it will not give you the good feelings you wanted from it, which is to say that unearned wealth is impossible.

If, therefore, you are going to earn it, what do you have to do? The answer comes with an answer to another question. ...

What will people willingly pay for?

There are countless correct answers to this question. If you doubt this, go to a shopping mall, look at the shops, and observe what is there and what people pay for. Look around you almost anywhere, and you will see things which have been bought and paid for, by choice. Even in the countryside, there are fields of crops which are only growing there because people happily pay for the produce.

Given so many possible answers, how do you choose a relevant one? In amongst them, there has to be one to which you can contribute. Once you have found it, you have found a way in which you can contribute your efforts to supplying what someone else will willingly pay for.

Supplying it

Then you do the work involved, always remembering that you are, in the final analysis, working for a customer who wants what you are helping to produce, whether it is a material thing or a valuable service.

If there is something you want, you can obtain it by force, threat of force, or dishonesty, thereby destroying your chances of happiness. Alternatively, you might be able to make it yourself by working on things you already own; this can be consistent with happiness. Best of all, supply by your own efforts something which someone else will willingly pay for, working with other people to do so if this is appropriate, and trade your efforts either for the thing you want or for the money with which to buy it; this too is consistent with happiness.

This brings us back to the subject of trade, and therefore to money, which is the subject of the next part of the book. Material things and money are linked in many ways and are to some extent interchangeable, and it is by means of money that we can indirectly swap one material thing for another (sell one and buy the other with the proceeds), but money is much subtler than that, as we shall soon see.

Whether money is involved or not, what people actually want is for the material world to fit with their requirements. It is up to you to get the material world to fit with your requirements, either by moving bits of it around by your own efforts and directly for your own purposes, or by moving bits of it around for other people's purposes having agreed with them that they will in turn move other bits of it around in ways which help to meet your purposes. This may seem like an odd way of putting it, but if you look carefully at what actually happens when people work or engage in trade, that is what it all comes down to.

"If you give all that, the money will fall into your hands; you can't get out of it."

Henry Ford

PART FIVE

Being Happy About Money

Life without money is possible. All other species manage it. The human race managed it until only a few thousand years ago. Some remote tribes still manage without money. A few people in the modern world try to live their lives without it, but they have difficulty. For most of us, money is very important, and a good understanding of what it is and how it works will help you in your quest for happiness.

Money was invented as a medium of exchange. Before it, the only system of trading was by barter, swapping some of what you had for some of what someone else had when you both believed that you'd be better off after the swap. After money was invented, you could sell what you produced and use the money to buy things from people who did not themselves need or want what you produced. This gave you more flexibility.

It also allowed you to introduce a time delay. You could sell something one day and keep the money for a while, even for years, and then use it to buy something else. Barter did not allow for such a time delay. It is the existence of this time delay which allows us to keep wealth in the form of money, and which makes money such a complicated subject. If you just see money as a medium of exchange in trade, it is quite a simple concept, but the time delay allows in ideas like investment, borrowing, interest, inflation, devaluation, and all the other things which make money hard to understand.

To be happy about money, however, you do not need to understand high finance. You just need to understand how money affects your life and the lives of other people, the basics of how to get the money you need without making yourself unhappy in the process, and the relationship between wealth and happiness. I think you will find this easier if we start by dismissing a few misconceptions about money.

*"I've been rich and I've been poor,
but rich is better."*

Pearl Bailey

Chapter 28

Misconceptions About Money

Most misconceptions about money seem to me to come from distortions of a simple truth. The basic truth is that only human beings have money. This is true, but it is too simplistic to be very useful. The whole truth about money and humanity is probably too complex for anyone to understand fully. (After all, economists have been trying for a long time to devise a complete and consistent theory, with a most remarkable lack of success or agreement.)

When you have a subject on which the only things you can say with complete confidence are too simple to be very useful, and of which the whole is too complex to be grasped, misconceptions are inevitable. Nevertheless, some of the commoner ones can be identified and dismissed, and that is what I hope to do here.

Poverty and Unhappiness

There is certainly a link between poverty and unhappiness. It is a matter of self-perception. People who see themselves as poor are usually unhappy about it, even if they have more actual wealth than many other people. Likewise, there are people who have very little in terms of material or financial wealth, but who do not see themselves as poor, because they are happy that they have what they need to live life as they are happy to live it.

If you see yourself as poor, you believe that you are unhappy because you are poor. This may well be true. You may also believe that, because poverty is making you unhappy, wealth would make you happy. This is very unlikely to be true.

This great fallacy is such a common mistake that we must look at it in more detail. How can such a gross error be so widely believed?

Logic
The human race has made great strides since discovering the rules of logic. Amazingly, many people do not deliberately use logic, and very few people take the trouble to study it systematically. Yet, without at least a few people using logic carefully, most of what we take for granted in a civilised society would be impossible. We are not concerned with the general principles here, just with the particular error of logic which leads to this terrible mistake about wealth, poverty, happiness and unhappiness.

The hypothesis is that poverty causes unhappiness. This implies that happiness means that poverty is absent. It does not imply that wealth causes happiness. Unhappiness can have a number of causes, of which poverty is just one. Wealth therefore takes away just one possible cause of unhappiness; it therefore allows happiness, but it does not cause it: other causes of unhappiness may remain even when you have wealth.

In this chapter, however, we are not concerned with other problems. Whatever other problems you may have, it is still true that ...

Poverty does cause misery

Misery and unhappiness are not quite the same thing. In a happy life, you can go through short periods of misery. Nonetheless, if misery is your constant companion, unhappiness is inevitable.

When poverty is a problem for you, you are likely to feel miserable. Much of this feeling comes from the perception of yourself as helpless, and forever stuck with your poverty. This is more likely to be a problem of focus than anything else.

Shortage, helplessness and misery

One danger is that you can get to focus on the lack of some particular thing. Another is that, in your helplessness, you can end up focusing on the belief that other people should look after you. Neither of these is helpful.

If your problem was a life-threatening shortage of food, water, or shelter, you would not be likely to be reading this book, and if you are short of anything else, I have to observe that there are people who are managing without it. The belief that your shortage is what causes your misery is therefore a belief which you have chosen, rather than an absolute truth.

If you focus on what you believe that other people should be doing for you, you are unlikely to think of those things which you can do for yourself. You may be able to accept help from other people, but it is what you do for yourself that will help you to overcome your misery. Some of the people "helping" you might not be very good at helping you towards independence, because without you being in need, they would be out of a job. Be particularly wary of those who work in unemployment benefit offices: their bosses have made the rules in such a way that it is very difficult for you to be better off by getting work. The so-called poverty trap may not be an accident!

Rich people are often miserable

Even if you are rich enough to buy anything you might need or want, this does not guarantee that you won't be miserable. There are plenty of rich people who are miserable. The number of suicides and cases of drug addiction amongst the rich and famous is proof enough that wealth does not always bring happiness. So, if ever you are tempted to think that you might be happy if only you were rich, remember that some rich people are unhappy too, and study the rest of this book before committing yourself to the search for riches.

Powerlessness

There is a link between poverty and unhappiness, and, as far as I can see, there is also a link between wealth and happiness. It is true that people who have become rich dishonestly do tend to be very unhappy, but those whose fortunes have been made honestly are often happy folk. There are happy people who are financially poor, but they are rather the exception.

There is therefore something specific about poverty which tends to make people unhappy, and it is too simplistic just to say that it is shortage of money. We have no reason to suppose that the whole human race was unhappy before money was invented, so we must ask what it is about money which makes shortage of it so miserable.

To answer this question, we have to look at a fundamental aspect of human nature. The most important human characteristic, the one which more than any other distinguishes us from the animals, is the power of choice. Put very simply, the more money you have, the more choices you have, and, if you have very little money, your power of choice is limited.

The real cause of the misery of poverty

There is no real difference between the power of choice and power itself. Powerlessness and lack of choice are the same thing. It is this which is the main cause of the misery of poverty. If you feel that you have no choices, you do not feel human.

Note this particularly. It is a matter of feeling. If you feel that you have no choices, you will feel both poor and sub-human. It is not a matter of thinking! The belief that you have no choices is always arrived at by feeling rather than by thought. As soon as you start thinking, you will start finding choices and will feel more human again, but before we get on to solutions, let's look at the problem in a bit more detail.

Powerlessness corrupts

There is a well-known saying that power corrupts and absolute power corrupts absolutely. There is truth in this, but it is also true that powerlessness corrupts and absolute powerlessness corrupts absolutely.

Recall that power and choice are essentially the same. Someone without choices is powerless, but what happens to people who are deprived of all choice? They become dehumanised. This is usually only caused by torture, the most cruel combination of force and threat of force the human race has ever devised, and one which dehumanises the perpetrators as much as their victims.

Yet having very limited choice is almost as dehumanising. Look at the conditions in the poorest parts of our cities if you doubt this. Go and listen to what the people there say, and watch carefully how they behave. I suspect that something similar happens to people in places where famine is a real problem too, but I must confess that I have not witnessed this first hand, nor even made a systematic study of it.

Lack of choice causes irrational behaviour

I found the clue to this problem when a very poor resident of a run-down town in the North of England said to me one day, "When you've got no choices, you don't think: you feel." Not many people in his position think clearly enough to come out with such a profound statement, but he was an intelligent man, suffering very difficult circumstances. (Things got much better for him later, but that is another story.)

The point he was making was not so much about thinking and feeling as about behaviour. If we think about what we are doing, we behave rationally, and can go about making things better. If we are feeling, but not thinking at all, our behaviour is determined irrationally, and our circumstances tend to deteriorate. What happens then is ...

Vandalism, crime and rebellion

Vandalism is often called "mindless vandalism" and it is one of the first symptoms of behaviour being determined irrationally rather than chosen after thought. Can you imagine a vandal thinking to himself, "I shall throw this brick through this window in order to feel that I have some power"? That is, of course, why he does it, but the behaviour is not chosen rationally. It is mindless, and its origin is in the corrupting effect of powerlessness, which is to say poverty.

Crime is not far removed from vandalism. A few crimes do require detailed forethought, but most are committed by incompetent people reacting to the pressures of their circumstances and without careful thought about the consequences and the alternatives. Many criminals fail to appreciate that there are alternatives. Most start from a condition of poverty, and most remain poor too.

What about rebellion? History has shown that when the poor are seriously oppressed but see that their rulers are very wealthy, violent rebellion often follows. The consequences of rebellion have led to the German proverb "Selt kommt was besseres nach", meaning that what comes afterwards is seldom any better. Violent rebellion proceeds without much thought on the part of the people engaging in the violence, and it seems to have a great deal in common with vandalism, only it involves killing as well as random destruction of property. It is irrational behaviour on the grand scale, and it follows from a widely held belief that no choices are available. It also opens the way for a new tyranny to start, but that is a separate problem.

Is comfort a cure?

People who work for the relief of other people's poverty tend to concentrate on the physical needs of the people they work with, rather than on anything else. This is, of course, helpful, but it does not, in itself, help to overcome the sense of dehumanisation which comes with poverty. If you are being fed, clothed and housed at someone else's expense, but you still have no choices, you are not much better off than a farm animal, which may be physically quite comfortable, but is still not human.

It is difficult to think clearly while in great physical discomfort, so the provision of comfort can help to overcome the most important problems of poverty, but it is not a complete cure. In order to be fully human, you not only have to have the opportunity to think, you also have to use that opportunity in order to choose your behaviour rationally.

Choosing your behaviour rationally starts with the choice of focus, what you choose to think about. Even when things are difficult, the most fully human thing you can do is to focus on the choices which you do have, and to work out as best you can what the consequences would be of the various actions which you might choose to take. You lose this ability only when acting under threat of force or when in serious physical discomfort. Shortage of money may make your choices more limited, but it does not completely eliminate your power of choice, even if it sometimes feels like that.

Freedom

The often mistaken belief that wealth will make you happy is also supported by the observation that freedom and happiness are linked. As we have seen, poverty curtails freedom, and total loss of freedom is dehumanising and makes for unhappiness. Does it follow that greater wealth means greater freedom, and that greater freedom means greater happiness? Let's look at this idea in a bit more detail.

Wealth brings choices

It is certainly true that if you are rich, you have discretionary wealth, that is to say that you have money which you can choose what to do with, or you can obtain such money. This is as good a definition of being rich as you will find. The richer you are, the more discretionary wealth you have.

It is possible to live in relative luxury, but think that you are not rich in this sense, if your income is only just adequate to maintain your standard of living. This can be an illusion. You could choose to lower your standard of living. This is such an unconventional thought in the modern western world that it might come as a shock. If you are wealthier than many people in the world, in the sense that you have possessions which they cannot afford or in the sense that your income is higher than that of many other people in the world, then you have some choices. Even if your income is committed up to the hilt, you are not without choices. If you choose to lower your standard of living in the material sense, then, by selling some of your possessions or by living more economically, you can free up some of your wealth, and thus buy yourself some other choices.

Choices bring freedom

Freedom and the power of choice are the same. If you are in a position to make choices, you are to that extent free. The more choices you have, the freer you are. If you have to make decisions, you may not feel as free as you are. This can be because such freedom brings responsibility with it, as we shall see later. It remains a fundamental truth that if you have choices, then you have some freedom, and the wider the scope of your choices, the greater is your freedom.

Freedom removes a cause of unhappiness

At last, we get to the fundamental link between wealth and happiness. Unhappiness can be caused by a number of factors, as I hope I have made clear in other parts of this book. Lack of freedom is just one such factor. If other factors in your life are making you unhappy, no amount of freedom or wealth will overcome this. Thus happiness depends upon having enough wealth and therefore freedom to avoid becoming dehumanised by lack of choice, but it depends upon other things as well.

You could note at this point that it doesn't take great riches to give you enough choices not become dehumanised through lack of choice. All you need is not to be reduced to dehumanising grinding poverty. Once you have some choices, you can use them to build your range of choices.

Not a means of escape from problems

Happiness depends upon factors other than freedom. If you have other problems, freedom will not provide you with a means of escape from them. Wealth will therefore not make you happy if you have something else to be unhappy about. It might provide you with the opportunity to spend some time on addressing and solving the other problems in your life, but it is not a solution itself.

A means of achieving certain aims

If you are wealthy enough to have plenty of choices, you can use this freedom to help you to achieve anything you think is worthwhile achieving. It is in this way that money can really help you to be happy. We have seen that severe shortage of money can make you unhappy, but this is not the exact opposite.

Money can help you to be happy if you use it to help you to bring about changes which you think are good and worthwhile. Provided that it is money which you have acquired honestly, this will help you to be happy. Money which has been acquired by other means will not make you happy no matter how worthwhile the application of the funds.

It is up to you to judge how your money should be applied to things you believe that it is right to apply it to. You must also respect other people's identical rights over their own money. You may see something which you think money should be spent on, and you may see someone else who seems to have plenty of money. You might suggest that they spend their money on your ideas, but you have no right to force them, nor to encourage anyone else to force them.

Freedom, happiness and responsibility

Wealth brings choices and choices mean freedom. Lack of freedom causes unhappiness. Freedom therefore allows happiness, but it does not cause it. If you have freedom, you therefore have choices, but choices mean decisions, and decisions require responsibility.

When you commit yourself to a choice by making a decision, you take responsibility for that consequences of that decision. Less obviously, but just as importantly, if you fail to make a decision you take responsibility for the consequences of that failure.

This burden of responsibility has implications for your happiness. If you are to be happy, you must be reasonably sure that the majority of your decisions are good ones. Everyone makes mistakes from time to time, so you will not get everything right all of the time, but you must be happy that you can cope with the ongoing responsibility of continual decisions. The richer you are, the more important this is.

Dangers of Choice

Now we have the better known of the two sayings quoted above. Power corrupts. There is very little difference between freedom, choice and power. Wealth brings all of these, and it brings concomitant problems.

Wrong choices

The greater the power of choice you have, the greater is the danger of making wrong choices, wrong decisions. These come in two varieties: mistakes and evil.

Mistakes

Mistakes are inevitable. Sometimes you will not have the best information with which to make the best decisions, sometimes you might misunderstand that information. Sometimes you might give instructions which are misinterpreted, and then you will have someone else doing something wrong on your behalf.

How do you feel about making mistakes? Will it upset you if you make a single error? Are you such a perfectionist that that would destroy your happiness? Such perfectionism is itself a matter of choice, and, if you are to be happy with the freedom to make your own choices, you must also choose not to destroy your own happiness by the interpretation you put onto genuine simple errors.

The way you look at your mistakes is vital for your happiness. The opposite extreme from perfectionism is denial of responsibility, which would also make you unhappy in the longer term. Whatever you choose to do, the responsibility of that choice is yours, whether the outcome was what you intended or not. Take responsibility for your errors, therefore, have the guts to say "my mistake", and correct the error and its consequences. This can be painful and difficult, but it is the way to be happy with the freedom and power of choice which comes with wealth.

Evil

When you have enough wealth and power to be free to make more or less any choice in any circumstances, you actually have more capacity for evil than when you are relatively poor. This comes very simply from the power of choice. The more things you can choose, the more wrong choices you can make.

If you deliberately choose to do something which you know to be wrong, you will make yourself unhappy. The way back to happiness from deliberate wrong-doing is very hard, as we have seen, and it is particularly so if you assume that it is going to be easy. If you are used to wealth and power, you can be tempted to think that you can easily do anything you choose, including undoing the damage done by your own wrong-doing. This is a dangerous illusion.

Almost as bad as deliberately choosing evil, is failure to choose good. Freedom, wealth and power can lead to moral laziness. Remember that happiness comes from doing what is right. This is quite different from just not doing wrong. If you can't be bothered to work out what is right, perhaps because life is easy, all the wealth in the world will not help you to be happy.

Less happiness?

Does all this mean that the more wealth you have the less happiness you will have? All these things that can go wrong are indeed more of a problem for rich people than for poor people, but does that mean that riches would bring you unhappiness? You must answer this question for yourself, but here are a few guidelines to help you.

Can you take the responsibility of the power of choice? Will you choose wisely most of the time? When you make mistakes, will you be able to admit them and correct for them? Will you resist the temptation to positive evil? Will you resist the temptation to moral laziness? Will you have the strength to try to discern what is right, and to do it?

If you can answer "Yes" to all these questions, you might be a wonderful person or you might be kidding yourself. If you honestly answer, "I do hope so and I will try", then wealth will probably not cause you to have less happiness, but will it bring you ...

More happiness?

If you are frightened of the responsibility that wealth would bring, what is the solution? Could it be deliberately to avoid material success in order to avoid having to make the hard decisions that money brings with it? No! To do this would be deliberately to reduce your power of choice, which would be to choose to become less human.

Happiness means being fully human. Being human means having the power of choice. It follows therefore that more wealth actually does mean more happiness, provided that you do not let it compromise your humanity, either in the getting of it or in the using of it.

There is no escape from this. As you go through life, you make choices because you are a human being, and we have no choice but to make choices. If you make good choices, you will be happy, and if you don't, you won't. Any choices you make which increase your power of choice will tend to make you happier, unless you damage someone else in the process, and thereby dehumanise yourself. Any choices you make which decrease your power of choice will tend to make you unhappier, as they dehumanise you too.

No-one else to blame

Before we leave this section, I must just mention one final mixed blessing. If you are rich enough and powerful enough not to have to take orders from anyone, you have no-one else to blame when things go wrong. This is an inevitable consequence of responsibility.

Now, responsibility is purely human. Animals are completely irresponsible, and cannot be blamed for the way they behave. If you make a bad choice, the properly human thing to do is to take the blame. If something goes wrong and you blame someone else for it, you might be right, but this doesn't help you to be more human or happier.

If something goes wrong, and you take responsibility for putting it right, you prove yourself to be more human, *even if you did not cause the problem.* When you are rich and powerful, you can take responsibility for correcting the consequences of bad decisions even when those decisions were not yours. If you can do this without blaming anyone else, you will show yourself to be the very finest of human beings, and you will be happy too.

More Wealth, More Freedom?

You might think that the more money you have the freer you will be. Many people do believe this, and, as we have seen, there is an element of truth in it. There is, however, great danger associated with this belief, and that is the ...

Danger of addiction to making money

It is possible to get hooked on money-making. You can start with the perfectly reasonable belief that if you had more money, you would have greater freedom and therefore a greater sense of your own humanness. You get more money, it feels good, so you go all out to get more. After a while, the pursuit of more and more money becomes a compulsion.

Compulsive behaviour is the very opposite of freedom. Once you're hooked on money-making, or on anything else addictive or compulsive, you have lost your freedom. There is no point in chasing more and more money all your life, or more and more of anything else for that matter. With things like this, the key is ...

Knowing when to stop

Once you have got into compulsive behaviour, it is usually too late. You can't stop to think how, why and where to stop. Before you start getting seriously rich, or even seriously committed to the process of getting any richer than you already are, you must place a limit on how much you want. You can review this from time to time, but having a limit of some sort is vital for your sanity, because the alternative is the dangerously simple idea of wanting more. If you just want more, you will always want more, no matter how much more you already have.

This brings us to the next chapter. We have dealt with some of the misconceptions about money and wealth, so I hope you can approach what is coming in a realistic frame of mind. In a civilised society, you do need some money to achieve what you want to achieve in life. Probably the most important question you will ever ask yourself about money is ...

Chapter 29

How Much Is Enough?

This is not an easy question. You want money. That is natural enough. You want more than you have at present. That too is understandable. If you had more, would you want more still, and then more and more and more? If so, you have a never-ending problem. This problem is not uncommon, and it is shared by both rich and poor people.

The only solution is to work out how much is enough for you. You may then find that you already have enough, and that there is no point in making yourself unhappy chasing after wealth which you do not need. Alternatively, you might decide that you do require a certain amount more for some reason, in which case you can set your mind to getting that amount without worrying about the danger of getting addicted to making money.

If you do believe that you need more money than you have now, then you have to find your own private answer to the question of how much would be enough. There is no single answer to this question, and your own answer is your own answer, totally individual, and not for sharing with anyone else. Of course, to answer such a big question for yourself, you need to start by finding the answers to some smaller ones, of which the first is ...

What do you Want it For?

If you have no answer to this question, it follows that you already have enough for your needs. Maybe you would do better simply to allow yourself to feel happy about the fact that you do not have financial worries.

More likely, when you ask yourself what you want more money for, you will find your mind flooded with so many answers that you feel overwhelmed by the problem of getting enough money to meet all your requirements. Do not despair: there is a way through this muddle.

The first thing is to forget all the detail of all the myriad little things you would like to buy but can't afford at present. Then set aside, for the time being, those things which you would like to have purely for your own enjoyment: we will come back to them later. Finally, postpone for later consideration things you need for day to day life, which we will also come back to later.

Now things should look a little simpler. If you are left with anything, you are left with a need for some limited number of things or limited amount of money which you want for some particular purpose about which you care deeply. This brings us back to a subject we covered in some detail in an earlier chapter.

Remember your goals

You will recall that an examination of your goals in life leads you to a list of material things which you need to have in order to achieve those goals. Those material things have a financial cost, and the time has come to estimate that financial cost.

Non-material goals

You may also have one or more goals which require little or nothing in the way of material things but for which you need time. Money can buy you time too. It won't make you live longer, although rich people do live a little longer on average, but, if you have enough money, you don't need to spend time earning it in order to survive, and if you have plenty, you can often save some time by spending some extra money, especially if you have to travel.

Non-material goals come in two varieties, which I call definite and indefinite. A definite goal is one which can completely attained, whereas an indefinite goal is one where improvement is always possible. Consider marriage as an example: if you want to get married, this is a definite goal, but once you are married, you can have the indefinite goal of making your marriage better and happier. Indefinite goals always carry the risk of compulsive behaviour, but even this can amount to a "magnificent obsession" if the goal is well enough chosen.

Whatever your non-material goals, they are likely to have a financial cost. Do not try to deny this. At the very least, they cost you time, time which you could in principle spend making money instead. More significantly, if you are going to spend time on a non-material goal, you will do it better if you do not also have to worry about financial matters: the money which you need to live is part of the financial cost of going for your goal.

Don't be too self-indulgent

Getting back to the question of what you want money for, you probably found, when you asked yourself that question, that many of your answers had more to do with your own enjoyment than anything more serious. There is nothing wrong with this. It is good to enjoy yourself.

However, if your only objective in life is to enjoy things, and your only purpose in getting money is in order to indulge in whatever it is you most enjoy, you are unlikely to become happier if you get enough money to be able to afford all the things you might enjoy. This is selfishness of the feeblest kind. It is not as bad as the kind of selfishness which causes people not to care about harming other people as they seek their own objectives, and it is not quite as destructive of your chances of happiness.

Enjoy things by all means. Lack of fun can make you unhappy, but fun alone is not enough. Include in your goals some things which are purely for your own enjoyment, but let that not be all. Have some self-indulgence, but only as much as you need to stop your spirit from dying for lack of enjoyment. With a lively spirit, you can make a better contribution to the human race as a whole, or maybe just to a few individuals: this is where your happiness will come from.

How Much do you Need for That?

Let us suppose that you have identified some goal which you care deeply about. It doesn't matter what it is. Whatever it is, it will have a financial cost. This may be very small, or it may be very large, but whether it is pennies or billions, the next thing to do is to ...

Count the cost

You may not be able to do this precisely at first, but any definite goal does have a definite cost, and it is vital to have at least a reasonable idea of that cost before you go for the goal. The last thing you want is to run out of resources without having achieved what you were trying for. Know what you need, get what you need, then go for your goal: that way you are much more likely to succeed than if you just proceed in hope without a clear idea of the resources you will require.

Indefinite goals are much harder, and many authors recommend that they be avoided completely. I don't agree with this. As long as you recognise that a goal is indefinite and that therefore its costs are open-ended, you can make allowances for this. In such cases, the best thing is to budget for a definite proportion of your income to go to support your efforts on this indefinite goal: do the best you can with that allowance, and accept that it might always have been possible to do better. A perfect job on an indefinite goal is impossible: recognising this will protect you from the unhappiness that might otherwise come from always being faced with more to do.

Even if your goal is definite, it might not be necessary to accumulate all the money you need to attain it before you go for it. As long as you are reasonably sure that you will have what you need when you need it, you don't have to have it all in advance.

Non-financial costs too

Whenever you try to achieve anything, it costs not only money but also time. The time you spend on it takes time away from other activities. Think through the implications of this and budget your time accordingly.

Do not underestimate

It sometimes seems that whenever people undertake a large project, the budget is exceeded. There are exceptions, but computer projects and construction projects more often than not take longer and cost more than was originally estimated. Probably the largest factor in this is the triumph of optimism over experience: things do go wrong, but we always like to think that they won't go wrong this time. Two other major factors are forgetting to include estimates for some of the details, and assuming that a greater proportion of your time is spent on the project than is actually the case.

When you form your own plans for some goal, be aware of these problems. Try to think of everything. Make allowances for unforeseen problems, and for the fact that some of your time and your financial resources will get diverted into other things.

What More do you Need?

Let's look at some of the other things which will take some of your time and money. First and foremost, ...

You have to live

I admit to stating the obvious here, but it is not unknown for people to underestimate their cost of living with disastrous results. If you are starting some kind of project which is going to take some financing, you must know how much money you need to live on. Know, do not guess.

You can work this out by monitoring your expenditure (every penny) for three months, and adding in everything you can remember which you pay for less often than that, the big things like annual insurance premiums, the car you replace every few years, and so on. Alternatively, you can get from any high street bank a set of leaflets about starting your own business: these usually include a guide on how to calculate your cost of living.

Better not to have to worry

If much of your mental energy is spent on worrying about shortage of money, you might find it difficult to get anything else done very efficiently. This is one of the problems of relative poverty. If you are short of money but not actually completely destitute, you can make yourself quite unhappy by focusing on your financial difficulties.

If, instead, you want to focus on something which you believe is more worthwhile, you have to have sufficient money that you will not worry about paying for the things you need to pay for.

Of course this is more easily said than done. If the main cause of unhappiness for you is shortage of money, it may well be that your principal goal in life is to get sufficient money that you will no longer have to worry. This is a perfectly worthwhile goal, and can be attainable if you can quantify the amount of money you need for it, rather than just thinking in terms of having more. You may be more concerned about how than about how much, and we will come to this soon.

You are allowed to enjoy yourself

"All work and no play makes Jack a dull boy", says the old proverb. The same is just as true of grown men and women as it is of children. As, I said earlier, you need some fun to stop your spirit from dying. Whatever you enjoy is likely to have some financial cost, even if it is only the cost of the time you take to enjoy it. Budget for that cost, or risk the unhappiness which can come from never being able to afford to enjoy yourself.

You'd better give some away too

When you have enough money to enjoy yourself, to live, and to strive for some other worthwhile goal, you are in a better position than a great many other people. If you ignore the plight of the genuinely helpless, you will make yourself unhappy.

Do not let yourself be fleeced by every collector for every so-called worthy cause. Contribute to what you believe in. Don't just try to buy good feelings; this does not work. Do not give money to people who will not be helped by it. Even if you have some to spare, your resources are still limited, so spend as wisely as you can.

Remember the division of the world into producers, parasites and genuinely helpless. Watch for parasites. Many administrators of charities are not actually parasites: many do indeed work as hard as they can to ensure that as much as possible of your money goes to help the otherwise helpless, but there are exceptions. Some of them live quite well by playing on people's emotions, holding up the suffering they say they are helping to overcome, whilst actually depending upon the continuance of that suffering for their own livelihoods. It can be difficult to discern how much of a donation to a charitable cause goes to such parasites and how much to make a genuine difference for the genuinely helpless, but the task of this discernment is your responsibility as the giver.

On no account be put off giving to the genuinely helpless on the grounds that parasites do exist. If you do this you will make yourself bitter and unhappy. It is better for your own happiness to give what you can as best you can to help the genuinely helpless, and accept that there are some people who are so stupid in their parasitism that they will feed off your generosity to others without understanding that this cannot make them happy. Do not let their stupidity disturb your happiness. Some of what you give will be wasted in this way. Just accept this with equanimity.

What about your old age?

If you do not budget now for a time in the future when you will no longer be able to make enough money to support yourself, then the time will probably come when you will be numbered among the genuinely helpless. If you are bargaining upon someone else supporting you when that time comes, then you are planning like a parasite, and you will make yourself unhappy.

Plan always to support yourself. This is the way to be happy about your old age. If you get your plans wrong and someone loves you enough to look after you despite this, then you can still be happy, but if you plan to be supported by someone else, you will be unhappy whether they support you or not.

Therefore, when you are working out how much money you need for any purpose, always include the money you will need in your old age.

How are you Going to Get it?

By now you should have at least some idea of how much money you want and what you want it for. I am not going to give you a get-rich-quick scheme here, but just give you a few points to bear in mind when you are working out how to get the money you need.

Of course, you understand by now that anything you do in order to get money must be completely ethical, simply because, if it isn't, it will make you unhappy, and the objective here is to end up happy, not unhappy. What else do you have to bear in mind?

The difference between getting money and making money

Money can be obtained honestly by any number of means. Broadly, these fall into two categories: trade, and good fortune. You may be fortunate enough to inherit money or to be given it, but relying on this kind of thing will not do much for your self-esteem, unless you use the wealth you get that way very wisely indeed.

Most of what most people get honestly is by way of trade, in its widest sense. I do not mean that you have to go into business on your own account. When you accept paid employment, you are engaging in trade, in the sense that you agree to supply some of your time and effort in exchange for your employer's money.

Likewise, if you run a charity, you accept money from people on the understanding that you will apply the resources you have available to something that they care about. This is a form of trade, even if it is not often identified as such. When people give money to a charity, they are buying an assurance that something will be done. You can earn an honest living in this way, at the same time as doing something that you care about. You could also earn a dishonest living in much the same way, essentially selling sticking plasters for other people's damaged consciences, but that would not make you happy, even if you were to use the money for something else which you did care about.

Fortunes are made, not paid

If you wish to make a very large amount of money, the most effective way to do it is in your own business. Many rich people have wealth which they have inherited; of those who do not, there are a very few who have won their money by gambling and a great many who have made their money in their own businesses. The gamblers also tend to lose their money almost as easily as they won it, perhaps because they discover that it doesn't buy happiness after all.

Admittedly, many businesses do fail. I have observed two phenomena concerning business failures, which are not widely publicised. Firstly, businesses which concentrate on the needs of their customers seem to be much more robust than businesses operated by people who are obsessed with their own needs, and who see customers as a means of satisfying those needs. Secondly, many (if not most) rich and successful business people suffer the failure of one or more of their businesses before they manage to run one which succeeds.

But who needs a fortune?

There is nothing wrong with wanting to be seriously rich, if that is what you really do want. It is quite a natural desire, but it can also be an illusion.

In the western world, there is almost a cultural expectation that one should long for riches, even when one is already comfortable. It is even considered bad taste to admit to being sufficiently wealthy: you are expected to pretend that you have some financial worries even when this is not the case.

There is a trap here, which can lead to unhappiness unless you recognise it and avoid getting caught by it. It might be pleasant to have more money than you now have, but it does not follow from this that you have a genuine desire to be seriously rich, a desire strong enough to put in the honest hard work necessary to achieve it.

You may have a genuine reason for wanting some particular amount of capital or level of income. That is fair enough, even if the amount is very large by most people's standards. If, on the other hand, you have a vague idea that it would be nice to be richer, you have probably fallen in to the trap of thinking that you want what you are expected to want, in which case, it is time for a re-think.

Making money

Your money must be earned or getting it destroys you. Any money which you acquire by any dishonest means will only serve to make you unhappy. Even money which you acquire honestly but without earning it, such as gifts or inherited wealth, can undermine your happiness, especially if it was acquired dishonestly by whoever gives it or leaves it to you.

If you earn your money by working for an employer, you can be happy with what you get only if you are sure that your rate of pay is fair. Unreasonably low pay and unreasonably high pay are both demoralising. Being paid by an employer whose work does not benefit customers is just as demoralising.

If you make your money in your own business, the most important rule to follow to keep your own happiness is ...

All transactions must benefit all concerned

Win-win situations do exist, and they are the stuff of all successful and happy businesses. You can do for your customers things which they cannot do for themselves, and they benefit from this. They pay you, and you benefit. Some of the money goes to your suppliers, who benefit from it, whilst supplying you with things you couldn't make yourself, thus benefiting you again. Even the parasites who come along and demand their slice of the cake get some benefit, in that they get to eat, even if they are never happy.

Your competitors may not be too happy about your success, but it could even benefit them. Competition in business spurs people on to doing a better and better job. (You can see this most clearly by comparing the standard of living of people in countries where competition is the norm to that in countries where it is not.) If your business did not pose a threat, your competitors could get lazy, knowing that their business was not threatened by competition, they might not put in the effort necessary to do the very best for their customers. (You can see this in any nationalised monopoly.) Failing to do the very best for your customers is a way to become unhappy.

Chapter 30

How Much Is Too Much?

Could you be too rich? Could you be aiming at getting too rich? Your first reaction may be to dismiss these as silly questions, because you have no clear concept of what "too rich" might mean. That is what this chapter is for. Remember that happiness depends upon being rational, and that requires clear thinking. If you are to be happy about money, you must understand it well enough to have a clear notion of how much is too much.

There is no numerical answer to this question. It is very much an individual matter. What may be too much for you may not be for your next-door neighbour, or vice versa. To get to the answer which is right for you, I suggest you start with ...

Some Questions

Having read the preceding chapter, you shouldn't find these too difficult to answer, although they may be uncomfortable to face.

Why might you need more than you need?

This is, of course, a rhetorical question, which admits of only one answer. By definition, you do not need any more than you need. Nevertheless, thinking about this question can help you to have a better understanding of what you do need, or genuinely want, and what you do not. On this subject, you will probably get greater enlightenment from the next question.

If you had more than you need, what would you do with it?

There can be any number of answers to this one, but they can be categorised. The simplest is, "I don't know"; if this is your answer, then you have successfully found the answer to the bigger and more useful question of how much you actually need and want. Other answers can be categorised according to how easily you can answer the next two questions.

What good would that do?

If you can answer this question readily, then perhaps you haven't set your sights high enough. You can think of the good you could do if you had the money, but you are still held back by the belief that this is beyond you.

What harm would it do?

This may the most painful question of all to do with money. If your resources were unlimited, how would you actually spend your time? Just enjoying yourself? If so, where would the harm be in that? The answer to that is simple:

enjoyment does not bring happiness. Happiness comes from honestly doing the best you can with your life. If plenty of money would encourage you not to do that, then you don't want too much money!

Causes of Misery

Another way of looking at the question of how much would be too much is to look for the causes of unhappiness in people who have plenty of money and who seem to be troubled by this. The problems I will mention here are not very common, but they are reasonably well-known, and very enlightening.

False expectations

Money can be very helpful in solving certain types of problem. It is all too easy to generalise from this fact to the idea that all problems can be solved by means of money. They can't. If you make the mistake of believing that they can, you are in danger of falling into a trap. The trap is more often sprung by the very few gamblers who win than by people who make their money by other means, but anyone can be caught by it.

It happens like this. You observe that money can help solve problems. Without contemplating its limitations, you put your faith in the idea that money solves all problems. You buy some lottery tickets. Unlike the vast majority of people who do the same, you win a huge amount of money. You now expect all your problems to be solved. Only later do you discover that they are not. In particular, you are still left with your basic problem of philosophy, the tendency to believe without careful thought, which will lead you into yet further unhappiness.

Aimlessness

Imagine that you had enough money for all your needs, but scarcely any more. What do you do? How do you spend your time? You don't have to work to earn money, since you have enough. You can't spend your time applying your surplus wealth to causes you believe in, because you haven't much surplus. Perhaps you could spend your time on something you believe in, but that would doubtless cost money too, and (Oh, dear!) you haven't got any money to spare. Your life is wasting away, and no good is coming of it. You are unhappy.

Poor little rich girl

Now imagine the same situation, except that you do have plenty to spare. You can have anything you want, except, perhaps the one thing you do want, happiness. As Lennon and McCartney observed in one of their greatest lyrics, "Money can't buy me love." Implicit in that lyric was the idea that love leads to happiness.

This situation, known as the poor little rich girl phenomenon because heiresses can be particularly prone to it, is not terribly uncommon. It carries with it some peculiar problems in the area of romantic love. Few people understand that love is inspired by values and the ability to produce things or services which people value. The poor little rich girl is unlikely to be particularly lovable unless she understands that she must use her life in such a way as to make things better for the rest of the world, just the same as those of us who have to earn our livings do. If she fails to understand this, her main worry in any potential romantic relationship will be whether the man involved is one of those who is so ignorant as to believe that he will be happy if he marries into money.

Thus, the poor little rich girl can easily become the rich and crabby old spinster, or the cynical multi-divorcée, more concerned about who is after her money than about anything else. These are caricatures of unhappiness, but I'm afraid they are not uncommon.

Waste

Suppose again that you have more money than you know what to do with. You can afford to waste it, or can you? If you waste so much that you cease to be wealthy, you will be plagued by regrets. If you waste less, your regrets will be less, but whatever you waste, regrets will come, as this is in the nature of wastage.

Unethical mode of acquisition

Finally, it bears repeating that if you acquire your wealth dishonestly, it will bring you no joy. Quite the reverse, in fact. Deep inside you there will always remain the knowledge of the people who suffered so that you could get your wealth. You may hide from this knowledge, thus cutting off part of yourself from the rest of yourself, but the barriers you erect are never perfect, and they always also cut you off from true happiness, which depends upon the self-knowledge which you deny yourself.

Solutions

None of these problems are insurmountable. Wealth is, on balance, a good thing, although it carries risks with it, as do many other good things. The philosophical errors associated with wealth, that is to say the common mistakes about money, are the basis of all the unhappiness associated with wealth. The key to happiness here is understanding and action based on understanding. In this respect, money is no different from any other subject. Now, let's look at how such understanding can solve some of the problems we have mentioned.

Jesus' extreme answer

You may be aware of a story about Jesus in which he is approached by a rich young man who is obviously not happy. When this young man asked Jesus what he should do, Jesus at first reeled off a summary of the Ten Commandments, but the young man said he kept all those, but he was still wondering what else he should do. Jesus' answer was that he should sell all he had and give the money to the poor. This was too much for the young man, and he went away even unhappier than he was when he came.

I believe that Jesus was trying to get this rich young man to grasp the fact that wealth does not of itself lead to happiness. Contribution does. If you cannot contribute by work, but you can contribute by giving things away, then this is what you must do. The rich young man's problem was that he was so wedded to the idea that wealth is necessary for happiness that he could not grasp that it is not having wealth which matters, but how you acquire it and what you do with it.

Read the rest of this book

You can be both rich and happy. If you understand what happiness depends upon, and if you always act in accordance with that knowledge, you will be happy. Whether or not you are rich is incidental to this. In fact, it is almost irrelevant. If you understand the rest of this book, and act on it, then happiness can be yours, whether or not you are rich.

Find a worthwhile goal

As we saw earlier, one of the greatest dangers for rich people is the risk of becoming aimless. There is a simple solution to this. Find a worthwhile goal, and pursue it. This will come quite easily if you set aside time for thinking and reflection, as recommended earlier.

Face your responsibilities

Finally, remember that wealth always carries responsibility. This is such an important subject that the whole of the next chapter is dedicated to it. Turning away from your responsibilities leads to unhappiness. If you are to be happy, you must face them.

Chapter 31

Responsibility

Money brings you the power of choice. Power implies responsibility. You can't get away from this. If you have money, you have to decide what to do with it, how much of it to spend and on what, how much of it to give away and to whom, and how much to keep and where. Even if you do not make any such decisions consciously, you are responsible for the consequences.

Responsibility is not a bad thing. In fact the proper exercise of your responsibilities can positively help you to be happy. Running away from money because you are afraid of the responsibilities it brings will not help you to be happy. Better then, to look at the responsibilities you have as a consequence of the money you have, and to think about those you might have when you get more money.

If you are responsible, to whom are you responsible? Everyone, I'm afraid! You may choose not to use your money to support any individual, or cause, or group, or anything, but let that choice be deliberate, not a mere failure. You have various responsibilities, so let's look at these from the point of view of asking who you are responsible to.

To Self

According to the Preamble to the American Constitution, you have an inalienable right to life, liberty and the pursuit of happiness. This right is no good to you unless you do pursue happiness. Some people regard this idea as selfish, and they see selfishness as evil, but this combination of ideas can lead to the conclusion that pursuing your own happiness is evil. It is not, but we need to look more carefully at the logic to understand why not.

If you pursue what you believe to be your own short-term interests without any regard for the consequences for other people, you will doubtless do evil, both to other people, and, in the longer term, to yourself. It is this kind of selfishness which has given the word "selfishness" a bad name.

If you honestly aim at happiness for yourself, you will discover that you cannot attain it by harming others, and that benefiting others will positively help you to be happy. It follows that the pursuit of your own happiness, provided that it is done honestly, is the greatest possible good.

You therefore have a responsibility to yourself, and you have to take this into account when you consider how your money is to be applied.

A little self-indulgence but not too much

There is no reason why you shouldn't enjoy yourself. Fun is a vital part of life. It is also self-limiting. If you keep well in touch with your conscience, which you must in order to remain happy, you will know when you have had enough fun for the time being and need to get on with something else worthwhile. You will, for example, know when you are in danger of spending more money on your hobby than would be consistent with the other things you care about.

This kind of knowledge is only semi-automatic: you do need to keep to your habits of reflection and self-examination, and you do need to keep an ear open to your conscience, but you will be doing this anyway, as part of your habit of pursuing happiness.

There is, by the way, a form of fun which need not be so limited. If you do work which you care about, and which benefits people in a way you can feel good about, you should enjoy your work. Work can be fun, and profitable too. Don't let yourself get so hooked on it that you become a workaholic, but by all means enjoy it.

Greater goals

Of course, you have in your life some aims which are more important to you than enjoying yourself. You can enjoy pursuing them, but that enjoyment is not the objective. You pursue these goals even when the going is tough, but you know that you will feel happier as a result of the effort.

Are you putting the effort in for your own benefit, or for something you regard as more important? There is no correct answer to this question, because it is a false distinction. There is no difference between going for something because you think it is important and going for it because you know you will feel better for having tried for it. However you choose to look at it, it is good, and you have a responsibility to apply your resources, including your money, to that which you believe to be important.

Contribution will make you

One of the recurring themes of this book is the idea of contribution. We have seen that the most relevant contribution you are likely to make is through your work, but what about contribution in the sense of giving money to some worthy cause, such as a charity, or contributing to a body such as your local church?

When you give money, there is a sense in which you give of yourself. Money is precious, and parting with it can be hard, but if you care deeply about what you are giving it to, you will be happier for it. If you are pressurised, conned or embarrassed into parting with your cash, you will not be happier for it. If you feel any such pressure, draw attention to the tactics being used, and help the person applying the pressure to see that that is not the way to improve anything for anyone. If the person applying the pressure stands to gain personally from what you part with, have nothing more to do with them.

When you do find a case where genuinely helpless people can be truly helped by money which you can give, then give. You will know in your heart how much would be right. Remember that there is nothing wrong with the good feelings you get when you give voluntarily: they are an effect of doing what you know to be right, and they will serve to strengthen you to do other things which you also know to be right. Do not, however, try giving just in order to get those feelings: it doesn't work!

Self-sufficiency

Self-sufficiency is a worthwhile goal in its own right. It stops you from being a parasite and protects you from the guilt you might feel at being a burden to others. If you are capable of meeting your material needs from your own resources, you need not be a burden on anyone else. If you do become a burden when you need not have done, you are unlikely to be happy, and you will do nothing for the people who end up supporting you.

Therefore, when you give time or money to some cause you care about, feel free to lower your standard of living, but do not reduce yourself to destitution, lest you turn yourself into a parasite. In particular, avoid parasitism on your own family: you will make nobody happy, least of all yourself, by deliberately arranging your life in such a way that you end up dependent upon your relatives, in the belief that they have a duty to look after you.

This brings us to the next set of responsibilities. If you owe it to yourself not to become dependent upon your family, what responsibility do you have to your family?

Responsibility to Family

Your responsibility for other members of your family is an issue which can lead to much strife. Do you have a duty to look after the weaker members, especially if they become incapable in old age, or what? What do they have a right to claim from you? Only you can answer these questions for yourself, but I will offer a few thoughts which I hope might be useful as guidelines.

Firstly, if any member of your family claims that you have a duty to support them, you will naturally feel less inclined to do so, and the more they demand, the less you will feel inclined to give. Conversely, the more they struggle to remain independent and not to burden you, the more you will feel inclined to help and support them.

Secondly, you will be happier if you decide what to do for them on the basis of thought rather than feelings, although you must take your feelings into account when you do your thinking. In particular, look out for guilt: if you think you might feel guilty for not supporting your relatives, ask yourself rationally whether that guilt would be justified or whether it would be false guilt which they have tried to induce in you in order to manipulate you into supporting them. Having thought about it, decide rationally what you want to do.

Thirdly, remember that people's situations keep changing, so what you decided last week may not be the right answer today. Furthermore, people, perhaps especially old people, can repent. Always be ready to forgive someone who might have tried to manipulate you in the past but now admits the error of their ways. Forgiveness leads to happiness, whereas grudge-bearing never does.

So much for the guidelines – are there any more absolute rules as to what you should do for your family? Yes and no. I will now give you some ideas as to what you should actually do for members of your family. These suggestions are not absolute rules, but I think they are very widely applicable. Remember that it is your happiness which is paramount: you cannot supply happiness to anyone else, but you can give your own happiness a better chance by solving other people's problems where they can't solve them for themselves.

Avert real hardship

If you have a near relative who is on the point of destitution and you can prevent them from suffering the worst ravages of poverty without destroying yourself in the process, then you will probably be happier if you help them. This is true even if they have hurt you in the past and they owe you an apology. You won't make yourself happier by refusing to help a desperate person who happens to have done you wrong in the past.

But do not demean

If you do help out someone whose position is desperate or nearly desperate, it can be quite hard also to let them keep some element of self-respect. It can be very demeaning to be wholly dependent upon someone else, but you must resist the temptation to make that part of their problem even worse.

If you can possibly help someone to a position where they can make more of their own choices and maybe get back to being self-supporting, everyone involved is likely to be happier.

Fourth commandment

To save you looking it up, let me remind you that the fourth of the Ten Commandments is the one about honouring your father and your mother. What does this' mean? Strangely enough, a useful contribution to this debate comes from Confucius, who points out that this kind of injunction means more than just feeding them and housing them: "People do that much for their dogs and their horses," says Confucius.

Quite what you do beyond feeding them and housing them is, of course, up to you. If you do no more, you are unlikely to be happy about the little that you do do, but, equally, you are unlikely to feel happy about doing more if you are only doing it because they argue that it is your duty.

Look at their real needs

The hardest thing to discern when people need help is what their real needs are, as opposed to their perceived needs. What they think they need may be quite different from what they actually need. Just as significantly, you may need to review in the light of experience your first thoughts as to what they need, especially if you find that your early efforts to help make no real difference at all.

Responsibility to Friends

If you have plenty of money, the people least likely to be much affected by it are your friends, so how does the responsibility which comes with money impinge upon your relationships with your friends?

Keep them

If your standard of living changes, either for better or for worse, it can be difficult to maintain good relationships with people whose standard of living is now different from your own. Your truest friends will not be much disturbed by your change in circumstances, as the best of friendships are not dependent upon money. Keeping your old friends is good for your mental health and happiness; so, too, is making new friends, but that is not the issue here.

If your standard of living improves, do not abandon your old friends, even if they cannot share some of your newfound expensive pleasures; continue to share, as far as you are able, the things you always used to share. On no account embarrass them with your wealth, either by expecting them to pay more than they can afford to join in with your lifestyle, or by undermining their self-respect by offering to pay for things for them.

If your standard of living declines, be prepared to let go of your wealthier friends, but do not feel that you have to abandon them if they obviously feel that they still want their relationship with you.

Don't attempt to buy them

If you become wealthy, you may find that you gain some new friends. Some of these are genuine, and others are just after what they can get from you: it should be easy enough to tell the difference.

You may also find yourself wishing that you had a particular individual as a friend. As a wealthy person, you might be getting into the habit of thinking that you can buy anything you want. This does not include friendship. If you try to buy someone's friendship, neither of you will be happy about it. I refer you back to Part Three for ideas on how to win friends.

Emotional relationship more important than material wealth

Your material and financial position is important, but it does not usually have much bearing on your relationships with your friends. A friend is someone with whom you share emotional things. It is up to you how explicit this is, but it is as well to remember that that is what friends are for, and that money has little, if anything to do with this.

Lending money to friends

What do you do if a friend asks to borrow some of your hard-earned money? Be very careful, because debts between friends can be very destructive to the emotional relationship. Often the best answer is to give, make it clear that your gift is a gift and that you expect nothing back, but allow your friend to repay as and when he can, if he can, and if he wants to, and even accept interest from him if he wants to give it to you and he can afford it. Do not let the existence of a debt of any sort sour your friendship.

If one of your friends does get into financial difficulties, it is probably better to help him to find a new self-sufficiency than merely to give him short-term support. If you have a friend who does not understand the difference between getting money and making money, he will eventually thank you much more for teaching him the difference, than he could ever thank you for just letting him get money from you.

Never patronise

If you let a poorer person think that you think less of them because you are richer and they are poorer, you will cause a grave hurt, which can destroy a friendship. If you wreck an old friendship by patronising an old friend in that way, you will never be happy about it. People can be valuable without being rich: value them for who and what they are, and don't make them feel they are inferior.

To Society

Should it be for you to decide how much responsibility you take for society, or should other people decide what your "duties" are to be?

Taxation

Would you be happy if you paid no tax at all? Probably not, because you do benefit from some things which are paid for from taxes, and it is hard to be happy about benefiting from anything taken from other people by force or threat' thereof. Are you happy, then, about the amount of tax you pay? As society is currently constituted, the more productive and richer you are, the more is taken from you by other people in the form of taxes, and, usually, the less productive you become as a result of resources having been taken away from you.

You may take the view, as many taxpayers do, that you do not mind paying a reasonable amount of tax to pay for necessary things which cannot be paid for in any other way. You may even think that the amount of tax you pay is actually reasonable, given the benefits. More likely, you believe that you are forced to pay more tax than you think is reasonable. In every other area, you pay what you accept as a reasonable price for what you get; when it comes to taxation, you have very little choice about what you get, and no choice about how much you pay for it. Why is this?

Politics

Career politicians have no real interest in reducing taxes. They claim to wish to do so in order to get elected. They want to get elected in order to increase their power base, or at least to maintain it. To maintain or increase their power base, they need to maintain or increase taxes. Politicians claim to be public servants, but it is very hard to find politicians seeking to give themselves less power rather than more, whereas true servants do not seek power, least of all power over the people who pay them.

Politicians in power claim that they have the support of the people because they got more votes than the opposition. This is another illusion: they got more votes than the opposition because the majority thought that the opposition would be even worse, not because they thought that the party currently in power would be any good. The problem faced by the elector is the choice between slightly different varieties of career politician, all of whom are hoping to live as parasites feeding upon those who have elected them.

What can you do about this? If you have made enough of a fortune to be able to afford to go into politics without depending upon tax money, then perhaps you might do so. Enough business people doing this might help to solve the problem without the system collapsing, which otherwise it probably will. Alternatively, if you can find any honest politicians, vote for them.

Local influence

The way you live your life impinges upon the lives of people who live near you. Whatever you do, you have a local influence. The kind of influence you have, the effect you have on your neighbours, is up to you. It is a matter of choice, and it therefore has a bearing upon your own happiness. You have a responsibility, which you cannot duck, to live your life in such a way that people who live near you remain happy to do so. If they can positively delight in having you as a neighbour, then so much the better.

Share your Skills and Knowledge

You can help other people to be happy by sharing with them not only the results of your work but also the skills and knowledge which make your work and your happiness possible. This does not mean that you should go around preaching to people about how they can be happy if only they follow your example, but it does mean that you should be happy to have other people learn from you.

Having read this book, you will know a great deal more about happiness and how it can be achieved than most people. If you share your knowledge with people who want to know, you will help to make everyone happier, yourself included.

The church?

Are you a member of your local church (or mosque, or synagogue, or whatever)? If not, you might think about joining. If so, you might wish to become more involved. I mention this because I have a subjective impression, not verified statistically, that a higher proportion of churchgoers are happy than non-churchgoers. Within the church, those who put in more effort seem happier than those who are only there for what they can get. In this respect, your local church can be an enlightening analogue of the world as a whole.

Responsibility to the Poor

Are you your brother's keeper? What responsibility do you have to poor people? Do you accept the idea that no man is an island? If you harden your heart to the extent that you can refuse to do anything for genuinely helpless people, how can you be happy?

It is that last question which is the most relevant here. If you have real difficulty supporting yourself, then it might be possible for you to remain happy whilst concentrating on solving your own problems. Once you are rich enough not to have to worry about yourself, however, your happiness will depend in part upon what you choose to do for those who cannot support themselves. There is no getting away from this; it is just a fact of human nature.

Help to self-help

You will not make yourself happy by helping to trap poor people in their poverty as is done by most so-called welfare systems, and by some charities. Professional helpers can be tempted to do this in order to secure their own livelihoods: as long as they can point to a problem they can get money from people, so they make sure that the problem continues to exist. This is much commoner amongst the professional parasites in governmental organisations than in privately run charities, where there is a higher level of honesty on the whole.

Your greatest joy will come when you see people who were destitute through no fault of their own become self-supporting again. You may also be happy to ease the suffering of people who are and will always remain completely helpless, the very old, the terminally ill, and those so handicapped that self-sufficiency will always be out of the question.

Charities

A charity is a business which sells good feelings. When you give money to a charity, you get a feeling of having helped, and this can help you to feel happier. There is nothing wrong with this, although many workers in the charity sector might be irritated by the definition, because they would prefer not to look at their organisations from that point of view.

There is nothing wrong with it, that is, provided that the charity's officers are honest about what they do. They get money from you on the understanding that they will use as much of it as they reasonably can to help genuinely helpless people, or to do something about something else which you care about. If they do this honestly, then the good feelings you get when you give them money are quite proper. If they cream off as much as they think they can get away with, whilst ensuring that the problem which gives them the excuse to ask for money always remains, then the good feelings are counterfeit and will make nobody happy in the long run.

Do not be afraid to get good feelings from giving money to charities, but always be as discerning as you can about the activities of those charities.

Do-it-yourself charitable work

You may be personally acquainted with someone who is in need of help. Do you refer them to your local social services department? What about tipping off a charity to their plight? What about doing something yourself? The last of these is most likely to leave you feeling happiest about what you have done. Do-it-yourself charitable work can be the most satisfying way to spend your time (and money) that you ever find.

Give your time and skills

It is all too easy to think of giving only in terms of giving money, but there is more to you than your money. Some people who have genuine needs cannot be helped much by money alone: they need people's time, perhaps yours. The time you spend might just go into conversation, or you might use some particular skill or other strength you have, which is not shared by the person you are helping.

If you are wondering about examples of what I have in mind, you need think no further than the immediate needs of an elderly neighbour. Elderly, lonely people can sometimes be helped by the simplest things, such as an hour or so's conversation, or some help in the garden, or perhaps just carrying the shopping.

At the other end of the age range, you might be able to teach a young person some skill you have, and thereby improve their prospects of supporting themselves.

In all such matters, you must make your own decisions as to what is right. You can listen to anything that anyone says about their own or other people's needs, but never allow yourself to be manipulated. If you do, you will not only make yourself less happy, but also everyone else involved.

What about employing them?

If you are in business in your own right, or you have hire and fire power in the company you work for, you could give some thought to employing people from difficult backgrounds. Not all poor people are poor because of the decisions they have made themselves, and even those who are might learn better.

There is no real point in employing someone just on the basis of their need: it won't help either you or them. But you can always be ready to help people to a fresh start if you think that there is a real prospect of them grasping the basic idea that a living is to be earned rather than just got. This can lead to greater happiness for everyone, and greater wealth.

"God is not a potentate ordering this or that to happen, but the world is full of chance and accident, and God has let it be so because that is the one sort of world in which freedom, development, responsibility and love could come into being."

Bishop John V. Taylor

PART SIX

Being Happy With
The Big Questions

Throughout this book, I have been encouraging you to think for yourself and to choose what you do on the basis of decisions taken after careful thought. When you think about everything, you come across some very big questions. Why are we here? What is truth? What happens when we die? Does God exist? How can people believe in a loving God when there is so much suffering in the world?

These are just a few of the Big Questions, and it is not the purpose of this book to answer them for you. In many cases, I would not even recommend trying to get an answer. Remember that happiness is your objective, not necessarily understanding for its own sake. Understanding something well enough to make intelligent decisions about it does help you to be happy, but failing to understand something which cannot be understood need not make you unhappy, although running away from an attempt to understand something difficult is likely to reduce your chances of happiness.

The point of this part of the book is to help you to face the existence of these big questions, and to remain happy in the face of everyone's inability to find completely satisfactory answers to them. Many people manage this; therefore it is possible; therefore you can do it.

"It ain't what you don't know ... it's what you know that ain't so!"

Chapter 32

Unanswerable Questions

Is there much point in seeking an answer to a question if you cannot prove that the answer you get is right? Many big questions are of that type: if proofs existed, rational people would be bound to agree about the answers. Given that there is no such agreement, it follows that no proof has yet been found, despite, in many cases, much of the greatest work of the greatest thinkers.

Limitations of Science

Science has helped us to understand and control so much of the world that it is tempting to believe that there may be no limits to the knowledge which can be gained through the scientific method. Broad as its success has been, the scientific method still has limitations. These are of two kinds.

Firstly, the basic method is of limited application. The way it works is this. You observe something. You think up a theory which might explain it. Then you think up some experiments to test the theory. The experiments, if carried out properly, either tell you that the theory is wrong, or that it might be useful. They never tell you that the theory is right, only that it is useful: it might even continue to be useful after a more sophisticated experiment has shown that the theory is not exactly right! This is a truly wonderful method, but you cannot apply it in all situations: it doesn't help you to decide whom to marry, what to call your children or how to write your will.

Secondly, even within its own sphere of applicability, the scientific method is not a perfect tool of prediction. The idea of a scientific theory is that, given knowledge of the state of a system at a given time, you can calculate its state at a later time, and how it will behave if acted upon in various ways. This is a fine idea, and very helpful for calculating the motions of planets (not that many people do that) and for designing structures and machines. In fact, the whole of engineering depends upon this type of prediction. Nonetheless it is imperfect: to understand why, it might be helpful to find what some famous scientists and mathematicians have thought about this.

Laplace

Pierre Marquis de Laplace (1749-1827) held the view that the time would come when science would be able to predict anything with any desired accuracy, given sufficiently accurate information about the starting conditions. The only limitation would be the accuracy with which measurements could be made, and even this could be overcome with well-enough built apparatus and sufficient care. This belief about science seems to remain quite popular, despite being fundamentally flawed.

Heisenberg

Werner von Heisenberg (1901-1976) pointed out that there is an absolute limitation on the precision with which measurements can be made. This is known as the uncertainty principle and comes from the observation that it is impossible to measure anything without disturbing it at least a little bit.

Although Heisenberg was referring to physical measurements, his idea has been popularly generalised to include the notion that you cannot observe people's behaviour without affecting that behaviour. This idea is not directly due to Heisenberg himself, but it is a useful idea, placing limitations on the knowledge obtainable by psychologists and sociologists.

Penrose

The contemporary mathematician Roger Penrose has more recently pointed out that, even if it weren't for Heisenberg's uncertainty principle, the predictions made by some theories in certain circumstances are non-computable. That is to say that, even if you knew everything about the starting conditions of a system and had a satisfactory theory to predict what should happen next, it is in principle impossible to do the necessary calculations.

Even if it is in principle possible to do the calculations, in practice it may be impossible to do them with sufficient accuracy. The classic example of this is weather forecasting, for which the results of the calculations can be very greatly affected by tiny variations in the starting conditions. It is impossible to measure the starting conditions (the weather today) well enough to make it possible to make usefully accurate predictions more than a few days ahead.

Gödel

At an even more fundamental level, Kurt Gödel (1906-1978) proved in 1931 that there can exist statements which are true but which cannot be proved. Admittedly, his argument was in pure mathematics and a bit obscure, but the principle is general. It follows from his theorem that there can also be false statements which can never be shown to be lies. In mathematical jargon, they say that some propositions are undecidable. It seems to me that many of the proposed answers to the Big Questions are actually undecidable propositions.

Pippard

Professor Sir Brian Pippard, the former Cavendish Professor of Physics at the University of Cambridge, was once heard to say, "I consider it the height of arrogance to suggest that science could ever disprove the existence of a Creator." This is just one example of an eminent scientist saying, in effect, that the idea of the existence of God is an undecidable proposition, in that it can't be proved either way.

Criteria for Belief

This leads us to the question of why you should believe anything. If Pippard is right and the existence of God can neither be proved nor disproved, is agnosticism the only honest position, or is it reasonable to be a believer or a convinced atheist? You can ask the same kind of question about any number of Big Questions, to which we want answers, but where no proof can be found to show that a particular answer is correct.

At a less fundamental level, we need to make judgements where the evidence is insufficient to constitute proof. In other words, we need to believe things which we cannot prove, even if proof were possible, which sometimes it isn't. If you could not make judgements, decisions would be very much harder, and happiness depends upon following through decisions which you have made on the basis of the best judgement you can manage.

So, on what basis do you make judgements about what is true? In other words, why do you believe what you do believe? There are several answers to this question, all of them valid, and all of them bear more careful consideration.

Proof

If something has been proved to you, you cannot help but believe it. You might not like it, but proof is proof, and there is no getting away from it. Furthermore, if it has been unquestionably proved, then you should be able to convince any other reasonable person of the truth by presenting the proof. If you have proof of something, you have the best possible reason for believing it.

Even so, mistakes are possible. When you are satisfied that something has been proved, continue to believe it, but never close your mind to the possibility that there might have been an error. If new evidence comes along which purports to show that what you believe is incorrect, do not dismiss the evidence on the grounds that you have already made up your mind: that is bigotry, which never makes anyone happy. Examine the evidence and see what you can learn from it.

Feelings

Many of the judgements we make without complete evidence are judgements as to whether we will trust another human being to behave in an acceptable way. Much of the time, we do this on the basis of whether we feel that the person is trustworthy.

This is not as irrational as it might seem. Your subconscious mind is constantly taking in information about people and their behaviour, and it is ready to weigh all the available information about people in general and about a particular person, and to deliver an instant estimate of any characteristic of that person, including an estimate of their trustworthiness. It delivers its judgement in the form of a feeling! It may not be a perfect judgement, but it is usually pretty good, and it is the best you can get quickly, which is when you usually need it.

When you have formed a judgement on the basis of feelings, it is always wise, if you can, to follow it up with rational thought, to examine how your subconscious mind reached its conclusion. This can be hard work, but it pays dividends. Everyone has a tendency towards trust or mistrust: this tendency can bias the results delivered by the subconscious, but you can correct for it to some extent by thought.

The process of thought can thus partly protect you from being tricked by people who are skilled at sending out signals to convince your subconscious that they are trustworthy, but whose intentions are dishonest.

Honesty

One of the judgements you most often make about someone else is whether they are honest. An individual's commitment to honesty is either absolute or non-existent. There is no middle ground. As soon as you find that an individual has been dishonest in one respect, you know that you cannot be sure of their honesty in all circumstances.

On the other hand, if you have regular dealings with an individual, and their commitment to honesty seems absolute, your faith that they will never deceive you will gradually grow.

Honesty, of course, is not quite the same as trustworthiness. An honest person can let you down, not by deliberately deceiving you, but by failing to achieve what they have undertaken to achieve. Promising to do something and then failing to do it is not necessarily a sign of dishonesty, although it might be; it is more usually evidence of incompetence or of unforeseen circumstances.

Experience

As you go through life, you will gradually form opinions and beliefs which are based, not on an intellectual examination of evidence, but upon your subjective experience of patterns in your life. You might express these as vague generalisations, or you might just base your behaviour on these beliefs without ever enunciating them, or even thinking about them.

As an example of this, it is not too difficult to find experienced farmers who can look at the sky in the morning and make a good estimate of what the weather is likely to do for the rest of the day. They do this without any formal training in meteorology, and very often they do it without rational thought: they just make a judgement on the basis of years of experience. They then base decisions as to what should be done that day on the basis of their judgement of the probable weather. Their judgement may not always be perfect, but it is useful!

Usefulness

This brings us to a whole new criterion for belief. If you don't know whether a notion is true or false, you can still choose to believe it on the grounds that believing it is useful.

If you don't know whether you can do something, but you believe that you can't, then you certainly can't. On the other hand, if you believe that you can, you are more likely to be able to. The belief that you can do something is therefore empowering. It is a useful belief. It may not actually be right, but you can believe it simply because believing it is useful. It might even become right, perhaps only as a consequence of your having believed it because of it being useful. This is an example of faith being causal, a useful idea which we shall return to in the next chapter.

Criteria for Disbelief

Although there are exceptions, most people are not deceitful most of the time, so why should you disbelieve anything you hear or read? There are a number of reasons. Firstly, some people do try to deceive you for their own purposes. Secondly, incompetence is very common, and many things are said or written in the mistaken belief that they might be true. Thirdly, wishful thinking is even commoner, and many people assert as true things which they would like to be true, without them necessarily being so. Fourthly, some superstitions are so persistent that they keep cropping up, seemingly justified on the basis that they must be true simply because so many people believe them.

Knowing all this, however, only tells you that much of what you hear or read might be wrong: it doesn't help you to sort out what is true and what isn't. So how do you decide what to disbelieve?

Disproof
The strongest reason for not believing something is if it can be proved to be false. If you know of any contrary evidence, the process of disproof may be quite easy; contradictions are impossible, and if two statements cannot be both be true then at least one of them is false. Logic will help you to sort out which is which.

Logic also comes into its own when thinking about a statement over which you may have some doubt. Ask yourself, if this is true, what else would follow. Look at the implications of what is said, and if you derive an impossibility or a contradiction, then you know that the statement you started with was false.

Having deduced that a statement is false, you cannot correctly deduce that the person who made it is a liar. They might just as well be mistaken, misinformed, incompetent, ignorant or just plain stupid. You do know, however, that they are not wholly reliable.

Mistrust
If you know or suspect that someone is not reliable, you may be more inclined to mistrust what they say. The same is true if you simply feel that you cannot trust them. A feeling that someone can be trusted is sometimes illusory, but a feeling that they cannot be trusted is much more likely to be reliable, unless you have a tendency to mistrust absolutely everyone.

If you feel that someone cannot be trusted, it does not follow that everything they say is false. Nobody is a completely consistent liar! It does follow that you should weigh everything they say very carefully, and be very much on your guard as to the costs to you if you should be misled by them.

Who is conning you?
If someone is going to mislead you, there is a sense in which they they are trying to act as a leader, to get you to follow them. It is very tempting to have a

leader to follow, someone who does all the thinking and decision-making and all that difficult stuff for you. There are plenty of people around who do very nicely out of other people's wish for leadership.

There are leaders who are good and honest and trustworthy, whose leadership is valid, but there are others who are just taking advantage of the fact that there are many people who do not wish to make the effort to do their own thinking. You can recognise these false leaders most easily by their tendency to offer certainty where none exists, and to discourage their followers from thinking for themselves.

Do not be tricked by these people. They are after power, and they want power over you. Although you might be tempted by their charisma, and also tempted to rely on them to show you the way through life, their way does not lead to happiness. You have to be a self-leader, and make your own decisions, rather than just blindly taking instructions from someone who offers to save you the effort of thinking.

So, if someone offers you certainty where you suspect that none exists, question them, and if they challenge your right to do so or simply assert that they know better, get out of their sphere of influence as quickly as you can, and trust nothing which comes from them or any of their followers. The alternative can lead all too easily to such horrors as the massacres at Jonestown, Guyana and Waco, Texas.

Happy atheists?

Not all religious leaders are evil, and you may have religious faith, or you may not. I have the impression that happiness is commoner amongst people who do have a religion than amongst those who do not, but I have no formal statistical evidence for this. You may regard the existence of happy atheists as sufficient reason not to believe in God. What about regarding the existence of happy believers as sufficient reason to join them?

Honest agnosticism

Is agnosticism the only truly honest position? I ask this not just about the Big Question of whether God exists, but about all such unanswerable questions. The agnostic says, "I do not know." The believer says, "I believe." (Even an atheist is a believer in this sense, saying, "I believe that God does not exist.")

The opposite of an agnostic is a gnostic. The gnostic says, "I know", rather than saying, "I believe." When it comes to unanswerable questions, gnostics are wrong. They may be wrong for a number of reasons, not just dishonesty, but if a proposition is truly undecidable, then there is no room for a gnostic, although there is room for believers of each persuasion and for those who have no opinion.

Thus, when it comes to unanswerable questions, including those of religious faith, an honest and competent person can say one of three things: "I don't know, but I believe", "I don't know, and I don't believe", or "I don't know, and I have no opinion." In this context, belief is to some extent a matter of choice, so what will you choose to disbelieve?

Damaging belief systems

The thing to avoid is any belief or set of beliefs which will harm you. It is not obvious, but many popular mysticisms, such as astrology, can be very damaging. Why is this?

If you believe that you should make decisions on the basis of what someone tells you is written in the stars, you are opting out of the responsibility of thinking properly for yourself, and unhappiness is the only possible long-term consequence.

The same criticism can be laid at the door of Tarot readings, runes, and other such occult fortune-telling systems. They all deny your power to think for yourself and your responsibility to make your own decisions on the basis of your own thinking. Your future is what you make it, not what the mystics would tell you it is going to be.

However, there is more to their power than you might think. If they do make a prediction for you, it is quite likely that it will come true. The way this works is that they implant their ideas in your subconscious in such a way that it influences your behaviour so as to bring the prediction to reality. It is therefore not safe to let them get to you: you can't just choose to ignore what they say. Never let them say it in the first place!

Chapter 33

Faith

When you are confident of the truth of something which you cannot prove to be true to someone else, you have faith. Faith is not necessarily irrational, although blind faith, which ignores contrary evidence, always is. In fact, it is normal to have faith in ideas, in ourselves, and in other people, without being able to prove that that faith is justified.

Everyone has Faith

You will not find anyone alive who does not have faith in something. Even if you were to find someone who refused to believe anything without proof, such a person could be said to have an irrational faith in the power of reason. It is, of course, right to have faith in the power of reason, but not to the extent that you refuse to believe anything which is beyond proof.

You have a belief system

If you had no faith, you would be paralysed with doubt over virtually every decision. You may not have thought about it explicitly but you have a belief system, a set of things which you believe without being able to prove them. Even if you claim to be a complete agnostic, ...

You trust people you've never met

Many of the decisions you make in ordinary everyday life are based on trust. When you do something as simple as drinking from a bottle of milk, you trust your life to the people who take responsibility for the hygiene in the bottling plant. Do you know these people? Have you met them, checked their procedures, and satisfied yourself that they are trustworthy? Likewise if you ever travel by air, you trust hundreds of people to co-operate successfully in ensuring your safety.

You could argue in both of these instances that there is plenty of evidence to show that these people are reliable enough to be trusted, but the principle holds good in such a wide variety of circumstances that it is clear that most people have a basic faith in human nature. We all understand that there are people out there who cannot be trusted, but on the whole we are confident that, when we buy something, we will get what we paid for, and when someone promises to do something for us, they will at least try to do it.

This principle of trusting other people is the very foundation of society. If it were not justified, civilisation would collapse. Of course, other people have to be able to trust you: they trust you to be decent, honest and reliable, and they trust you not to try to get something from them for nothing, in the same way as you trust them. If you betray this trust, you are working for the destruction of civilisation, and for your own diminution as a human being. Your happiness depends upon you yourself being trustworthy.

Faith as opposed to belief

There is more to faith than believing things you can't prove, such as the trustworthiness of other people. There is always an element of the unprovable in any matter of faith, whether it is faith in human nature, faith in yourself, or a religious faith.

Faith affects your decisions. You base your actions upon faith. This is what distinguishes faith from mere intellectual acceptance of the truth of an unprovable notion. You may accept the theory that black holes exist without being able to prove it, but unless the belief affects your decisions in life, it can hardly be called faith.

If on the other hand, you believe in God, in a final judgement and in eternal life ending in Heaven or in Hell, you are likely to base your decisions on these premises. Indeed, you would be crazy if you didn't. You may not be able to prove the truth of what you believe to someone else, but likewise they cannot prove the contrary: you are therefore not crazy to believe what you do, but you would be mad not to act in accordance with what you believe.

Faith is causal

It is for this reason that faith is causal. What do I mean by this? Events are caused by people's beliefs, including their religious beliefs.

If you believe that something can and should be done, and that God will help you to do it, you will certainly try very hard to achieve it. If you do try very hard, the chances are good that you will succeed. When you have succeeded, it will be clear that it was your faith which was the most important factor in getting things done.

The realisation of this does not explain away the power of prayer any more than the understanding of science explains away the existence of a Creator. It is true that prayer has a profound psychological effect upon the person doing the praying and that this can have an effect upon their success in life, but that does not mean that God is not personally having an influence: it merely describes the form of that influence.

It may also be true that God's influence affects more than just the person doing the praying, and a great many people do believe that this is the case. If it is the case, then it is also true that the extent of that influence is in some way related to the strength of faith of people who pray. When something truly remarkable happens as a result of this, we describe it as a miracle. Do miracles occur? If they do not, why do we have a word for them?

Faith does change things. It has real physical effects in the real physical world. Even if the only effects you observe are in the behaviour of people who have faith, these effects are none the less real.

Great Religions

Faith is usually thought of in terms of religious faith, and there is good reason for this. If you believe something which you cannot prove to be true and that belief affects your behaviour, you have a religious faith in it, regardless of whether it conforms to the teaching of any commonly recognised religious creed.

Regardless of that, most people who have a religious faith adhere to one of the great religions. In fact, the majority of people adhere to one of the great religions. About a fifth of the population of the world is at least nominally Christian. There are fewer Jews, Muslims, Buddhists, Hindus, Taoists, believers in Shintoism and other minor religions, but collectively they amount to substantially more than half the human race.

What they have in common

All of these religions involve faith in unprovable assertions. All of them have a code of conduct, or set of ethics. With the possible exception of Islam, whose record on the rights of women and non-believers is not impressive, they all promote human rights and the idea that no human being should be cruel to another human being.

All of the great religions forbid murder, dishonesty and theft. All of them have people who claim to be followers but who still live by means of dishonesty or force.

What divides them

Although there is broad agreement on ethics, there is fundamental disagreement on the basis of the ethical code.

Judaism, Christianity and Islam all have the Ten Commandments, said to have been given directly by God to Moses, but Christians claim that Jesus, as the Son of God, said that the whole of the law was founded on love: if you love God and love your neighbour, you will always obey the Ten Commandments anyway. Of course, Judaism and Islam reject the idea of Jesus as Son of God.

Meanwhile, Buddhists are trying to live rightly without hurting any other living being, in order that, when the time comes for reincarnation, they will get a better life, and might eventually reach Nirvana.

Hinduism is such a broad philosophy that it claims to include all other religions. A Hindu can accept the idea that a Christian's faith may be true, whilst failing to accept that Christian teaching says that Hinduism is wrong.

There are tribal religions where people believe what their ancestors believed without understanding how their ancestors came to have the belief in the first place. Many of these beliefs are incompatible with those of any other religion.

The battle of the memes

A set of religious beliefs is in fact a set of memes. Memes, as we saw in Chapter 7, compete for accommodation in meme vehicles such as human brains. Many religions have a mission to convert as many people as possible to their faith, and this is the observable manifestation of this competition between memes.

The complex of memes which makes up a religious creed usually carries with it a promise that if you accept all of the memes, you will get certain benefits. All religions include a sense of belonging to the community of people who share the faith. Most also include a promise of happiness, either in this life, or in an everlasting life after death, or both.

Religious persecution

It only takes a slight distortion of the teaching of any religion to get to the idea that there is an everlasting fate worse than death for non-believers, and that therefore any means are permissible to save people from this fate. From this comes religious persecution, and many of the bloodiest wars of human history.

The people guilty of all this cruelty and institutionalised murder have failed to grasp two facts, and your happiness depends upon your grasping them. Firstly, cruelty and killing never lead to happiness for anyone. Secondly, if you attempt to wipe out a belief by force or threat of force, the effect is to strengthen the resolve of the people who have that belief: thus the tendency of their memes to be spread is increased rather than decreased.

Self-surrender?

Many religions carry the idea that self-surrender, or self-sacrifice is a good thing. To the extent that this leads you to contribute to society as a whole by your own choice, this idea will help you to be happy. If you let other people push the idea on to you, to the extent that you are diminished as a person in your own right, it will make you less happy.

Power to Move Mountains

Jesus said that if you have faith the size of a mustard seed, you can tell a mountain to be uprooted and planted in the sea, and it will happen. He wasn't recommending that you go around changing the landscape by psychokinesis. He was, as he often did, speaking figuratively, simply trying to convey the power of faith to change things.

If you believe that faith changes things, does this mean that you believe in miracles? Not necessarily. If miracles do occur, it may be that they are caused in some strange way by the direct action of faith upon the physical universe, but the very fact that we call such events miracles shows that this is not the way that things usually happen. What usually happens is that your faith inspires you to do the things you have to do in order to make the changes you believe should be made.

A good example of this principle can be seen in the only case I am aware of in which a mountain was uprooted and planted in the sea.

Osaka airport

One of the human race's biggest construction projects ever was the building of Osaka's new international airport at Kansai. A large airport requires a good area of flat land, and none was available at Osaka, although the city was much in need of a new airport. The solution was to build an artificial island just off the coast, with road and rail bridge connecting it with the mainland. Building the island required not just one but two local mountains to be removed and planted in the sea.

This was not done merely by faith. The architects, engineers and builders did not move these mountains just by sitting and believing that their faith alone would be sufficient to cause the miraculous movement of two mountains into the sea. They used bulldozers, trucks, boats, cranes, and so on.

Nevertheless faith was necessary. If none of them had believed the project to be practicable, it would not have got done. Faith does not of itself move mountains, but if you are going to move a mountain, you do need faith!

How things really get done

The building of Osaka's Kansai Airport is just an example of how things really get done. Whatever you want to do, you have to believe in it first. In the famous words of Napoleon Hill, "What the mind can conceive and believe, the mind can achieve."

Faith without action rarely achieves anything. Once you have thought of the possibility of something, you must believe it to be possible. Once you have a clear belief in the possibility of something, you must see how to do it. Then do it.

Part of the process of getting things done often involves the co-operation of other people. If others are going to co-operate properly, they need to share your faith. Getting other people to share your faith is part of the process of getting things done from your point of view, and it too depends upon your belief that it is possible. If you really believe in the value and possibility of your plans, persuading other people to share your faith should not be too difficult. Having got them to share your faith, getting them to join in with the action required should be relatively easy.

The mystery of prayer power

Does prayer help? In 1988, the cardiologist Randolf Byrd led a study in which 393 heart patients were randomly divided into two groups, one of whose members were prayed for, the other not. Not only did fewer patients in the prayed-for group die, but they had fewer complications too. This could not be accounted for by the placebo effect, since this was a double-blind experiment, in which neither the patients nor the medical staff knew who was in which group.

There is also plenty of anecdotal evidence to support the contention that prayer is effective. Although there are also counterexamples showing that prayer does not always bring about the desired result, if you have a religious faith and you pray for God's help in carrying out some project you believe in, the probability of a successful outcome is almost certainly increased.

Chapter 34

Life After Death

Death itself is not one of the Big Questions. It is an incontrovertible fact that your present life is temporary. Unless the end of the world comes before you die, you will have to face death; and, even if the end of the world does come before you die, it remains true that your present life is temporary. If you try to deny that this life is temporary, you will lead yourself into self-deception which can never help to make you happy. You must therefore admit it, face it, and decide how you will cope with the fact: you don't have to be pleased about it, but equally, there is no reason why it should make you unhappy. It is just a fact.

The Big Question is whether any part of your consciousness persists after the death of your physical body. In other words, do you have an ...

Immortal Soul?

The idea of an immortal soul is so wrapped up with connotations of ancient teachings of the Roman Catholic Church that it is easily rejected more on grounds of prejudice than logic. The idea does, however, bear some examination. I invite you, therefore, to set aside any preconceptions you might have and consider the whole subject afresh.

The first thing is to separate the idea of the soul from the idea of immortality. The question of whether you have an immortal soul breaks down into two separate questions. Is the concept of a soul a valid concept, and, if so, what is it? If the soul is a valid concept and every human being has one, does it survive the death of the body? Let's look at these questions one by one.

St. Augustine's definition

When Augustine of Hippo was challenged by someone who did not accept the concept of a soul, he asked, "Are you identical with your corpse?". Of course you are not identical with your corpse, and the difference between you and your dead body is, in Augustine's definition, your soul.

Forget anything you think you know about your soul. Forget also any religious teaching about it which you may have accepted or rejected in the past. Just hang on to Augustine's definition for the time being: your soul is the difference between you as a whole, and your body, just as a material object. There is a real difference; you can call it what you like, but in this book it is called your soul.

291

Separable?

The next question is whether body and soul are in any sense separable? Can your soul have any existence apart from your body? As Ayn Rand pointed out in one of her books, a body without a soul is a corpse and a soul without a body is a ghost: both of these things connote death.

Despite this, there are many people who claim to have had "out-of-body" experiences, in which they seem to be able to experience the world from some place outside the body. Although this seems to be experienced most often in traumatic circumstances, there are even claims that it can be done deliberately, by means of what is referred to as "astral projection".

You are at liberty to dismiss any such claims, as they are, as yet, unproved from a scientific standpoint. Nonetheless the claims exist, and, if they are valid, they support the contention that body and soul can survive a temporary separation.

Immortal?

What about a permanent separation? The evidence that the body does not survive this is clear. Dead bodies decompose, and ultimately disintegrate altogether. If you do not believe in life after death, it follows that you believe that your soul cannot survive without your body any more than your body can survive without your soul.

If you do believe that your soul can survive without your body, it follows that you believe in life after death. This is not the same as believing that the afterlife is everlasting. It is perfectly consistent to believe that life after death is temporary, and followed either by non-existence or by reincarnation.

Nevertheless, if you do believe that your soul will survive the death of your body, this does beg the question of what you think it might not survive! Immortality does seem to be the most logical consequence of life after death.

What about the animals?

Do animals have souls? Of course, St. Augustine's definition works just as well for an animal as it does for a human being. A live dog is not the same as a dead dog, and the difference is the soul of the dog. The soul of the dog therefore exists, but does it continue to exist after the death of the dog?

It seems to me that the best approach to this question is to ask whether it is a useful question. I cannot see how such a question could ever be answered with any degree of confidence. I also fail to see what use any answer could be put to. On these criteria, I do not personally find it to be a useful question.

You are welcome to disagree. The only implication I can see for your happiness is that you could run a risk of making yourself unhappy by wasting a great deal of effort pursuing the answers to unanswerable questions of this kind, and thereby not using your life in a way which could make you happy.

Reincarnation?

There are many people in the world who believe that after the death of the body each soul acquires a new body, not necessarily of the same species. It is not for me to say that such a belief is right or wrong, but I have to point out that it does have implications for happiness.

Your happiness depends upon what you do in this life, not upon what might have happened in previous lives, if any, nor upon what you will be doing in any subsequent life. Live in the present, or at least in the present life: that way, you will remain in touch with reality, which is necessary for happiness.

Evidence

There is some evidence that the soul does in fact survive the death of the body. This evidence does not constitute proof, but it is still worth considering.

Near death experiences

There is a long history of people having very strange experiences when close to death. According to Raymond Moody, one of the leading researchers in this field, there are documented cases dating back thousands of years, but the phenomenon of the near-death experience has become much better known in the last few decades because of improvements in resuscitation techniques. More people now return from death or near death than ever before in history.

What these people report is very hard to explain in psychological or neurological terms. What is significant is that, as far as I am aware, everyone who has made a serious study of near-death experiences has ended up convinced that there is life after death, even if they had no such belief beforehand. It also seems that people who have had a near-death experience share the same belief.

Ghosts

There is also a long history of stories of the sighting of ghosts. There is no satisfactory physical explanation of this, but there appear to be some patterns to the claimed observations. The manifestation of a ghost is usually correlated with the death of someone who was not ready to die. When a ghost appears to someone, the appearance is not readily explained simply as an hallucination.

Hallucinations are correlated with a person suffering from a psychiatric disease, and two different such sufferers have their own individual hallucinations. Stories of ghosts are correlated with a particular place and its history, and the anecdotes seem to suggest that similar appearances are observed by different people, even when they do not know the history.

Regression

Under hypnosis, people sometimes appear to recall events from long before their birth. This is sometimes proffered as evidence for reincarnation, it being alleged that they remember a past life. This is called regression. The evidence is very weak, but there are people who accept it.

Not Proof

The evidence which there is to support the idea of life after death is only evidence; it is not proof. You could say that there is proof of life after near-death, but that is by no means the same thing! What would constitute proof?

If you think of the notion of life after death as a scientific theory (which it isn't), the way to test it would be to look for observable consequences beyond those which are already known. As far as I am aware, no such consequences can be derived from the theory, so we can't look for new evidence to support it. Even if we had a way of testing the theory like this, and we ended up with new evidence to support it, this would not absolutely prove that there is life after death: all it would show is that the possibility is not ruled out.

Would you believe it if it were?

Let us suppose, however, that we could have such overwhelming evidence of life after death that most people would accept it as proof. Would you believe it then? I ask this question, not because I am trying to persuade you one way or the other, but just so that you understand that this kind of belief is a matter of choice.

As Jesus pointed out in his story about the rich man and Lazarus, even if someone were to return from the dead, people would not believe what they had to say. Now that returns at least from near-death, if not from death itself, are commonplace, perhaps he is being proved right. Christians have traditionally believed that he was referring to his own forthcoming Resurrection.

What about the Resurrection?

It is clear from the historical record that something very strange happened shortly after Jesus' execution. Whether or not you believe that he came back from death, the fact remains that about a billion people believe that he did, and that the course of history was changed by his life, death, and whatever happened next. Whatever did happen next was enough to convince a great many people that he had indeed come back.

Given the other evidence which suggests that the soul can indeed survive separation from the body, it seems to me that the most reasonable explanation of the events following Jesus' death is indeed that a few days after he was dead and buried, he came back. You are welcome to disagree, as there is no incontrovertible proof, but whether you agree or not, is a matter of choice on your part, and it may be ...

Your Biggest Choice

What are you going to believe about death? Ducking this question would be running away from reality, and, as we have seen, happiness depends upon dealing successfully with reality, not with illusions. The only certain thing about life is death, and if you try to deny this, you will undermine your chances of happiness.

What is going to happen to you?

At the end of your present life, are you going to go on into some other life, or is this all there is? If this is all there is, then you might think that the best policy would be to take what you can get now, without regard to the long-term consequences, or for the implications for other people, but that would not actually help you to be happy in this life. Whatever might or might not come next, you still have to live with yourself now!

Happiness, even just in this life, is not achieved by unenlightened self-interest. If you know that you get what you get at someone else's expense, this will make you unhappy now, ...

And maybe for ever

One of the commonest occurrences in near-death experiences is what has become known as the "life review". It has been known for a long time that people who have come close to death have suddenly had their whole lives flash before their eyes, as it were. It seems, however that, if there is an afterlife, you will carry knowledge of everything you have done in this life forward into the next. This could be both your Heaven and your Hell.

Later may be too late to change

If you want to be happy, and you can see that you need to change your life in order to be happy, change things right now. If you see the need to change, and you postpone it, you will have to live with the knowledge that you should and could have done things better, and you may have to live with that knowledge for ever. Even if you don't, you will still find death easier to face, if you can face it knowing that you have done your best.

Chapter 35

God?

No-one has rigorously proved the case either for or against the existence of any deity. You may be convinced one way or the other, and it is not for me to tell you what you should believe. Nevertheless, your belief system does have a bearing on your happiness, and what you believe about God is potentially one of the biggest influences in your life.

A great many people don't believe in God. Amazingly, the God they don't believe in is also rejected by people who do believe: the believers and the atheists have very different ideas of who or what God is, or might be if He does exist. There are many good reasons for not accepting someone else's religious ideas, not least of which is the fact that there are criminally-minded people who wish to profit from getting their apparently religious teachings accepted.

Conversely, there are enough good reasons for believing in God that a very large proportion of the human race does believe, and these people are not just the poor, ignorant and uneducated, as is sometimes claimed by ardent atheists. Most believers stick with their beliefs not for intellectually justifiable reasons, but because they find that their faith is empowering and that their happiness is bound up with their beliefs.

The God you Don't Believe in

If you don't believe in God, you have probably quite properly rejected someone else's image of God.

Despite all the efforts of theologians over the centuries, nobody really knows anything very much about God at all. Even so, some believers are apt to claim certainty, and to assert that they know that what they believe is true. This is not only not completely honest; it is also to some extent destructive.

If you do believe in God, you have some incomplete, inaccurate image of Him. If you assert that your image is correct, and your image is rejected by someone else, that rejection may well carry with it not just your image of God, but also the very idea of the existence of God at all.

An old man in the clouds

As an example of this, consider the old idea of God being like an old man sitting up in the sky on a cloud. This image is now the stuff of cartoon caricatures, but for centuries it was an image which had real meaning for people. Apart from young children, nobody now finds this to be a useful image, but there are still people who reject the whole idea of God because this particular image is now seen as infantile.

An all-powerful loving God who allows suffering

Most believers assert that God is omnipotent and loving. Yet there is still great suffering in the world. How can an omnipotent, loving God permit this? Doesn't the existence of such terrible suffering show that God does not exist or, if He does exist, that He is either not omnipotent or not loving? These are challenging and important questions, but the fact remains that many people do maintain their faith despite such questions.

There may seem to be a paradox here, but suffering is a complicated subject, as we shall see in the next and last chapter of this book, and it does not actually follow that love requires prevention of suffering. The idea of an all-powerful God caring or not caring about people's suffering is just too simplistic to be useful.

What is the alternative?

If you dismiss other people's images of God as being too childish or too simplistic in some other way, what idea of God are you going to accept or reject? The problem is that all images are wrong. This was recognised as long ago as the fourth century, when John Chrysostom wrote of the "incomprehensible nature" of God.

It is fair enough to believe that God exists, and to have certain other beliefs about God, but it is wrong to claim complete understanding, and also wrong to claim that what you believe is undeniably accurate. Yet it is very hard to believe in God without having any sort of image in mind, so what sort of image should you have?

Just choose the useful ones

As we have seen, your beliefs affect your behaviour, and consequently your happiness. Any image you have of God affects you in this way.

You may gain strength from belief that God will help you. You may gain self-confidence and self-respect from the belief that God loves you. You may gain the courage to do what is right from the belief that God will reward you eventually. If you have such beliefs about God which you can honestly accept, in that they are consistent with reality as you know it, you will find that they help you to live a happy life.

But these beliefs about God are not the same as images of God. An image of God is something which you might hold in mind while you pray. As such, it is a very personal thing, and it is not for anyone else to tell you that you should not have an image which you find helpful. If you personally find that old image of a father-figure to be helpful, even though you may understand that it is inexact, you are entitled to maintain that image. If anyone tries to tell you that you are wrong to do so, you should be suspicious of their motives.

Your right to your beliefs

You will probably find that there are people who dispute your faith. As long as you are not being dishonest, you are entitled to believe what you believe, but it is always worth asking why someone should wish to change your faith. They may genuinely care about you and believe that you would ultimately be happier if you shared their faith, but they may have other reasons.

Beware of Prophets who Profit

From time to time you will come across people trying to persuade you to join their religion. One of the first things to try to understand when this happens is the motivation of the people doing the persuading. What's in it for them? More significantly, what's in it for the people further up the hierarchy? If, at the top of the pile, you find someone living the life of the spectacularly rich, your next question should be, "What are the costs?"

You will not get the answer to this in straightforward financial terms. Look instead at the lifestyle of the average member. Do they earn their living in the normal way from productive work? Do they live with their own families in ordinary houses in ordinary towns, or are they in an allegedly happy commune away from the rest of society?

There is always a financial cost of membership of any organisation like a church, but this should be, and normally is, under the direct control of the members. When the plate comes round on Sunday morning, no attention should ever be drawn to how much or how little, if anything, you choose to put into it. Finance does matter, but there is a much bigger question, and that is ...

Who owns your mind?

As we have seen, your happiness depends upon your ability and willingness to use your own mind, to think for yourself, and solve your own problems. There are religions which deny this, and which promise eternal happiness if only you will follow the instructions of the leaders. This is a lie, and a power ploy. Once you have surrendered your mind, you are nothing, you have nothing, not the happiness you have been promised, nor the ability to do anything about it. You are just a pawn in someone else's power game.

Can you think for yourself?

Thinking for yourself can be hard work. It is always rewarding, but the fact that it is hard work makes it easier for people who wish to rob you of this faculty to tempt you with an easy life without thinking. If you ever find yourself tempted in this way, remember the Nazi philosophy which held that no individual was to blame for following orders, no matter how evil the orders, and remember the unhappiness that this caused, not only to the victims of atrocities, but also to their perpetrators. Remember too the unhappiness of people entrapped by the Moonies. Better to do your own hard work, and think for yourself.

Benefits to non-members

If you join a church or other religious organisation, you are much more likely to be happy if that organisation has a positively beneficial effect on people who are not members. An introverted organisation, concerned only with the affairs of its immediate members, and possibly regarding the rest of society as an enemy, is never as happy. How will you assess an organisation from this point of view? That is up to you. You have a mind. Use it!

Rewards to senior members

Look also at the senior members of the hierarchy. Do you see happy people living modest lives, or do you see people who are materially very well provided for, but whose lives show signs of unhappiness, or what? How do you interpret what you see? What sorts of people rise in the hierarchy? Who is likely to replace the present leader when he (as it almost always is *he*) eventually dies? An ambitious person, or one who just accepts the burden of responsibility?

It is up to you to decide how to interpret the answers you find to these questions. All I am doing is pointing out that the questions are relevant to your happiness, and that it is up to you to find and interpret the answers for yourself.

How cults work

We humans have a natural craving for automatic guidance. This makes us vulnerable to cult leaders who offer such guidance. Politicians use the same trick, as do some of the less respectable business people in the world, and quite a number of academics. Accepting other people's guidance can help you to be happy, but only when you have the opportunity to examine their reasoning.

You should know you are being tricked when you are assured that there is no need for you to think for yourself, that the answers will be provided. That is the way to unhappiness, even though it is often sold as the easy way to happiness.

A disguised version of the same trick comes with the use of sleep deprivation: you are not told not to think, but you are prevented from doing so, and also deprived of the opportunity to practise reflection.

How to be Happy with God

If you do not believe in God, you are presumably happy without Him, and so you can skip the remainder of this chapter.

Happiness and faith in God are compatible, but not all believers are happy with God. If you do believe in God and you are not happy with Him, then you need to change something. Being happy with God depends primarily upon your being happy with the way you live your life, and the rest of this book should help you with that, but there is more to it than that.

Don't depend on other people's rules

Happiness with God is not dependent upon following a set of rules laid down by other people. Of course, you must behave ethically at all times, but this need not include slavish adherence to a set of traditions which have no direct relevance to your life and your relationship with God.

If you do belong to a church or other such community, there is a lot to be said for following the traditions of that community, but it is a purely human thing. Never let anyone try to convince you that your relationship with God is dependent upon following their code of practice in respect of things which are morally neutral, in the sense that, if you do break the rules, no human victim can be identified. Don't let them convince you that you will hurt God by eating the wrong sort of meat on the wrong day of the week, for example; God is bigger than that!

Get a real relationship

Your happiness with God is dependent on your perception of your relationship with Him. You will damage this if you behave unethically. You will enhance it by prayer, but if you get so carried away with the joy which comes with prayer that you neglect other things which you know you should do, then you will damage the relationship, or at least your perception of it.

Allow God to forgive you

Of course there will be times when you don't manage to live up to the standards you have set for yourself. In the same way as you forgive yourself, you must allow yourself to feel forgiven by God. There is no evidence to suggest that God bears grudges. You may feel sure that God can forgive you for anything for which you can forgive yourself.

Knowing that you can always be forgiven should not lead you to presuming that you can get away with anything. Deliberately doing something which you know to be wrong on the assumption that you can repent later and be forgiven simply does not help you to be happy. Whatever you do has consequences, and you will always regret anything you do wrong, especially of you do it deliberately and presuming future forgiveness: forgiveness doesn't work that way.

Remember you're free

Belief in God should not constrain your decision-making, except in so far as it will make it easier for you to avoid wrong-doing. You have free will, and you can choose what you want to do within the constraints of ethics and morality.

You may have the idea that you should at all times carry out the will of God, but this begs the question of how to discern it. Apart from the signals you get from your own conscience, which we have discussed elsewhere, there is no way, as far as I am aware, of telling what God wants you to do. It follows that, if the idea of the will of God is an invalid concept, then the only way to follow it is to follow your own conscience.

Make your own decisions, following your own beliefs as to what is right. That is the way to happiness, and to a good relationship with God too.

You are loved

Theologians of various backgrounds have different opinions about God, but they all seem to agree that God loves His creatures, which is to say you, me, and the rest of the human race. Quite what this means in practice is unclear, but there is no reason why you should not feel loved by God.

Give God time

If you are to experience the love and forgiveness of God, the one extra virtue you will need is patience. There may be times when your experience of life seems to conflict with your faith in God, or your beliefs about God. You may learn to change some of your beliefs about God, all of which are always in some way inadequate or inaccurate, but if you keep your basic faith, you may trust that in the longer term this will be shown to be justified. Give Him time!

Chapter 36

Suffering

One of the most difficult things to understand about happiness is that it is possible to be happy despite suffering. Certain events in life cause emotional pain, and physical pain can strike anyone. It is easier to remain happy when one's suffering is purely physical, but emotional pain need not destroy your happiness. Your happiness depends upon the attitude you take to suffering, whether physical or emotional. The first thing to recognise is that suffering is a consequence of ...

Problems

You might think that suffering is itself a problem and, of course, you would be right, but suffering doesn't just happen without a cause. Suffering is a consequence of something, and that something is a problem. Now let me remind you of ...

Weinberg's definitions

You will remember from Chapter 1 that a problem is best defined as a difference between the situation as observed and the situation as desired. Leaving aside the question of phantom problems, which are caused by errors of observation, let us concentrate on real problems, where the situation really is not as you would wish it to be.

If you have a real problem, it is natural to suffer: that is what suffering is, after all, enduring a situation which is not as desired. You already understand that the healthiest approach to a problem is to find a solution to it; but some problems just cannot be solved, and even those that can often take quite a time, during which time you continue to suffer.

What you want, however, is to manage to develop that attitude of mind which allows you to continue to be happy despite the suffering which comes from having problems. Firstly, you must believe that this is possible. Observe that there are happy people who have problems which they cope with: therefore it is possible, therefore you can do it. All you need to know is how. I recommend that, as a first step, you ...

Classify your problems by type of cause

There are three types of cause of problems. Some problems are inevitable: you don't have to like it when a dear old friend dies, but such things do happen and there is nothing to be done about it. Some problems arise from bad choices: there is someone to blame, or someone to forgive, perhaps yourself. Some problems arise just from bad luck: accidents will happen, and sometimes there is no-one to blame. We will go into each of these in quite a lot more detail shortly, but first let's have a quick look at ...

Coping with problems

When you have a problem, an undesirable situation, and you have identified its cause, the next thing is to establish whether you can do anything about it. You must distinguish what you can change from what you can't. If you can't change something, you just have to accept it, but if you can change something, or prevent a new similar problem from arising, then you must do what you can.

This is where anger comes into its own. Anger is the emotion which helps you to change things which need changing so as to solve a problem or to prevent it from recurring. However, there is no point in feeling anger at something which you cannot affect. Remember that your emotional reaction to a situation is a matter of your own choice, a consequence of the interpretation you put on what you observe.

Now, let's get back to the various types of causes of problems and how to approach each.

The Inevitable

Some problems are inevitable. Everyone has problems of one sort or another, and, of course, this entails some suffering, but it need not imply unhappiness. If you can't affect the situation, your only approach is to change your attitude to it. Accept what cannot be changed. Do not focus on the problem. Instead, focus on things which are good in life, and most importantly upon things which you can change.

All inevitable problems are of the type that you can't solve, in the sense of being able to change things. In particular, ...

You cannot change the past

Do not waste your life wishing that you could go back and change the past. You can't, but do not despair: the past is past, and no matter how bad it was, you have some power of choice over the future, and that is the way that happiness lies. The writer Napoleon Hill often remarked that every adversity carries the seed of an equal or greater benefit: the past, no matter how bad, can help you to make a better future. Even if the past is a source of great pain for you, you can choose to make it an asset.

Perhaps you can learn from one of the central themes of Christian belief. Death is followed by resurrection. However bad things get, something will follow which will be much better than you could ever have expected.

You cannot change the laws of physics

If you drop something, it will fall because of gravity. Left to themselves, most things rot or rust away, on account of the second law of thermodynamics. The physical universe follows regular laws which forbid things like perpetual motion machines and levitation. This is the way the world is, and you will not change it no matter how much you might like it to be different.

Why do I mention this? Simply because it is important to live in the real world. Anything else is delusion, and delusion does lead to unhappiness. If you find someone claiming to offer some benefit to you which depends upon the laws of physics (as you understand them) being changed or suspended, test the claim: you will probably uncover some dishonesty, and then you will know not to get involved.

Death

The only certainty in life is death. Bereavement is painful, and it is necessary to grieve properly when you lose someone you love. Eventually, however, you must let go of the pain of separation and let it become part of the past. Remember that the principal purpose of pain is to teach you to do something differently, but when someone has died there isn't anything you can do differently to bring them back.

The only thing you can do differently is to prepare yourself better next time. Other people close to you will die in the future. Prepare yourself now. Say those things to them which you might later regret not having said, and do your best to reconcile your differences while you have time. Face the fact that people do die: the alternative to this is denial of reality, which, as we have seen, makes for unhappiness, especially when the death eventually occurs of someone you wouldn't let yourself believe could die.

Bad Choices

A great deal of suffering arises from problems caused by bad choices, bad decisions. Indeed true unhappiness seems to me always to arise from this, the inappropriate use of free will, the choice of evil rather than good. As I have argued throughout this book, the only long-term solution to this is to make good choices, but this does not relieve the short-term suffering caused by the bad choices of the past, whoever made those choices.

Being happy despite the fact that people, yourself included, have made, and will continue to make bad choices, is a matter of attitude, and you choose your attitude, but just stating that is too simplistic, because so much depends upon whose decision is to blame for the problem.

Whose choice?

Who made the bad decision which led to your problem? If you want to express it that way, who is to blame? Placing blame and condemning people for their choices is not often useful or constructive, but asking who is to blame is a useful way of characterising the type of cause of the problem you have.

If you are inclined to blame God, then, unless you are dodging your own responsibility, your problem arises either from bad luck or from the nature of the universe. If you are inclined to blame God for your suffering, then the only solution is to change your attitude. Either you are pretending that you are not

304

responsible for something which followed from your decisions (in which case you are prevented from being happy by your refusal to face reality), or you have chosen rules which prevent you from being happy with the laws of physics as they are (in which case you have to change your rules), or you are blaming God for your bad luck (in which case you need to change your attitude to risk).

If you recognise that you are to blame, that the suffering is due to your own bad decisions, then you have a problem which can be solved. As you will have learned much earlier in this book, what you need is that old-fashioned idea known as repentance, or re-programming the mind, as it is known in modern parlance. I refer you back to the beginning of the book. You will find your own way from your present suffering to undeniable happiness, no matter how bad things are now.

If there is someone else to blame, then the natural response is anger. What you need is for someone else to repent of their bad decisions. There is a difficulty here because anger tends naturally to lead to violence, but if you try using violence or a threat thereof to persuade someone to repent, it won't work. The reason for this is that the mind tends to go numb when the body is threatened; people don't think clearly when attacked or threatened, but clarity of thought is necessary for repentance. Your approach must therefore be gentle, carrying an obvious readiness to forgive along with a clear presentation of your view of how their decisions led to pain and suffering, and pointing out that their happiness depends upon them changing their ways, as no-one can be happy whilst causing suffering to other people. You may not get the response you hope for, but you can be happy that you have done your best.

You can learn from the past

Whoever is to blame for your present suffering, there is something for you to gain by studying the past. You can learn from your own mistakes, and from other people's. This can be a painful process in itself, especially if it means facing the fact that you have made some bad choices yourself, or reacted destructively to bad choices made by others. Because looking at the past can be painful for these reasons, it can be tempting to try to forget, to deny the past and to shut it out of the present altogether. This is not a good idea, because if you deny the past you will never learn from it: as the saying goes, those who are ignorant of history are doomed to repeat it. It is also not a good idea because the brain is not good at blocking out chosen subsets of knowledge: what happens if you shut out part of the past from your conscious knowledge is that you also suppress other parts of your personality too, and this can of itself leave you unhappy and possibly even in need of professional help.

No matter how painful the past, there is always hope, because anyone can repent. Change is possible. You need not be set in your ways, and nor need anyone else who needs to change in order to be forgiven. If you are determined to believe that change is impossible for you or for anyone else, you can trap yourself in an unhappy state of bearing a grudge. Believe in the possibility of change, and be ready to forgive, whether it is you that needs to change and be forgiven or anyone else. Always allow a way forward into happiness, remembering that that way forward involves learning from the past, no matter how painful.

Bad Luck

There is a great deal of risk-taking in everyday life. Most of the time, we don't think consciously about the fact that things can go wrong for no readily apparent reason, but they do. As we go through life, we take risks, usually without ever making any kind of numerical estimate of the probability of things going wrong. Then, when an accident occurs, or we suddenly get ill, we complain about our bad luck.

Conversely, many people are disproportionately afraid of things which are relatively safe. There are many people who are afraid of flying, but not afraid to travel to the airport by car, regardless of whether they are aware that they are much safer in an aeroplane than on the road. There are even people who smoke cigarettes but are afraid to eat beef: when they get lung cancer, they think they have been unlucky.

Rational risk assessment

It is easier to be happy about any risk if you know what it is. Irrational fears can do a lot to make you miserable, and the solution is to try to get as good an understanding as you can of the risks you take in life, and then make your decisions consciously and as rationally as you can, having assessed the risks as well as you can. If things then go wrong, you can say, "That is the risk I took." That kind of realism will make you better able to cope with bad luck.

The best way to understand risk is to study probability and statistics. Unfortunately, the language of these subjects is mathematical and many people find it obscure, but if you do have some mathematical skills, even just simple arithmetic, you can learn to use a basic understanding of probability and statistics to help you to make better decisions. The better your decisions, the happier you are likely to be.

Dealing with bad luck

No matter how good your decisions, you will sometimes suffer from bad luck, and so you need to know how to cope with it when it does strike. If you can accept what has happened as being part of the risk you consciously took, you will cope with it quite easily, but what if you had not thought of this possibility in advance?

The most important thing is to recognise bad luck for what it is. Don't try to blame anyone if there is no-one to blame. Least of all, don't waste your life trying to get compensation, as no monetary compensation extorted from anyone will ever help you to be happy, even if they are to blame.

Having recognised bad luck for what it is, learn what you can from it. Maybe what has gone wrong was more probable than you originally thought, and maybe you can organise your life so as not to fall victim to that kind of accident again. Equally, there is no need to fear lightning striking twice in the same place if your rational assessment of the situation tells you that there is a low probability of the same kind of bad luck striking again.

The crucial thing is the matter of how you will approach future risk-taking. Denying that any risk exists is denying reality, which leads to unhappiness. Facing the risks which exist and assessing them as rationally as possible is the way to be happy about them: this too is the way to make rational decisions, which is to say good decisions.

Pain in Heaven

Can you be happy and still have pain? Yes, you can. In fact, you cannot have true joy unless you have experienced and understand suffering.

Joy and pain inseparable

As Kahlil Gibran said in "The Prophet", "When you are joyous, look deep into your heart and you shall find it is only that which has given you sorrow that is giving you joy. When you are sorrowful, look again in your heart, and you shall see that in truth you are weeping for that which has been your delight." He also said of joy and sorrow, "Together they come, and when one sits alone with you at your board, remember that the other is asleep on your bed."

The ability to feel joy depends, as does the ability to feel pain, upon having real feelings, and happiness depends upon this too. If you repress your feelings in an effort to overcome pain, you will also suppress your capacity for joy and happiness. The alternative to feeling is numbness, and although it often comes about subconsciously, it can be achieved by an effort of will, but it doesn't make for happiness.

Therefore you must have pain, but you can make pain your friend. Pain, emotional pain, is at least real, and you can listen to what it has to say to you. In the same way as physical pain tells you to do something different in order to avoid injuring yourself or making an injury worse, emotional pain gives you information about how you are living your life and the decisions you are making.

When you feel your pain in all its fullness and analyse where it is coming from and why, you can work out how to change your life so as not to cause such pain in the future. Alternatively, if the pain came as a result of bad luck after a rationally chosen risk, you might still choose to run the same risk again if you judge that the prospective benefits are worth it. When you make any such decision, and run your life accordingly, you will find true and lasting happiness, but only because you made friends with your pain, rather than trying to get rid of it.

Death and Resurrection

When you go through pain and come out full of joy, you re-enact in a small way the Christian story of Death and Resurrection. Many people have trodden this path before you and found the lasting happiness which comes from finding a pathway through pain, both physical and emotional. So, when you find yourself facing pain so terrible that it seems like death, look for the coming resurrection:

do not fear the pain itself, for the pain can be your friend, look for the pathway to new life which the pain will help you to find.

Between the pain and the joy, you may find a patch of numbness. The pain is over but the joy hasn't come yet. It is a bit like Holy Saturday, after the Crucifixion on Good Friday, but before the Resurrection on Easter Sunday morning. If you enter numbness having faced your pain squarely, rather than having repressed it, the numbness will pass, and will be followed by joy greater than the pain which preceded it.

Suffering ennobles

It is sometimes said that suffering ennobles, that anyone who has suffered greatly will be both stronger and better able to support other sufferers, and there is some truth in this saying, but there are hidden dangers here too.

First of all, it may be true, but it is not helpful to say it to someone in the midst of their pain. If you are helping someone to face their pain, concentrate on the realities of their pain, its causes, and what they can do about it. Do not talk in such flimsy abstractions and clichés: it helps no-one.

Secondly, it is a mistake to seek suffering for the sake of the good which might come from it. This may seem rather a bizarre idea, but some people do choose such a way of life, and it doesn't help them or anyone else to be happy. It is true that a little fasting can help you to strengthen your will, but if you fast to the point of damaging yourself, you will be no stronger for it. Likewise, if you accept the suffering which naturally comes your way as you live your life as best you can, you will have suffering enough: there is no point in seeking more.

Doing what is right does involve experiencing some pain and suffering. It follows from this that some pain is acceptable. As you experience pain, and learn from the messages it gives you, you will grow stronger, and better able to bear more and more, better able, in fact, to do what is right, no matter what the difficulties are.

Pain is not unhappiness

You will understand by now that pain is not the same thing as unhappiness. Nonetheless, there is still some potential for confusion, because you cannot have unhappiness without pain. In fact, in the same way as happiness can be described as a state of non-contradictory joy, so unhappiness can be described as a state of consistent sorrow. It may be relieved by occasional enjoyment of something, but the underlying state is one of sorrow, and this entails sustained pain.

The pain of unhappiness, not to be confused with the unhappiness itself, is a useful signal. It tells you to live your life differently. It doesn't tell you exactly what to do differently; you have to work that out for yourself, but it does tell you that change is needed. This pain is therefore your friend: proper attention to it will lead you eventually to happiness, the state of non-contradictory joy which will last, maybe beyond the grave.

Solution

So there you have the solution to the problem of pain, how to be happy with suffering. At all times, no matter what joy you have or what evil you suffer, remember that ...

You always have the choice of focus

A very poor person once said to me, "Things are looking up. When you're in the gutter, the only way to look is up." He eventually solved his problems, but if he had been looking down, into the gutter, as it were, I don't think he would have done. Advocates of the idea of the power of positive thinking may use this as an illustration of the value of that idea, and correctly so, although positive thinking, while very helpful, is not sufficient in itself.

Positive thinking helps you to concentrate upon the good outcome which you are eventually seeking, but you also need to focus upon the choices you have now which will help you towards the good outcome you ultimately seek. The key to finding your way to happiness is to choose the ethical path to greater choices. You do this by focusing upon what you can do now. Change is always possible.

"Accept it now faithfully and trustingly, and at the last end thou shalt see in truth and in fullness of joy."

Lady Julian of Norwich

Bibliography/Further Reading

Berne, E.: *What Do You Say After You Say Hello? The Psychology of Human Destiny,* Corgi Books 1974

The Bible, any translation or edition you like!

Braudel, F.: *Civilisation and Capitalism 15th -18th Century (tr. Siân Reynolds),* Collins 1981

Brooks, F.P.Jnr: *The Mythical Man-month,* Addison Wesley 1995

Chrysostom, John, Saint: *On Marriage and Family Life (tr. Catharine P. Roth & David Anderson),* St. Vladimir's Seminary Press 1986

Chrysostom, John, Saint: *On the Incomprehensible Nature of God (tr. Paul Harkins),* Catholic University of America Press 1984

Collier, P. & Horowitz, D.: *The Fords, an American Epic,* Collins 1988

Confucius: *The Analects (tr. Arthur Waley),* Quality Paperback Book Club 1992

Defoe, D.: *Robinson Crusoe,* Daniel Defoe 1720

Dominica, Sr. F.: *Just My Reflection, Helping parents to do things their way when their child dies,* Darton, Longman & Todd 1997

Edwards, B. & Sturgess, W.: *How to be Happy,* BBC Educational Developers 1996

Gibran, K.: *The Prophet,* Heinemann 1926

Hill, N. & Stone, W.C.: *Success through a Positive Mental Attitude,* Thorsons 1990

Hofstadter, D.R.: *Gödel, Escher, Bach: An Eternal Golden Braid,* Penguin 1980

Jaynes, J.: *The Origin of Consciousness in the Breakdown of the Bicameral Mind,* Allen Lane 1979

Karbo, J.: *The Lazy Man's Way to Riches,* Joe Karbo 1973

Lambert, T.: *The Power of Influence,* Nicholas Brearley 1996

Moody, R.A.: *Life after Life,* Bantam 1976

Norwich, Lady J.:*Revelations of Divine Love, tr. James Walsh,* Anthony Clarke 1980

Orbach, S.: *What's really going on here?,* Virago 1994

Peale, N.V.: *The Power of Positive Thinking,* Cedar 1953

Penrose, R.: *The Emperor's New Mind,* Oxford University Press 1989

Peter, L.J. & Hull, R.: *The Peter Principle,* Pan 1969

Pirsig, R.M.: *Zen and the Art of Motorcycle Maintenance,* Corgi Books 1976

Rand, A: *Atlas Shrugged,* Random House 1957

Robbins, A.: *Awaken the Giant Within,* Simon & Schuster 1992

Shone, R.: *Autohypnosis,* Thorsons 1982

Shone, R.: *Creative Visualisation,* Thorsons 1984

Skynner, R. & Cleese, J.: *Families and How to Survive them,* Mandarin 1983

Sutherland, S.: *Irrationality, the Enemy Within,* Constable 1992

Wallace, F.R.: *The Neo-Tech Discovery,* I&O Publishing Company 1990

Weinberg, G.M.: *Are your lights on?,* Ethnotech 1979

Xenophon: *The Cyropaedia (tr. J.S. Watson & H. Dale),* George Bell & Sons
1905

Afterword

This book has taken years. It is my profound hope that the more people read it, the commoner happiness will become and the better life will be for everyone.

I have done the best I can, but I am the first to admit that any such work is capable of improvement. I expect that the time will come when I want to have a new edition published. Perhaps you can help with this. If you think you can make a positive contribution to a later edition by means of constructive criticism, please feel free to write to me care of the publishers.

It is not usual for authors to reply to such letters, and I wouldn't expect to reply, but don't be too surprised if you get an implicit acknowledgement in the form of a recognisable change between this edition and the next.

Finally, if you do wish to criticise, please be constructive and make a positive contribution. If you merely attack my work, no-one will be the happier for it, least of all you yourself.